LIGHT (

Brief Reflections

C000264316

Hans Urs von Balthasar

Light of the Word

*Brief Reflections on
the Sunday Readings*

Translated by Dennis D. Martin

IGNATIUS PRESS   SAN FRANCISCO

Title of the German original:
Licht des Wortes:
Skizzen zu allen Sonntagslesungen
Second edition
© 1992 Johannes Verlag
Einsiedeln, Freiburg im Breisgau

Cover art by Donald J. Rooney
Cover design by Roxanne Mei Lum

© 1993 Ignatius Press
ISBN 978-0-89870-458-7
Library of Congress catalogue number 93–78538
Printed in the United States of America

CONTENTS

5

TRANSLATOR'S PREFACE

FATHER VON BALTHASAR based his "sketches" on the German and Latin lectionary texts. In the present translation, where German terminology in phrases set off in quotation marks by von Balthasar diverges significantly from the translations of the same passages in either the New American Bible or the English Lectionary for the Mass, I have translated the German and dropped the quotation marks. Where von Balthasar's German phrases in quotation marks differ less significantly from the English language versions, I have translated them and retained the quotation marks.[1]

One might also note that one of von Balthasar's common metaphors is taken from one of his favorite areas of endeavor: music. The imagery he intends when he uses the term *Auftakt* ("upbeat") is lost if the word is translated more generally as "prelude", "opening phase", or "introduction", since an *upbeat* is the unaccented moment before the *downbeat* that launches the music. It is not the opening note, rather, it is the moment of anticipation and rhythm-setting that is necessary if an orchestra or ensemble is to make music together successfully. In light of this, I have translated *Auftakt* with the noun "upbeat", even though this word is most often used as an adjective and with a completely different meaning in contemporary American English.

For the reader's convenience, I have added references in instances where von Balthasar makes direct and extended allusions to Scripture passages outside the lectionary text at hand. Where Father von Balthasar's references to other scriptures

---

[1] N.b.: In some cases, especially where a Scripture citation begins a reflection, quotation marks have been reinstated to show that it was a direct quote, even though it differs somewhat from the corresponding English Lectionary text—ED.

follow a divergent Vulgate numbering system, I have silently modified them to conform to the numbering used by the New American Bible and other modern versions.

— D.D.M.

INTRODUCTION

THE REFLECTIONS on the three Scripture readings of each Sunday Mass presented here are not intended to provide complete models for homilies or for personal meditation. Their purpose is to provide stimuli for homilies or personal meditation, stimuli among which each reader can choose according to taste. Above all I have attempted to draw the two readings (usually from the Old and New Testaments) and the Gospel into an inner coherence that seldom dawns on those attending a celebration of the Eucharist, since listeners may more often be confused than edified by hearing more than one text. As many people know, the passages from the Old Testament and the Gospel have for the most part been selected because they relate to each other. Since the second reading derives from a sequential reading of New Testament epistles, it occasionally is tangential to the line connecting the Gospel and the Old Testament reading. That explains the present attempt to lift out motifs that pervade all three readings and reveal an easily remembered thematic unity. Although the reflections thus provide for masses in which all three readings are heard, they can equally well be employed when only two are read. Given the purpose outlined above, the reader can understand why a more penetrating interpretation of the texts, including the Gospel readings, was not possible, although the attempt has been made to come to terms with the most important exegetical demands of each pericope. What is offered here is, of course, based on the assumption that even a homily directed at pastoral concerns of great immediacy will still be based on the readings that have been read, especially on the Gospel. Because the application of the readings will vary greatly depending on the age and character of those present, any such attempt at direct application has been avoided here in favor of emphasis on the central proclamations of the biblical revelation. In instances where the lectionary offers shorter versions of a reading, the reflection is always based on the full pericope, lest important themes fall into the cracks. Occasionally, however, even the full reading has been shaped in such a way that what follows or precedes it is essential to comprehension. In such instances we touch briefly on that which has been omitted from the lectionary selection. In any case, we offer here merely a quarry from which each person can cut to shape whatever suits his purpose.

— HANS URS VON BALTHASAR

YEAR A

[A] First Sunday of Advent

Isaiah 2:1–5; Romans 13:11–14;
Matthew 24:37–44 (29–44)

1. God comes. Before we can distinguish between God's first and second advent, we must grasp the comprehensive proclamation of Advent and the stringent warning it contains: God is underway toward us. This was the developing premonition that pervades the Old Covenant, which expected that the arrival of the Messiah would bring with it the End-Time. It was John the Baptist's direct premonition, for, according to all three of the synoptic Gospels, he wanted to do nothing else than prepare the way of the Lord in the wilderness and announce a divisive judgment: "Even now the axe is laid to the root of the trees" (Lk 3:9). That which would follow him would be God's final discernment of history. All three readings point toward this arrival of God: they want to rouse us from sleep and indifference, keep us on standby, dressed for action, awaiting the Lord with flaming torches or oil-filled lamps. In the second reading Paul is particularly insistent: one can see the signs of God's approach in one's own lifetime, because he has been drawing closer to us ever since the time of our conversion. The Gospel insists firmly on the sort of vigilance that does not try to study earthly circumstances for hints of God's coming, since God erupts into history vertically, from on high. Precisely because he comes at an hour when no one is expecting him, one has to be constantly expectant.

2. Expectancy. This necessary vigilance demands above all that one distinguish oneself from the routine of the unexpectant world. At most it has its own aims in mind, aims that have no real impact on daily patterns of "eating and drinking and marrying", since people normally do these things without the slightest awareness that God's advent might roll over them like the great Deluge. Paul calls this purely earthly activity "the works of darkness", because it is not oriented toward the dawning light. He does not devalue earthly things: eating and drinking continue but not "carousing and drunkenness"; marriage continues, but without "sexual excess and lust"; work in the fields and at the mill remains but "without quarreling and jealousy". Earthly life is regulated and restrained, reduced to necessities, when one expects God. This world's activity is sleep, and it is high time to awake from it. Awakening itself is light's dawning, an equipping of oneself with "armor of light" to fight the urge to doze off into the God-forsaken business of the world.

3. In the light of the Lord. Isaiah's great opening vision in the first reading reveals that those who expect God are a spiritual mountain whose light provides an orientation point for all nations. From this point alone can justice intervene in international strife, at this point alone is the incessant intra-worldly warfare quieted into God's peace, here alone can the world that by itself is darkened "walk in the light of the Lord". Of course, in the perspective of both Old and New Testaments, this does not take place without separation and judgment: one will be taken and the other left behind. For a deaf world, the very promise of a God who is coming contains a threat, yet a threat only in the sense of an admonition to be vigilant and ready. To the vigilant, God's advent is no cause for fear: at the advent of God "lift up your head, for your salvation is near" (Lk 21:28).

[A] Second Sunday of Advent

Isaiah 11:1–10; Romans 15:4–9;
Matthew 3:1–12

1. The Spirit-filled One. God now comes in an earthly form,
as a "shoot from the stump of Jesse". Yet his coming is a
unique and ultimate coming. According to the first reading,
three things characterize this advent: (1) the fullness of the
Lord's Spirit which enables the coming one (2) to exercise dis-
cerning judgment in favor of the helpless and poor against the
violent and wicked and (3) to complete a supra-terrestrial peace
that transforms all of nature and mankind. The Spirit of wisdom and knowledge that fills the One who comes is poured
out over the world so that the world is "filled with knowledge
of the Lord as water covers the sea". When he judges, the
Spirit-filled One practices that which he is and has; when he
fills the world with his Spirit he distributes what he is and has.
In the Bible, knowing God is no theoretical knowledge, rather,
it is a drenching of the entire being with inward understanding
of what God is. This knowledge is peace in God, participation
in God's peace.

2. Baptism with Spirit and fire. The Gospel portrays the forerunner in the midst of his activity. He prepares the way for
the coming One by hearing the confessions of sinners who
are being converted and by baptizing them into the advent of
the greater One who is to follow. They are being prepared for
the coming One; no one dare rely merely on the past, on ge-
nealogical membership among the descendants of Abraham.
The Baptist's words, "God can raise up children to Abraham
from these very stones" are oddly prophetic: for the Jews the
Gentile nations are stones, and the coming Spirit-filled One

can awaken them to become children of God. John falls down before him in the most profound humility, for he will baptize with the Holy Spirit and with fire rather than with water. He will baptize with fire that is God himself, with the fire of divine love, which he comes to "cast upon the earth", fire that will burn away all self-centeredness from souls. This same fire of love becomes a fiery judgment to those who will not love, who are chaff: "The chaff will he burn in an unquenchable fire." "God is a consuming fire", and whoever will not burn in the glow of his love will burn forever in that consuming fire. Love is far more than the morality of the Pharisees and Sadducees. Morality that does not fulfill itself and disappear into the Holy Spirit's fire of love will not survive the threshing-floor's winnowing.

3. "Accept one another." The flame of love brought by the Spirit-bearer flashes up over Israel to embrace the world. The chosen Jews and the hitherto unchosen Gentiles who are now admitted to God's people are brought into unity in this love. In the second reading Paul requires that both of these "accept each other"—because "Christ has accepted us", and because Christ has done so, for the same reason Jews and Gentiles must accept each other: to glorify the Creator who has created everything with reference to his Son. By fulfilling all prophecies in his earthly existence the Son makes present God's covenant righteousness, and also God's mercy toward all who know nothing of God's covenant. The Spirit-filled One whose advent Isaiah glimpsed will establish a genuinely divine peace on earth. If, as the prophet hoped, the nations should seek out this "shoot out of the stump of Jesse", the "Spirit of the knowledge of God" would also fill them, a Spirit in whose peace "shall be no harm or ruin".

[A] Third Sunday of Advent

Isaiah 35:1–6, 10; James 5:7–10;
Matthew 11:2–11

1. "Are you it?" It is part of the Baptist's approaching witness-to-the-death that even in prison he must put up with the darkness God has given him. He had expected a mighty One who would baptize with Spirit and fire. And now there appears in the Gospel this gentle One who "will not quench a smoldering wick" (Is 42:3). Jesus calms John's disquiet by showing him that the prophecy is being fulfilled in himself, in gentle miracles that still call for trusting faith: "Blessed is the man who finds no stumbling block in me." Perhaps the darkness that burdens John as a witness to Christ is the very reason why Jesus praises him to the crowd: he really is what he understood himself to be, the messenger sent in advance of Jesus to prepare the way. John referred to himself as a mere voice in the wilderness ringing out the marvel of the coming One. The least among those belonging to the coming Kingdom is greater than John, who assessed himself as belonging to the Old Covenant, yet, as "friend of the Bridegroom" he is showered with the light of new grace as he humbly makes way for Christ. On icons he joins Mary the Mother, who also comes from the Old Covenant yet steps across into the New Covenant, the two of them at the right and left hand of the world's Judge.

2. "The desert shall exult." In the first reading Isaiah describes the transformation of the desert into fertile fields at the coming of God. "See, here is your God!" The desert is the world that God has not yet visited, but now he is on his way. Blind, deaf, lame, and mute is the man whom God has not yet visited, yet now his senses open wide and his limbs loosen up. As the Psalms and the Wisdom literature depict, the idols people venerated instead of the living God are themselves blind, deaf, and dumb, and those who venerate them are their equals. These idol-worshipers had turned away from the living God, but now "those ransomed by the Lord shall return", shall be freed from spiritual death to find true life. After all, that is what Jesus is alluding to in today's Gospel when he describes his deeds.

3. Patience. But the return to God at his approach to us requires patient waiting, as James insists in the second reading. We are given the example of a farmer and the completely ordinary attitude his occupation requires. He awaits the fruit of the earth that grows of its own accord for him, produce that grows in a manner the farmer does not understand—according to one of Jesus' parables (Mk 4:27). The farmer does not try to conjure up the rain, rather "he waits patiently until the soil receives the winter and spring rains." James realizes that Christian patience is no leisurely waiting, realizes that it requires "strengthened hearts"—not through discipline for discipline's sake but "because the coming of the Lord is at hand". This is a patience that does not hurry anything, does not artificially accelerate things, but rather, in faith, faces up to everything God has decreed (cf. Is 28:16). If we know that "the judge is at the gate" we still have no right to throw the gate open. Wisely James refers impatient Christians who could not wait for the Lord's coming back to the prophets and their steady patience. One could just as properly point to Mary's patience as she awaited the Advent. A pregnant woman can and ought not hasten anything. The Church too is pregnant, but she does not know when she will give birth.

[A] Fourth Sunday of Advent

Isaiah 7:10–14; Romans 1:1–7;
Matthew 1:18–24

1. Mary in the twilight. Mary finally makes her appearance in
the Gospel, Mary, the door by which God will enter the world.
"She was found with child" even though she had never slept
with her betrothed. She is the vessel of tranquility and thus
she is not the one to announce the wordless affair taking place
between her and the Holy Spirit. Joseph, in whose house she
does not yet live, notices what is happening. It seems impossible that others would not also have noticed. Talk about her is
unavoidable, but she neither wishes to nor can silence it. People
will eventually come to the consensus, as the Gospel tells us,
that the child is Joseph's. Yet something about this child does
not quite make sense. God is not in a hurry. Decades later the
Gospels will cast light on the secret. For the time being Joseph
remains unenlightened and filled with the most profound disquiet. How could he on his own have come up with the idea
that God himself was underway within his bride? Joseph's plans
to divorce her quietly correspond to Mary's quietness. Yet he
would thereby expose her to shame. Thus, at the last moment,
he is enlightened and instructed to take Mary to himself. God
has time.

2. Jesus in the twilight. The second reading, from the opening of the letter to the Romans, has embarrassed many readers. Considered "according to the flesh to be a descendant
of David", only "by his Resurrection from the dead" is Jesus
viewed as "the Son of God in power". Yet both assertions agree
completely: as the son of David he is Israel's Messiah; only after the Resurrection, after stooping to life on earth, after his

slave's obedience unto death on the Cross, does he reveal himself as "the Son of God in power". In light of his unheard of teaching and miraculous power people are uneasy: "Is that not the carpenter, the son of Mary and the brother of James, Joses, Judas, and Simon?" (Mk 6:3). "Is that Joseph's son? Did we not know his father and his mother?" (Jn 6:42). When he "set himself equal to God", that alone was cause enough to seek to kill him (Jn 5:17–18) and eventually to murder him. "He ought to die, because he made himself the Son of God" (Jn 19:7). The Father does not intervene. It is all part of the divine plan. God has time.

3. The prophecy in twilight. The prophecy in the first reading has been called the most controverted passage in the Bible (Buber). In it God offers to give King Ahaz a sign; he refuses it because he does not want to tempt God. Isaiah scolds him for that and God gives him a sign anyway. No exegete has succeeded in unraveling the meaning of the sign itself. Who is the young woman or virgin (the word can mean either)? Who is the child who is to be called Immanuel, "God-with-us"? Is that a prophecy of salvation or damnation? God has time. Not until the Greek translation of the Old Testament, long before Christ, do we find a clear reference to a virgin, together with the clear expectation that the "God-with-us" refers to the awaited Messiah. And only after the unpretentious event took place in Nazareth did the ultimate meaning of the prophecy become clear. Later still the Gospel writers discovered the true coherence of it all through the Spirit's illumination. Even when revealing the meaning of his word God is unhurried.

[ABC] Christmas, Vigil Mass

Isaiah 62:1–5; Acts 13:16–17, 22–25;
Matthew 1:1–25

1. The promised king. The texts of the vigil Mass for Christmas center on the following theme: Israel's promised Redeemer will be its King. In the concept of a king two things are involved: the king representatively encompasses the nation yet also gives it transcendent meaning and direction. Three characteristics dominate the genealogy of Jesus as it is presented in the Gospel. First, it emphasizes Jesus' descent from David and his ancestry in Abraham, the founder of the nation and the nation's faith. Second, it underscores the reigns of Israel's kings in succession yet omits those who were wicked. Third, we find an unusual cluster of names of women and mothers: Tamar, Ruth, Bathsheba, ultimately, Mary. The Davidic line ends with "Joseph, the husband of Mary", from whom the Messiah descends. A Jewish father who acknowledges a child as his own is considered that child's legal father. Joseph does this, following the angel's instructions. That inserts Jesus into the royal line, and the Magi will then inquire about the "newborn King of the Jews".

2. The royal marriage. The text of the first reading also concentrates on this theme, connecting it with the theme of God's marriage with the chosen people, a marriage that shines like a light into the entire world, so that "all kings shall behold your radiant glory." In God's final turning toward Israel, which takes place in the sending of his Son, Israel becomes "a glorious crown in the hand of the Lord, a royal diadem held by your God". Yet this is no external bestowal of power, rather, it establishes an utterly intimate love affair as when a "young man marries a virgin" . . . "and as a bridegroom delights in his bride". The divine power that the nation takes to heart in Jesus, the power that permits it to partake of God's royal power, is the power of love, the love in which God pours all his matchless power into the creature who is thereby raised from a simple maiden to Queen: Jesus' humanity is just as worthy of worship as his divinity.

3. Homage. In the second reading Paul describes how men chosen by God behave in light of their having been graced by him. God alone has "exalted" the chosen people. Already as strangers in Egypt, Israel owed itself to his "outstretched arm". Then "he raised up David as your king." This exaltation stems from God alone, and it takes place in order that the one thereby exalted might "fulfill my every wish". Kingship by God's grace remains nothing but service to God. The King from David's line will fulfill this in that he, the King of the universe, is also the One who does "not his will but the will of the Father" in everything. This service comes to completion in the submissive attitude of the final forerunner, who declares himself unworthy to "unfasten the sandals on the feet" of the Highest King who will follow him. Even in Revelation it is those who have been exalted to royal dignity who are the most profound worshipers of the eternal King.

[ABC] Christmas, Mass at Midnight

Isaiah 9:1–6; Titus 2:11–14;
Luke 2:1–14

1. The sign of the child. For the central act of world history God's providence provides the requisite perfect constellation.

According to the Gospel, not only must the Messiah descend via Joseph from David's lineage, but he must also be born in David's city. The emperor's decree must obey this purpose. To satisfy the prophecy, "a child is born to us", the Messiah must be born as a child, and only because he is a child will his "dominion be vast". The child has to be born into earthly poverty (that there is no room at the inn is no accident) in order to partake of the world's poverty from the outset. And, even though all heavenly splendor spreads itself above the brutal poverty of stable and manger, the great hymn of praise merely serves to point simple folk toward an even poorer sign. There is only one proof that Israel's finest hour of consummation is at hand: "a child, wrapped in swaddling clothes, lying in a manger". In a sort of vertical universality complete unity and reciprocity rule the most sumptuous splendor above and the crassest poverty below.

2. *Warfare is crushed.* Immense messianic joy sounds forth in Isaiah's prophecy found in the first reading, as light shines on mankind dwelling in darkness. Humanity rejoices at the birth of the child as one rejoices when receiving a festive gift. The child is "born *for us*" and is "given *to us*". Everything he will be and do is "for us". The prophecies about the Messiah "on David's throne" that are now fulfilled tell us that unimaginable peace and perfect covenantal righteousness have finally dawned "now and forever". Because it has the power to eliminate warfare, such a peace was previously unimaginable; in order to eliminate warfare, the new ruler must carry both the name "God-Hero" and "Prince of Peace". And Jesus will say that he has come both to bring peace and the sword, but a sword whose power and task it is to destroy war and bring about "peace forever". This is a new kind of universality that exceeds all the powers and abilities of men: warring on behalf

of the child will be the path to his Kingdom of peace. "Death is swallowed up in victory" (1 Cor 15:54) and war is consumed by peace.

3. "To save all men." The final, horizontal, universality is announced in the second reading, from Titus. It expands the messianism of the child beyond Israel to reach all mankind. The "people cleansed for God himself" will no longer be one nation among many. Instead, all people anywhere in the world who decide to leave behind wickedness in order to follow Christ will belong to that "cleansed people". Thus it is that, here at Christmas, our glance is directed toward the Cross, toward Jesus' surrender of himself "for us [*pro nobis*], to redeem us from all unrighteousness" (v. 14). God's descent into poverty at Christmas is merely the conductor's "upbeat" for what would be completed on the Cross and at Easter—not merely the redemption of Israel but the salvation of all mankind. As the Church Fathers put it: "To be able to die he became man."

[ABC] Christmas, Mass at Dawn

Isaiah 62:11–12; Titus 3:4–7;
Luke 2:15–20

1. The confirmation. In the Gospel the shepherds obey the angel's instructions. It is not enough that they believe the angel's announcement is true, rather, they must also confirm it in their own experience. The entire story deals with this confirmation: first the decision they reach among themselves: "Come, let us go over to Bethlehem and see this event." Then, having confirmed things for themselves, they tell what they have experienced so that their own confirmation becomes a confirmation for those who had heard the angel and heavenly choir. Thus not only the shepherds but "all who heard of it were astonished at the report given them by the shepherds." Finally, as the shepherds return home, we are once more reminded explicitly that they thanked God both for the angelic apparition and their experience at the manger, "because all they had heard and seen" was "in accord with what had been told them". If we pay a bit of attention in our Christian life, we will find that we are not asked merely for naked faith, but that we continually receive confirmation that faith makes sense, that we are on the right path of God even in the midst of drab routine. Since such confirmations may be quiet and plain, a person who is expecting a tangible sign may not see God's nod. That is why he should imitate Mary, who reflected on all that had happened.

2. *"And she reflected on these things."* Mary treasures everything in her heart. She forgets nothing that has to do with the child. She knows that everything has meaning for her and for her mission. If one holds on to all the threads, in the end everything that takes place within a Christian's lifetime will yield a meaningful fabric. If one preserves what has happened and tries to extract its deeper meaning, he will not be unprepared for the unexpected. Mary's ongoing contemplation of every event in her child's life is not without significance for the constant renewal and deepening of her Yes—all the way to the Cross.

3. *"Justified by grace."* Both of the first two readings reveal how much the confirmations we experience are pure gifts of God. Our own deeds and striving would yield nothing if we did not have the grace, through the sacraments and renewal in the Holy Spirit, to receive and perceive God's "mercy". All of our existence is so permeated by his grace that we cannot merely look

lazily and haphazardly toward a life after death but must, in firm Christian "hope", anticipate "eternal life" with the living God. And the daughter of Zion is told that she should look forward to the coming salvation as an already accomplished reality. For she too is given confirmation: already she can see the first of God's trophies preceding him, "the redeemed of the Lord". For the people of the Old Covenant this meant that the prophets constantly confirmed that God really was on his way to us. For the Church this means that the saints within her tell her that God's Word in Jesus Christ makes sense— it can be and is lived. From this confirmation Christian hope draws strength.

[ABC] Christmas, Mass during the Day

Isaiah 52:7–10; Hebrews 1:1–6;
John 1:1–18

1. In the beginning the Word becomes flesh. The complete fullness of the divine plan of salvation is spread out before us in the powerful prologue to John's Gospel. To be sure we find within the story the witness who, as forerunner, points to that which is greatest, but what is greatest is the entry into the world of the One who was with God at the beginning before the whole world and who, as God, created, brought to life, and enlightened everything in the world. Christmas is not an event within history but is rather the invasion of time by eternity. So too Easter is not merely an event within history but is the Resurrected One's exodus from history into eternity. The law given through Moses was within history, but as a whole it too pointed ahead to the true expositor of God, to the "only one who is God and who has returned to the bosom of the

Father", the One who has "expounded" God exactly as he is, namely, as "grace and truth". Truth means "God is like that!" and grace means "God is pure love freely given." Today this First of All came into the world, into his own world, the world he created. Even if many do not recognize and receive him, those of us who do believe and love have been given the grace to receive him and, through him, in him, and with him, "to become children of God". Christmas is not only his birth, it must also be our birth from God with him.

2. *"Today I have begotten you."* The second reading, from the Letter to the Hebrews, speaks in similar language of the divinity of the Word made man. Where John emphasizes the Alpha more, here the accent is placed on the Omega: many words of God preceded this Incarnation. "In this, the final age", at the end of history, in the Omega, the Father has brought everything together in a single word. But this origin and consummation of all things is an event of "today". In God there is neither past nor present, only eternal Today, and this eternal Today becomes present in the temporal. That means not only that all the past, all that belongs to the Old Covenant, has always been the dawning of this Today, rather, it also means that, in God, the Today of the invasion of the eternal event can never become a matter of the past. The Now of God's coming into the world is not new and relevant merely at each recurring Christmas celebration, rather, there can be no moment of an ordinary day in which it is not a present reality. The feasts merely remind us forgetful people that God's arrival in history is always taking place right now. The Lord who is always coming remains constantly newly arriving, he never departs in order to come again. This is worth thinking about in regard to his eucharistic advent.

3. "All the ends of the earth will behold salvation." In the first reading the prophet adds two things: first, the existence of bearers of glad tidings who announce the Lord's coming. Without the messengers' constant cries and "shouts of joy" we might forget how real and immediate the Lord's coming is. The prophets were messengers, Holy Scripture is a messenger, and, in the Church, the saints and everyone who speaks under the Holy Spirit's leading are messengers. The second point is that the Church's message of joy is one that is open to the world. It is no secret doctrine learned in esoteric circles. Instead "the Lord bares his holy arm in the sight of all the nations, and all the ends of the earth will behold the salvation of our God." No part of Christ's revelation is hidden: Jesus will tell Pilate: "I have spoken publicly to the world, in synagogue and temple where all the Jews gather. I have said nothing in secret" (Jn 18:20). The depth of his revelation is, from the beginning, a "sacred open secret".

[A] Holy Family

Sirach 3:2–6, 12–14 (3–7, 14–17); Colossians 3:12–21; Matthew 2:13–15, 19–23

1. The bonds of love that hold a natural family together are modeled for us in the Gospel by a supernatural family in which the child is the Son of God. To that degree this unique union of husband, wife, and child is the norm for a normal earthly family's Christian life. The passage depicts above all *the father's* (and indirectly the mother's) *devotion* to the future of the child. All the instructions Joseph receives from the angel are aimed at the child's wellbeing. Nothing is said about how heavy a burden these commands place on the father. The orders are given in categorical terms: "Get up, take the child and his mother" (the child comes first) "and flee to Egypt." How you manage this is up to you; that you must give up your job matters not. We are told nothing of how Joseph reestablishes himself in Egypt and finds a way to provide for his family. In the story the next thing we hear is, once again for the sake of the child's wellbeing, a command to return, with precise instructions to avoid the region ruled by Archelaus, Herod's cruel son, and to settle in Nazareth. The foster-father serves the child and two future words of prophecy of which he had no notion: "Children ought not to save for their parents, but parents for their children" (2 Cor 12:14).

2. *The devotion of children* to their parents is such an obligation of gratitude that it is commanded as one of the ten chief commandments of the law. Jesus Sirach (in the first reading) describes this duty concretely yet with tenderness. Aging parents whose "minds fail" are to be cared for with respect; a son should not revile them "in the fullness of his strength". Whoever does not honor his parents will live in the fear that his own children will bring him no joy. Yet the command is elevated to acquire a religious component: love of parents brings about forgiveness of one's own sins, counts as "a sin offering", indeed, more than that, "whoever shows honor to his mother honors the Lord": behind the human parent stands God, without whose action no new human life can emerge. To conceive and bear children is a process possible only with God. That is why the grateful honoring of parents in the fourth commandment is inseparable from gratitude toward God. If, in the Gospel, the emphasis is on the obedience and obligation of the father, here the mother's care for the child is put on the same level.

3. *Reciprocity.* In the second reading, Paul reveals love's unity in the family. "Love one another", "forgive one another". Love

alone is the cord that holds the family together through all crises. And this takes place not merely on the level of natural feeling for each other, rather, "Whatever you do, whether in speech or in action, do it in the name of the Lord Jesus." Distinctions are made within the parents' mutual love: for husbands genuine love (like that of Christ for the Church, as the letter to the Ephesians specifies) without lust for domination or delusions of superiority is commanded; a corresponding obliging spirit is commanded for wives. The mutual love between parents and children is based on a remarkably profound psychology: children's obedience to parents is simply "the acceptable way in the Lord", who himself gave an example of this obedience (Lk 2:51). In contrast, the father is told exactly what to do: "Don't terrify your children, lest they lose heart." The purpose of unchallenged fatherly authority is to encourage the child's own courage for living, which, after all, is what the root meaning of *auctoritas* entails: augmentation, growth. The whole, delicate web of differentiated mutual love dare not be ripped apart: the Holy Family offers a model for successful achievement of that differentiated mutual love.

[ABC] January 1:
Mary, Mother of God
(Octave of Christmas)

Numbers 6:22–27; Galatians 4:4–7;
Luke 2:16–21

1. The blessing of the new year. The Old Testament's solemn formula of blessing in the first reading inaugurates the liturgy of the new civil year. The exact wording of this blessing was prescribed by God to Moses. Twice the blessing asks God to turn his face toward us and let its splendor shine upon us and thereby grant us grace and wholeness. That God looks at us is (according to Paul) much more salvific than that we see him ("He who loves God is known by him" [1 Cor 8:3]). According to Augustine, "to see the Seeing One" is the ultimate blessing (*"Videntem videre"*). At the same time, however, with limitless love the Mother of the Lord views us as her children and blesses us. In the New Testament this blessing cannot be separated from her Child's blessing and from the blessing of the entire triune God, so deeply is her motherhood grounded in and surrounded by divine fruitfulness. She blesses us both as the personal mother of Jesus and as the epitome of the "immaculate" Church (Eph 5:27) who is Jesus' bride.

2. Mary treasured all these things in her heart. The simple words of the Gospel about Mary treasuring all these things in her heart and reflecting on them are mentioned twice (Lk 2:19, 2:51). They show that she is the inexhaustible vessel of memory and exposition for the entire Church. She knows most profoundly about all the events and feasts of the Church that we celebrate throughout the year. This is also the significance of praying the Rosary: the mysteries of Christ must be considered and venerated through her eyes and her heart in order to understand them, as far as is possible, in their depths. And the devotion and feast of the Immaculate Heart of Mary is not something sentimental, rather, it is an entry into this inexhaustible source of understanding for all God's saving mysteries that affect the entire world and each of us specifically. To place the year under the protection of her motherhood means that we are asking her, as brothers and sisters of Jesus and therefore as Mary's children, for an enduring understanding of lasting discipleship of Jesus. Like the Church, whose core she is, she blesses us not in her own name but in the name of her Son, who in turn blesses us in the name of the Father and in the Holy Spirit.

3. The second reading places great emphasis on this *Holy Spirit.* It speaks of Mary as the woman through whom was born the Son who acquired divine sonship for us by his suffering. But because we are God's sons, "God sent the Spirit of his Son into our hearts, the Spirit who calls 'Abba! (Father!)'." If we did not have the Spirit and attitude of the Son we would not be children of the Father. It is this Spirit who permits us to shout to the Father gratefully, indeed, enthusiastically: "Yes, you really are our Father." But let us not forget that this Spirit was first sent to the Mother as the Spirit that brought her the Son, and thus as "Spirit of the Son" he is also the Spirit of the Father. Her rejoicing at this event, a joy that never ceases throughout the history of the Church, rings forth in the Mother's Magnificat. This is a prayer of praise that resounds to the Father entirely out of the "Spirit of the Son", a personal and at the same time ecclesial prayer that gathers up all thanksgiving from Abraham to the present. It is thus the best way to launch the new year.

[ABC] Second Sunday after Christmas

Sirach 24:1–4, 8–12 (1–4, 12–16); Ephesians 1:3–6, 15–18; John 1:1–18

ONCE AGAIN, AS IF TO DEEPEN the Christmas liturgy, we hear the most important texts of Scripture that center on the wonder of the Incarnation and peer into its profundity.

1. Wisdom dwells in Israel. God's wisdom, that is, God's entire plan of salvation for all of creation, constantly keeps the entirety of the world and its history in view but always accomplishes this universality out of the specific. Thus he directs his Wisdom, which is spread primarily over the entire creation, to find her "abode" within Israel and Israel's holy tent. God's Wisdom has been poured out over the entire creation and thus one ought not be surprised that many pious and God-seeking people have sought to honor God primarily in the marvelous order and beauty of the world, in the glory of the heavenly bodies (Wis 13:1–6). Yet only beginning with Israel has that same Wisdom become the ultimate self-revelation of God that finds its completion in Christ and his Church. Only the biblical religion knows of an Incarnation of God which in a unique way brings to light the deepest and most hidden Wisdom of God. Repeated incarnations in Gentile religions (Greek, Indian) are always relative incarnations that illuminate the being of the Absolute from a distance and can be supplemented by additional "Avatars".

2. *"Through the Word all things came into being."* According to the Gospel, in Jesus Christ the Creator-Word of God becomes "flesh", that is, a man like us. All things owe themselves to this Word but who it really is in truth is revealed to the world only if this most Universal becomes a single, specific, individual human person. This person had the power not merely to reveal to his fellow men by means of his entire existence that he is the all-creating Word of God, but to demonstrate that he is the eternal Word proceeding from his Origin and Father. No angel could have done that, for an angel cannot die, and the "word of the Cross" (1 Cor 1:18) was required to unveil the last mystery in God: that he is Love that extends all the way to giving up his most Beloved to death—out of love for the world (Jn 3:16). No religion has even distantly caught sight of this Word expressed in human form. True religion consists

in neither trying to become God (mysticism) nor persisting in creaturely distance from God (Judaism, Islam), rather, true religion is to attain supreme union with God precisely on the basis of the lasting distinction between Creator and creature.

3. The second reading clearly combines this into a *"praise of the glory of God's grace"*. From eternity creation by God's Word was the saving plan to incorporate us men, and with us the entire world, into the eternal Son's relationship of childhood to his Father—even though he had to pass through Incarnation and Cross to do this (Eph 1:7). This is so incomprehensible that the Apostle prays that we might receive the Holy Spirit in order to glimpse "how great a hope" we have been called to through the Son. No man could by himself have had any hint that such an incommensurate destiny was his. Only God's Spirit, which he has placed in our hearts, could make us bold enough to consider ourselves "heirs" of God's entire "glorious wealth". Here all thought simply must turn into a grateful hymn.

[ABC] Epiphany of the Lord

Isaiah 60:1–6; Ephesians 3:2–3, 5–6;
Matthew 2:1–12

DESPITE THE HEAVENLY HYMN OF PRAISE, the Christmas story was a quiet manifestation of God limited to a few. Yet it affected not only all of Israel, but the entire world. That is what is celebrated in today's solemnity: God's manifestation in the world is intended for the world as a whole, including specifically the Gentile nations who, unlike the Jews, had received no prophetic announcements, and who are now the first to arrive to pay homage.

1. The Gospel depicts the arrival of the *Gentile astrologers* who have seen the rising of the star of redemption and have followed it. Through an unusual star in the midst of customary constellations God sent a message to them that shocked them and made them ready to listen, while Israel had become so accustomed to God's Word that it had become deaf to such revelations, wishing not to be disturbed in the normal course of its dynasties. (So too it often is with the Church when a saint blindsides her with an unexpected message.) Directed at the Jews or the Church, the naïve inquiry of these outsiders: "Where is the newborn king of the Jews?" causes embarrassment, even fright. This results in a cleverly disguised plan of murder on the part of Herod, but, led by the star, the astrologers reach their goal: they pay homage and escape unharmed, led by God's providence. The event is symbolic, for it prefigures the election of the Gentiles—more than once Jesus will find greater faith among them than in Israel. Often it is converts, seldom welcomed, who reveal to the Church new and fruitful paths (cf. Acts 9:26–30).

2. "All from Sheba shall come." In the first reading Isaiah calls on Jerusalem to brighten up, since she seems unwilling to recognize her Redeemer. Thus he tells her, "Rise up in splendor, for your light has come." Jerusalem has no light of her own, even when she thinks she does, yet she shall see nations and kings coming with their treasures, not to her but to her light. And only in this light can she gather herself together out of the diaspora that has descended on her. She cannot reassemble herself by cutting herself off from the peoples who are now bringing her the "riches of the sea" from the most distant lands, rather, she can do this only in unity with them. What is brought together there will be a new people, the "Israel of God", over which Jerusalem will shine and feel her "heart throb". If "all from Sheba shall [now] come", this is now something other than the queen who traveled to find Solomon's wisdom, it is really a people of God chosen from all the nations of the earth and announced by the first arrivals, these astronomers who follow the light and pay homage to the child.

3. "Members of the same body." At heart Israel should have had some sense of the "secret plan" now revealed to Paul (in the second reading), namely, that ancient Israel would open itself to all peoples so that they might "share in the same promise in Christ Jesus" and be "co-heirs" with Israel. Yet, even though God told Abraham that the nations would be blessed in him, Israel did not grasp the hint and indeed resisted the "newborn King of the Jews". Only "through the Holy Spirit" was it revealed to the "apostles" and New Testament "prophets" that the ancient promise to Abraham and the even more ancient covenant of Noah with the entire creation were fulfilled in this newborn. It is in the Church of Christ that we first see what sort of star has risen and what kind of epiphany brightens the whole world.

[A] Baptism of the Lord

Isaiah 42:1–4, 6–7; Acts 10:34–38;
Matthew 3:13–17

1. "All righteousness." In the Gospel, John, the forerunner, shrinks from the task of baptizing the One whose coming he had proclaimed, but Jesus insists, because all righteousness must be fulfilled. This is the righteousness that God offered to his people in his covenant; it will be fulfilled if the chosen people return it to God perfectly. That is what is happening in this scene, where Jesus will become the perfecting covenant between God and mankind. But it will not happen without the involvement of Israel, which in faith has approached its Messiah and, in the symbolic figure of the Baptist, must bury its faith in God's act of grace. To the humble spirit of the Baptist it seemed quite fitting to leave the grace of fulfilling all righteousness entirely to God, but, if it is more fitting that his obedience be included, he "gives in". Thus, many years after the first epiphany through the homage of the astrologers, a second epiphany now follows—as the very heavens open up. The triune God confirms the fulfillment of the covenant: the voice of the Father reveals that Jesus is his beloved Son, and the Holy Spirit descends upon him to anoint him Messiah from heaven.

2. *Light over Israel.* In the text that has been chosen liturgically as the first reading, Isaiah speaks of God's chosen one who is not Israel in its entirety but a particular form within it. This is clearest where God says, "I . . . set you as a covenant of the people, a light for the nations." The covenant with Israel was established long ago but in the end was broken by Israel. Now this Chosen One is established to represent the covenant with Israel in a new and final way. Jesus is the epiphany of the completed covenant, he is God's Son and the son of a Jewish woman, God and man in unity, the perfected covenant that cannot be broken. As such he is both the light of all the Gentile nations and Israel's purpose in himself—to bring God's salvation to the ends of the earth. He will accomplish this mighty enlightening of the world in the humility and tranquility of a single man: he does not "shout", he uses no force, since he does not "quench the smoldering wick", but precisely in this peacefulness he does not tire until God's covenant-justice has penetrated all world history. He is the light that shines on Israel's

tragic history, but also on tragic world history as a whole. He is the One who "opens the eyes of the blind" and frees those who are captivated by themselves, who sit in darkness, to experience God's light.

3. In the second reading Peter testifies that Jesus' anointing with the Holy Spirit at his baptism by John was the upbeat not only for his activity within Israel, but *for mankind as a whole.* Peter says this after having baptized the Gentile centurion and after he has "in truth" grasped that "in every nation anyone who fears God is acceptable to him." Even Jesus' messianic activity within Israel, where he "went about doing good works and healing all who were in the grip of the devil, because God was with him", was already intended for the entire world, as the Gospels which report all of this show: they were written for all lands and all times. In the Baptist's baptizing Israel expands beyond itself. On the one hand it becomes the "friend of the Bridegroom" insofar as it rejoices to have helped Christ to find the worldwide Church as his Bride. On the other hand, Israel is willing "to decrease" in order that the friend might "increase" (Jn 3:29–30). In this humble "decreasing", Israel itself grows into the New Covenant and imitates Christ's "decrease" all the way to the Cross, which is tangibly visible in the beheading of John the Baptist.

[A] Second Sunday in Ordinary Time

Isaiah 49:3, 5–6; 1 Corinthians 1:1–3;
John 1:29–34

1. The witness. Jesus' baptism itself, to which two of today's readings refer, was considered last Sunday, which was also the first Sunday in Ordinary Time. In today's first reading Jesus is the beloved servant of God, who was "anointed" by the Spirit that descended upon him (anointing-chrismation-Christ-Messiah). Today's Gospel deals with John the Baptist's testimony to this event. It is so concerned with giving testimony that John the Gospel-writer, for whom "testimony" is a central concept (testimony of the Father, of Moses, of the Baptist, of the disciples for Jesus; Jesus' self-testimony), does not even mention the baptism itself. The Baptist is so intent on his testimony about the Greater One that he does not consider his own action worth mentioning: "He must increase, I must decrease" (Jn 3:30). All his action and being point to the future, to the being and action of Another; he himself is comprehensible only as a functional servant of another.

2. The situation of the testifier is odd. He probably knew Jesus as a man, who was his relative (according to Luke). If he nonetheless says "I knew him not" that must mean: I did not know that this unassuming son of a carpenter was the One Israel yearned for. He did not know that, but he has a threefold premonition of his own mission. First, he knows that the One coming after him is the important One, indeed, the only important One, since he "was here before me", that is, as One who comes from God's eternity. In that sense he knows of the *pro*visional nature of his mission as *fore*runner. (That he, the earlier, had received his mission already in his mother's womb from this later One, John does not know.) Second, John knows the content of his mission: that he and his water baptism were intended to acquaint Israel with the coming One. Thus he knows the content of his assignment even if he does not know the goal and completion of it. Third, he had received a criterion for recognizing the moment when this fulfillment began: the Spirit-Dove who descends and rests on the Chosen One.

With these three clues John can arrive at his total testimony: if he "was here before me" he must come from above, from God: "I testify: 'this is God's Son.'" If he is going to baptize with the Holy Spirit, then he is the One who will "take away the sins of the world as the Lamb of God". To have concluded this by the grace of God on the basis of the hints he had been given is the greatest achievement of the Baptist. He catches up with, indeed, he surpasses, Isaiah's prophecy: "I will make you a light to the nations, that my salvation may reach to the ends of the earth" (first reading).

3. The Baptist is a model for the witness of Christians, who, in another sense, are also forerunners and witnesses of the One who comes after them (cf. Lk 10:1). That is what Paul consecrates them to in the second reading. They know more of Jesus than John the Baptist did but they too must be satisfied with the clues they have been given, hints that are also promises. At the outset they know the One they testify of far less than they will someday come to know him in the course of carrying out their assignment. The better they carry out their mission the higher he will tower above their little deeds as the Always-Greater One. In the process they will realize their lack of importance and provisionality, but at the same time they will experience the joy that comes with being able, by grace, to help Christ's chief mission complete itself: "So this joy of mine has been made complete" (Jn 3:29).

[A] Third Sunday in Ordinary Time

Isaiah 8:23–9:3; 1 Corinthians 1:10–13, 17;
Matthew 4:12–23

1. The dawn of the light. Nothing is hurried. The light's rising
is gradual. In the Gospel, after the imprisonment of John the
Baptist, in proximity to whom Jesus had been active, Jesus first
withdraws to Nazareth (Luke 4 and the episode at Cana) and
then to Capernaum, since he had encountered resistance in
Nazareth. To Judaeans, with their zeal for the law and expectation that God's salvation would arrive in their land, Galilee
was a spiritually dark, half-Gentile region. Yet, accompanied
by "abundant joy" the light rose precisely over this "district of
the Gentiles" (first reading)—"can anything good come from
Nazareth?" (Jn 1:46)—rather than over the holy city. (Simi-
larly, it is often obscure corners of the earth that are the locus
of the activity of saints or apparitions of the Mother of God.)
That Jesus came from this half-Jewish, half-Gentile region and
began his ministry there is like a prophecy. Ultimately, however, both Jews and Gentiles have "dwelt in the land of gloom",
and only One can call himself the "light of the world" and the
"light of life" (Jn 8:12). The phrase "Rise up in splendor" (Is
60:1), directed at Jerusalem, is eschatological and was spoken
with the Messiah in mind. Those who returned home from the
Exile sobbed, "We look for light, and lo, darkness; for bright-
ness, but we walk in gloom!" (Is 59:9).

2. But Jesus, the dawning light, does not want to act alone.
Every man, even the God-man, is a fellow man. Thus he soon
has helpers and, at the outset, promises them that he will turn
them from mere fishermen to fishers of men. They follow him
without delay. For a while we do not see them acting on their

own, for they must first watch and learn to understand what he does. Only then can they proclaim the message of the Kingdom of God (of the "Kingdom of heaven") and through it heal men of their afflictions. They are present in contemplation in order that soon thereafter they might be sent out actively to accomplish Jesus' purposes (cf. Mk 3:14–15).

3. The assignments that they soon receive are both all alike and yet suited to each individual. In the community into which Jesus calls the disciples there is neither collectivism nor individualism. Paul drives home *the sense of unity* within the Church (in the second reading), even if elsewhere (Rom 12; 1 Cor 12) he emphasizes the specificity of the task given to each individual. "Quarreling" and "factions" that oppose each other and name themselves after specific leaders are to be completely excluded from the Church. "Has Christ then been divided into parts?" The stories of the calling of the disciples show that, for the sake of a single Christ, all who are called leave everything behind, including their former individual opinions, and, looking toward him, their only leader, are of one spirit. To accompany Christ will in the end necessarily mean the way of the Cross. If quarreling and strife dominate this path, the "Cross of Christ will be emptied of its power" (1 Cor 1:17).

[A] Fourth Sunday in Ordinary Time

Zephaniah 2:3, 3:12–13; 1 Corinthians 1:26–31;
Matthew 5:1–12

THE THREE SCRIPTURE READINGS fit together unusually well. In the center stands the Gospel, with the beatitudes—which can be understood only from the perspective of the form and destiny of Christ. The first reading reveals the prehistory that Jesus takes up and completes; the second reading reveals later history in the Church, which God has expressly shaped according to the archetype of Christ.

1. Christ and the beatitudes. Christ's teaching in the Gospel is directed specifically to his disciples, in other words, to those who are ready not only to listen to him but to accompany him. The ninth beatitude (Mt 5:11–12a) addresses them directly. What Jesus says here in programmatic fashion is no generalized morality that anyone could understand, rather, it is the pure expression of his most personal mission and destiny. He is the one who has become poor for our sake, who weeps over Jerusalem. He is the nonviolent one against whom all the world's violence rages and is shattered. He is the one who hungers and thirsts for God's justice, who reveals and accomplishes God's compassion on earth. He has the pure heart that always sees the Father; he is, as Paul says, "our peace" by virtue of having destroyed enmity with his crucified body (Eph 2:14–17). He is the one who is persecuted by the entire world because he has incarnated God's righteousness. In all of these he is the blessed one because he perfectly incarnates and mediates the salvation God intends for the world. He exults in this even in the midst of tribulation in the world (Lk 10:21) and he will eternally exult in this as the One who returns to the Father with his mission accomplished. He begins his ministry of proclamation with a self-portrait that invites his listeners to follow him.

2. The poor of Yahweh. The disciples could have understood none of this had they not had a preunderstanding of it, however incomplete. The Old Covenant was able to accept both poverty and wealth from God; each had its relative advantages

(Prov 30:8). Yet Israel did not think in a Stoic manner (see the first reading). Israel understood wealth as value and poverty as lack of value, yet Israel always understood more fully that the poor have the advantage of hoping and expecting everything from God, whereas the rich run the risk of relying on their own goods, oppressing the poor out of greed, and (like Ahab) robbing the poor of what little they possess. Already the law—even more so the prophets—excoriates such attitudes as violations of the covenant. The Wisdom literature and the later Psalms point to the perishability of all earthly goods, a point Jesus develops radically in his parable of the rich farmer. But the Old Covenant knows nothing of voluntary poverty, even as it knows nothing of voluntary mourning, voluntary renunciation of all violence etc. The widow's mite that Jesus marveled at was not a token of voluntary poverty (in the sense of the evangelical counsels [see Mt 19]), rather, it was an expression of spontaneous love of God and neighbor lived out of a radical understanding of the chief commandment.

3. Following Jesus. The second reading shows with precision what it means to follow Christ in his Beatitudes-existence. Paul lists the elements: foolishness (in contrast to intellectual wealth of wisdom), weakness (that cannot defend itself against overwhelming power), lowliness (that can never become sophisticated and distinguished), in sum: nothingness, that is, apparent worthlessness in every respect. God has chosen all of this in order to equate it to the wisdom of the Cross of Christ, who has overcome all worldly powers and forces in the power of his weakness. To "glory in the Lord" (Jer 9:23) means here precisely "to glory in the Cross of Christ" (Gal 6:14). The disciples who were listening to the Beatitudes would have to learn this gradually as they experienced Christ's Passion and Resurrection and the sending of the Holy Spirit.

[A] Fifth Sunday in Ordinary Time

Isaiah 58:6–10; 1 Corinthians 2:1–5;
Matthew 5:13–16

1. Three metaphors. The Gospel gives three images in a row, each of which is introduced when Jesus addresses his disciples with the words, "You are". This descriptive form carries with it, as the rest of the passage shows, a prescriptive implication: "You ought to be this", indeed, you must be this if you are to avoid "being thrown out". The metaphors are very simple and would enlighten anyone. All three have something in common. Salt does not exist for itself, but to season things; light does not exist for itself, but to brighten its surroundings; the city on a hill is constructed to be a visible orientation point for others. The excellence of each lies in its potential to give something to some other being. This theme, which was self-evident to Jesus, is itself expressed in the first reading, where light is mentioned twice and noonday once: light rises where someone shares bread with a hungry person, clothes the naked, takes the homeless into his house. In the second reading the Apostle's light and seasoning power is announced when he says that he "knows nothing" and wants to proclaim nothing "except the Crucified One". That is his spiritual gift.

2. Misguidedness. Jesus explains this when he mentions two of the three metaphors: the disciple who should be salty can go flat. In that case, he no longer seasons anything and the entire dish tastes flat to the community that surrounds him. When Jesus says, "you are", it can refer equally to the Church, or community, as a whole or to an individual Christian. A Christian who does not live out the Beatitudes, every single one of them, no longer radiates anything and should not be surprised if he is tossed out into the street and trampled on. In the parable of the vineyard, the vintner prunes the vine and throws the withered, fruitless branches away to be burned. Something of that sort can make a congregation, a church in one place, bloom—a sharp persecution may be the only means to restore its ability to give light and to season things. That is why Paul avoids spreading a false light through "sublimity of words or of wisdom" and chooses not to cloak his message with "persuasive words of wisdom", lest these induce the community not to build its faith on God's power and light. Were he to do that, instead of being a lightgiver in Jesus' sense, he would be inserting himself in light and thereby would do exactly what Jesus had in mind with the image of a man putting a basket over a lamp. Whoever places himself in the light immediately causes it to go out for lack of oxygen.

3. The purpose of radiance. So that men may "see goodness in your acts and give praise to your heavenly Father." A danger lurks in this: If people see our good works they might praise us as good, saintly Christians and then we would "have received our reward" (Mt 6:2, 5). Because he does not know Christ, the Old Testament righteous man runs this risk: "Your righteousness shall go before you and the glory of the Lord shall follow after you" (Is 58:8). But Christ never lets his light and wisdom shine forth from his own center. Instead he lets them radiate from the Father's light and wisdom. So too the Christian must always be inwardly aware that everything he is able to pass on comes from God for the benefit of others: "*Your* name be glorified, *your* will be done." Everyone who really prays (like the tax collector, not like the Pharisee), learns profoundly that he must shine forth as a whole, because God is the self-giving triune love within him. It is within this love that each person exists solely for the other and knows nothing of "being-for-oneself".

[A] Sixth Sunday in Ordinary Time

Sirach 15:15–20; 1 Corinthians 2:6–10;
Matthew 5:20–22, 27–28, 33–34, 37

1. The meaning of the law. At the beginning of the Gospel Jesus emphasizes that, far from doing away with the law given by God in the Old Testament, he fulfills the purpose God originally intended for the law. And he fulfills it down to the smallest detail, that is, down to the innermost meaning God intended for it. This purpose was given at Sinai: "You shall be holy as I am holy" (Lev 11:44). Jesus repeats it in the Sermon on the Mount: "Be perfect as your heavenly Father is perfect" (Mt 5:48). That is the point of the commandments: whoever wishes to be in a covenant relationship with God must match God's behavior and intent. All ten commandments say that. Jesus will show us that it is possible to fulfill the law and he will spend his entire life modeling its ultimate meaning for us, until "all (prophecy) has taken place"—all the way to the Cross and Resurrection. Thus we are not being asked to do the impossible, as the first reading explicitly says: "If you choose, you can keep the commandments;" "to do God's will" is nothing more than "loyalty", that is, our effort to respond in gratitude to what he offers. "The command which I enjoin on you to-day does not exceed your capabilities, it is not unreachable, . . . for my word is very near to you, it is in your heart" (Dt 30: 11, 14).

2. "But I say to you." In all these antitheses ("It was said to the ancients, but I say to you") Jesus certainly seems virtually

to replace the Old Covenant's law with a new law. But the
new law is nothing other than what is revealed by the ultimate
intent and consequences of the old law. Jesus eliminates the
rust with which man's laxity and a comfortable minimizing interpretation of the law has covered him, revealing the shining
purpose that God has already inserted into the law. For God
there never was any contrast between Sinai's law and Abraham's faith. To follow God's instructions is the same as the
obedience of faith. In their self-righteousness the "pharisees
and scribes" had not grasped this, and thus their "righteousness" had to be transcended in the direction of Abraham and,
more profoundly, of Jesus. The covenant is an offer of reconciliation between God and man. Therefore man must first
be reconciled with his neighbor before he can approach God.
God is eternally faithful in his covenant. Therefore marriage
between a man and woman should be a model of this faithfulness. God is truthful in his faithfulness. Therefore man should
stick to a true "yes" and "no". All of this has to do with an
ultimate decision: either I pursue myself and my success or
I pursue God and his service: death or life. "Before man are
life and death, whichever he chooses shall be given him" (first
reading).

3. Heaven or hell. The radicalism with which Jesus interprets
God's law brings access to the Kingdom of heaven (Mt 5:20)
or its loss, that is, hell (Mt 5:22, 29, 30). Whoever follows God
finds him and attains his Kingdom; whoever merely seeks his
perfection in the law, loses him—forever, if he persists at it.
In the second reading Paul says that the world does not know
this radicality: without the revelatory Spirit of God "no eye has
seen, no ear has heard" what God gives if one meets his expectation—"it has dawned on no one". But the Holy Spirit, "who
scrutinizes the depths of God" has revealed this to us, includ-

ing the depths of the grace that he offers us in his covenant-law: to become "like him" in his love and selflessness.

[A] Seventh Sunday in Ordinary Time

Leviticus 19:1–2, 17–18; 1 Corinthians 3:16–23;
Matthew 5:38–48

1. The catholicity of God. If God is love, he can hate nothing that he has created. The Book of Wisdom has already said this (Wis 1:6, 13–15). God's love cannot be led astray by man's hatred, aversion, and indifference: he lets his grace govern good and evil depending on whether men perceive his graces as sunshine or rain. He tolerates it when one accuses, scolds, or simply denies him, but he does not tolerate out of sublime indifference, for he is deeply affected by man's inclination toward him or aversion from him. If a man really rejects God's love, then it is not God who condemns him, rather he condemns himself by not recognizing and practicing what God is—Love. God's justice is not an "eye-for-eye, tooth-for-tooth" justice. Furthermore, a man who cannot transcend earthly punitive justice, as necessary as that justice is, has failed to understand God and therefore does not wish to be with God. God does not love halfway, he loves totally, which is the meaning of the word "catholic".

2. The catholicity of Jesus Christ. Jesus is the only Son of God and he makes known to us what he "has seen and heard" from the Father (Jn 3:32), namely, that God is not part love and part justice, rather, that he does not respond to the sinner's attack on him by retracting his love. Jesus portrays this in human terms when, refusing to counter force with force, he turns the other cheek in his Passion, when he travels the second mile, indeed all the miles, with sinners. He lets the soldiers take not only his cloak but also his tunic. All the force of sin rages over him precisely "because he made himself the Son of God" (Jn 19:7). But his nonresistance can outlast all earthly force. It would be a distortion to elevate Jesus' behavior to a political model, for it is clear (to him too) that public order cannot dispense with punitive force. (In his parables Jesus himself speaks of such force, for example, in Mt 12:29; Lk 14:31; Mt 22:7, 13 etc.). In this world of violence Christ portrays God's way of nonviolence, a way of meekness that he said was blessed for his followers (Mt 5:5) and which he invites them to practice.

3. The catholicity of the covenant. In the Old Testament love was primarily something for one's own clan (first reading, vv. 17–18) which constituted "one's neighbor" in that era. In Christ every man—for whom Christ lived and suffered—has become a neighbor. Therefore they too must follow Christ's example and surpass the limited sense of common humanity that characterizes the "tax collectors" and "Gentiles". In the second reading Paul reveals the form this covenant-catholicity takes. Christian wisdom realizes that it cannot be partisan, since, on account of the catholicity of redemption, all mankind, indeed the entire world, belongs to the Christian, yet it belongs to him precisely to the degree that he has made his own the catholicity of Christ, who himself reveals the Father's catholicity: "All these are yours, and you are Christ's, and Christ is God's." A Christian's true catholicity consists less in outward tolerance of developments than in an inner attitude: "Love your enemies, pray for those who persecute you, so that you might become sons of your Father in heaven."

[ABC] Ash Wednesday

Joel 2:12–18; 2 Corinthians 5:20–6:2;
Matthew 6:1–6, 16–18

1. The call to conversion and to a time of repentance issues (in the second reading) from the Church, whose spokesman is Paul, together with his collaborators: "We are ambassadors in Christ's stead: be reconciled with God." This has a dual meaning: Be reconciled to God both personally, each of you, and through us, the representatives of the Church. It is the "collaborators with God" who admonish us, who make us attentive: "Now is the time of grace! Now is the day of salvation!" Though we are free to repent whenever we will, obedience to the Church means that we do it now, within the framework of the liturgical year. The motivation the Church gives us is the action of God himself, who made his sinless Son "to be sin, so that in him we might become the very holiness of God". The enormity of the fact that Christ has on our behalf already taken the most extreme punishment upon himself should move us not to leave him isolated. It should also inspire us to rejoice that another has taken our place in representing sin before God —for not to rejoice at that would be a further enormity. Instead of leaving him alone, we should be moved to enter into his suffering for us, doing together with him what little we can do to atone for the world's sin.

2. Already the Old Covenant directed the people into a general period of "conversion" and atonement (first readings). Here too penance and fasting should be undertaken not as external actions but as an inner attitude: "Rend your hearts and not your garments." Here too it does not say "turn around for God's sake" but for our own sakes return to the gracious and merciful God. Here too there is a common liturgical activity: "Holy fasting" is viewed as the entire congregation's worshipful service (*Gottesdienst*) to God. Here too we find no magical attempt to manipulate God but rather a simple, intense prayer for divine compassion.

3. In the Gospel, *Jesus* does not eliminate this repentance, but ultimately shields it from being minimized by self-righteousness: everything must be shifted into the inner and invisible if it is to have meaning and value before God. Jesus' emphasis on utter invisibility toward the outside in each of his three admonitions (how we should give alms, pray, fast), an invisibility that will permit our action to retain its Christian purpose, by no means diminishes the necessity of doing these things. Instead the emphasis on invisibility underscores how welcome they are with the heavenly Father, who knows how to evaluate and reward them. Yet we do not repent in order to be rewarded by God, rather, we do it as a simple, grateful following of Christ and because we see clearly that the world in which we live cannot be profoundly helped in any other way than by our repentance. Jesus gives us three effective forms for this: alms, prayer, and fasting. One can fast in many ways: by abstaining from food, comforts of all sorts, sleep, or friends in order to give attention to the poor, needy, and handicapped, that is, those who cannot pay us back (Lk 14:14).

[A]   First Sunday of Lent

Genesis 2:7–9, 3:1–7; Romans 5:12–19;
Matthew 4:1–11

1. Temptation and fall. In the tale of the seduction of the first humans, the story of mankind's fall into sin (first reading) is explained as a temptation to be like God. The important elements of this narrative are, first of all, that God did not create his creature to be distant from him but to live in a relationship of grace-given friendship with him. Second, God must give a creature to whom he has given the most sublime gift (freedom), a chance to choose freely—one who has been "congealed" within the Good would not be free. And, even if God foreknew that man in this free choice would not resist the temptation to be like God, he also knew at a deeper level in his universal plan that the One whom he would send as his Son to face the same temptation would resist it and would thus, right in the midst of temptation, win the victory over temptation for all of mankind. The first humans fancied that knowledge of good *and* evil would make them more like God, but whoever wishes to search out "the depths of evil" (cf. Rev 2:24) loses taste for and knowledge of the good, which is God. Since the good is truth and evil is the lie (the serpent lies, the devil is the father of lies; Jn 8:44), sinful man falls into a deep ignorance.

2. Temptation and victory. The Gospel depicts Jesus' victory after forty days of fasting, that is, at a moment when naturally he was weakest and most vulnerable to temptation but supernaturally strongest and most confident of victory. His temptation is completely authentic—he experiences the excitement of evil not at the superficial level of sensual satisfaction but at the much deeper level of a temptation to disobey his divine mission. He could gain the favor of the masses by means of a spectacular miracle; he could gain power over the world (which he indeed will win for God) by going in on the deal offered by the one who presently is "the ruler of this world" (Jn 12:31; 1 Cor 2:6–8), but for this he would pay the price of being recognized as one of the same. No temptation was greater and more genuine, none more decisive for the fate of the world. Jesus, who recognizes in the temptation the power of evil as well as that of good (God), decides for the good out of genuine human freedom. Three of God's words from Scripture suffice to rob the devil's lying scriptural prooftexts of their force ("the devil can cite Scripture to suit his purpose", Shakespeare says). Obedience to God elevates free choice to perfect freedom.

3. The preponderance. By repeating the same thought five times, Paul shows (second reading) that the pervasiveness and even the intensification of sin in all mankind is outweighed by the obedience of the One who is no mere private individual, but who represents the entirety of humanity before God. His resistance to temptation, his perfect obedience, possesses such power that he brings "all mankind to acquittal". The statement is so categorical and universal that one might think that all men automatically become righteous through Christ's action. But that is not what Paul says. Rather, because of what Jesus has done, they are no longer slaves of sin but are offered the grace of righteousness, of being children of God. Instead of slavery to sin they receive the graciously given freedom to decide for righteousness. With that they also receive the freedom to choose to follow Christ in the time of penance that is coming.

[A] Second Sunday of Lent

Genesis 12:1–4; 2 Timothy 1:8–10;
Matthew 17:1–9

1. Traditionally the *account of the Transfiguration of Jesus* is read during Lent. This reminds us that this visible revelation of

Jesus' glory follows upon his having explained to his disciples that he was departing for Jerusalem to suffer and die. In addition, Luke reports that his conversation with Moses and Elijah centered on his approaching end in Jerusalem. Led by Peter, the disciples will face fear and flee, but even here, in the presence of unearthly revelation, they "fell prostrate, overcome with fear". In neither account does their fear keep them from grasping the essence of the event. On the mountain they experience the opening of heaven and an epiphany of the triune God—the Father points out his "beloved Son" to whom they are to listen, and the Holy Spirit, in the form of a bright cloud, draws them into the sphere of mystery. To truly hear and really be overshadowed will be their lot only after Easter. And Peter's fear during the Passion, similar to his confusion here when he wants to build booths, will only be removed by the Resurrected One's threefold question. In his letters Peter testifies to both events and to their interconnectedness (2 Pet 1:16ff.; 1 Pet 2:21ff.).

2. *Renunciation and fruitfulness.* In what happens to Abraham the first reading gives us something of a first, hidden hint of the Transfiguration and Passion. From the patriarch's utterly obedient willingness to leave everything he had—country, father's house, kinship—issues forth the promise of a universal blessing proceeding from his discipleship of God. Such a divine blessing can only radiate from a man who, for God's sake and following his direction, has left behind everything he owns. Otherwise the blessing would be restricted to him and his possessions, and his possessions would be secured and increased, as so often happened in the Old Testament and in blessings given to Israel. In the case of Abraham, however, we are told, "You will be a blessing". In perfect renunciation lies unrestricted fruitfulness. That is the insight and the title that

Israel places over its entire history, and it finds its perfect fulfillment in its Messiah.

3. "Bear your share of hardship with me for the gospel." These are
Paul's words to his "son" Timothy in the second reading. At
the time Paul was surrounded by suffering and doing without
as part of his deliberate following of Christ, the suffering and
resurrected One. God's plan to conquer death through Jesus'
suffering, to let "the light of immortal life" dawn in the darkness of God-forsakenness, became clear to the Church through
the Holy Spirit. From his conversion onward Paul understood
this unity well (the Transfigured One says: "I will show him
how much he must suffer for my name"; Acts 9:16). In the Acts
of the Apostles we see the entire Church realizing this; now
the generation after the Apostles, represented here by Timothy, and all subsequent generations, including our own, are to
understand it. The Transfiguration belongs in the middle of
Lent and the Passion belongs in the middle of the Transfiguration.

[A] Third Sunday of Lent

Exodus 17:3–7; Romans 5:1–2, 5–8;
John 4:5–42

NOTHING IS MORE IMPORTANT for a time of penance and fasting than the realization that God's grace precedes all our activity and that it was preceding our activity when we were still
sinners. Today all of the liturgical texts deal with this.

1. Water from the rock. Dying of thirst in the desert the people
grumble about Moses and, at a deeper level, at God himself.

This is clearly stated at the end of the first reading: the people did what was strictly forbidden, they challenged God, they "put him to the test". Likewise, in the wilderness the devil tries to seduce Jesus to commit this sin. Moses cries to the Lord; he sees no way out. God, who pursues his salvation-plan despite all human resistance, listens to the people's murmuring (how could one not be kind to someone dying of thirst) and makes water flow from the hardest, driest rock. In the march through the wilderness this constitutes an episode; in the New Testament text it becomes the central theme of salvation history.

2. "While we were still sinners." In the second reading the episode at the rock serves to buttress the Pauline teaching that we are blessed by God's grace apart from any merit of our own. Christ did not die for us because we were "good" and "righteous". Incredibly, he did it "when we were still sinners", while we were clamoring against God. Who would ever think of dying for an enemy? Only God would. He called us his "friends", that is, those for whom a man will die in order to prove his love (Jn 15:13). Yet it is only because of this death that we become friends, when "love is poured out into our hearts" from the wound in Jesus' side; when, from his spirit's surrender to death, the Holy Spirit is given.

3. Both readings prepare for the marvelous *conversation of Jesus with the Samaritan woman.* Her first encounter with grace is Jesus' request for something to drink. This is a gift that the sinner does not understand, even though she does not deny his request. We never find out whether Jesus received a drink from her. Second is the offer of living water, the heavenly gift of eternal life, which she cannot begin to comprehend. It is only the third grace that gains access to her closed heart: the confession that Jesus draws out of the woman through his own knowledge. This makes the woman open to the word of the "Prophet", which leads to a conversation about worship of God. In a few steps they have come to the theme of worship in spirit and truth and to the self-revelation of Jesus as God's Anointed One (Messiah). Here the water of grace has penetrated to the core of the sinful soul, cleansed it, and inspired it to apostolic activity. The woman's penance—admitting readily the guilt laid to her account—is almost meaningless in light of the grace that defines everything from the very beginning.

This finds such great confirmation in the Church that the true believer already considers his penance before God to be an effect of God's magnanimous grace. It is a "may", not a "must"; it is to take a few steps in the company of the Son who does penance for us all along his path of atonement.

[A] Fourth Sunday of Lent

*1 Samuel 16:1, 6–7, 10–13; Ephesians 5:8–14;
John 9:1–41*

1. "To make the blind see and the seeing blind." The Gospel's long and dramatically told story of the healing of a man born blind culminates in the following alternatives: whoever recognizes that he owes his sight (his faith) to Christ, ultimately enters the light through the pure grace of the Lord; whoever thinks he sees and believes on his own account, without owing it to grace, is already blind and will ultimately be blind. That is Jesus' parting shot at the Pharisees: "If you were [merely] blind that would be no sin. 'But we see', you say, 'and your sin remains'." The man who was blind from birth, who Jesus encounters at the outset, does not ask Jesus to make him see, nor does Jesus ask him if he wants to see. He is simply an object of demonstration in which God's power is to be made obvious. Then he slowly becomes a complete believer. Initially he obeys without understanding: "Go wash yourself. . . . And the man went off and washed." Then he has to face up to his healing without knowing who had healed him. When he faces the Pharisees he becomes bolder and confesses that he believes his healer to be a prophet and, when his parents reveal fear at his confession, he gains the courage to challenge his opponents ("Don't tell me you want to be his disciples too?"), indeed, he is prepared to be tossed out of the synagogue. With that he is ready to encounter Jesus and, when Jesus reveals who he is, to worship him in faith. From hopeless darkness he grows into the purest light of faith, entirely through the power of a gift of grace he never asked for; a faith whose logic he follows obediently, a faith that, like a mustard seed, grows in him until it becomes a huge tree.

2. When we consider in the first reading the events of the *choosing of David*, we find in them confirmation that the smallest one, the one of whom no one (neither Jesse nor Samuel) expected much, suddenly becomes the right one, the one chosen by God, the one who surpasses all his brothers. "Not as man sees does God see", the prophet seeking the one to be anointed king is told. "From that day on", not before, it reads, "the spirit of the Lord rushed upon David", a spirit that permitted him to develop into a symbol and ancestor of Jesus, a prophet who, in the tragedies of his old age anticipates something of the Passion of his descendant—much as the grace-gifted blind man was ultimately thrown out of the synagogue.

3. The second reading simply admonishes us to live as "*children of the light*". All of us have followed the path of the man born blind: "There was a time when you were in darkness, but now

[you are] light in the Lord", that is, through the Lord, who is the light of the world, you are taken up into his light, and therefore you must "live as children of the light". As such, like the man born blind, we should bring the darkened object to the Light and hand it over, so that, flooded with light, it can become visible and, if it lets itself be handed over, can itself become light. Here, as in the great narrative of the Gospel, it becomes clear that Jesus' light not only illumines but transforms what it illuminates into a light that radiates and enlightens alongside his light.

[A] Fifth Sunday of Lent

Ezekiel 37:12–14; Romans 8:8–11;
John 11:1–45

1. "I open your graves." As it comes closer to the Passion of Jesus, Lent raises the penitent sinner's hope to unmeasurable levels. Even if one is spiritually dead because of his guilt, the living God is greater than death and his power is mightier than any earthly decay. Nowhere in the Old Covenant is this expressed more completely than in the first reading, Ezekiel's vision of dry bones scattered in a field that are clothed with flesh and rise again to form a powerful army. Wisdom says that God "does not rejoice in the destruction of the living, for he fashioned all things that they might have being" (Wis 1:13b–14a). By turning away from the living God, Israel has hurled itself into death, but God's vitality is stronger and can give life and strength back to dead bones.

2. In the Old Covenant this is primarily a prophecy for the future of the people. It became an unhoped-for *reality through*

Christ's Resurrection. Now, in the second (Christian) reading, the matter at hand is the individual, who indeed must die but, on the basis of the Resurrection of Jesus and his Holy Spirit, has the sure hope that God will also "bring your mortal bodies to life" through this Spirit. The prerequisite, according to the Epistle, is that we let ourselves be led not by the flesh (meaning the worldly and perishing) but by the "Spirit of God" the Father and "of Christ". If that is so, the germ of divine, eternal life already lives in us with this Spirit and we hold a "down-payment", as it were, a ticket for admittance to God's life. Thus a Christian penitent making atonement for his sin, rather than being mournful, can be mysteriously joyful as he makes his way toward Life.

3. The raising of Lazarus from the dead is Jesus' last miracle before his Passion, and it becomes the immediate pretext for his arrest (Jn 11:47–56). The One who is making his way toward death wishes to stare death in the face in advance. That is why he deliberately lets Lazarus die despite the pleas of his friends. He wants to stand at the stone-sealed tomb of his friend and weep, "troubled, crestfallen, enraged" (however one decides to translate the word) at the fearful might of this "last enemy" (1 Cor 15:26), an enemy which can only be conquered utterly inwardly. Without these tears at the tomb Jesus would not be the man that he is. Then everything happens in rapid succession. First, the command to take away the stone, despite all protest. Then the prayer to the Father, for the Son still begs heaven for each of his miracles—they are never done by magic but by power granted him. Then the command: "Lazarus, come out!" His power over death is part of his mission, but it only becomes "authorization" for us if he himself dies, breathing out the Holy Spirit to God and to the Church. Death will no longer be the fate of the children of Adam, but becomes the revelation of God's ultimate devotion to humanity in Christ. Only because he dies this death of obedient love can he call himself the "Resurrection and the Life", and utter the death-surpassing words about himself: "Whoever believes in me shall come to life, even though he should die."

[A] Palm Sunday

Isaiah 50:4–7; Philippians 2:6–11;
Matthew 26:14–27:66

IF A HOMILY IS GIVEN, the first two readings could form the framework: Jesus does not shrink away, he stands firm against all the insults men hurl at him. That is his self-emptying even to death on the Cross, which takes place within history and makes him Lord of all history. What once happened in history —for the Passion is no myth, since it took place "under Pontius Pilate" on the firm ground of history—nonetheless makes visible what has been happening in the entire human tragedy, from beginning to end: God is "struck" and contemptuously "spat upon" as he humbles himself to the uttermost for us, as he takes our rubbish upon himself. A few main themes can be lifted out of the great Passion according to Matthew.

1. The meal. Jesus' eucharistic giving of himself takes place after he has pointed out the traitor (26:25) and thus in full view of the Passion that has already begun. It also takes place in full view of the fact that all his followers would take offense at him that night and fall away—Peter not excepted, indeed, precisely Peter would fail (26:30–35). Jesus knows that he must endure the entire business in complete loneliness, which is why the disciples fall asleep even in Gethsemane: prior to the completion of his Passion, he really has no following ("later you will follow me" [Jn 13:36]). The almost unbearable burden of the world's sin begins to weigh upon him in his lonely vigil as the Father begins to withdraw: overwhelmed he has to ask, "If it is possible, let this cup pass me by" (the cup is the Old Covenant's image for God's anger at sin). But the One who has already given himself eucharistically must, in accord with the Father's will, take upon himself the seemingly impossible, and he does it in our place, "for us".

2. *Betrayal and verdict.* The first betrayal is by a Christian, accompanied by an open repudiation on the part of the most trusted one, the spokesman of the coming Church; by refusal to believe that this gentle One can be the warlike Messiah expected by the Jews; by fear of really being taken for one of the disciples of the condemned One. The second betrayal is by the Jews: this man who claims to be the Messiah and Judge of the world (26:63–64) resembles not at all the image of a political Messiah that had been elaborated in what ultimately was a betrayal of the pure faith of Abraham. Just as Judas was thinking in Jewish terms when he betrayed Jesus, so the Jews are thinking in Gentile terms when they hand Jesus over to the Roman procurator. Now it is the chosen people who betray him. The arraignment before Pilate, the Gentile, can lead nowhere, since every form of mediation (through biblical revelation) is now lacking. Therefore Jesus, the Word of God, remains silent after his confession that he is "the king of the Jews". He neither can nor wants to halt, or even to steer, the fate that races toward him. It ends on the Cross where even the Father "abandons" him so that the suffering might be complete. Surrounded to the end by the world's mockery, he screams his last and sinks into death.

3. The end of the world. Only Matthew depicts the event of the Cross in eschatological hues: darkness, earthquake, open graves (although only after Jesus' Resurrection do the dead leave the tombs). The curtain in the temple is ripped open as a sign that Israel's sacrificial worship is a thing of the past. The Cross, which stands in the center of world history is simultaneously the end of world history: all history courses toward the Cross (Mt 24:30; Rev 1:7). It is here that the world's judgment takes place ("Now is the time of judgment come" [Jn 12:31]). Matthew's apocalyptic scene is not intended merely as colorful imagery, for in that death the world of death and the netherworld (Rev 1:18) are really unlocked, so that in the wake of Jesus' Resurrection mankind might be freed, to be "raised up with him" (Eph 2:6).

[ABC] Holy Thursday

Exodus 12:1–8, 11–14; 1 Corinthians 11:23–26;
John 13:1–15

THE LITURGY FOR THIS CELEBRATION is unusual in that the first reading describes the Old Testament prefiguration of the Lord's Supper, the eating of the passover lamb, while the second reading, taken from Paul's letters, describes the New Testament fulfillment of that prefiguration. Thus the Gospel need not retell the story of the institution of the Eucharist yet again but can concentrate on Jesus' inner attitude at his self-giving to Church and world. It does this through the gripping scene in which he washes feet. This drama, which certainly took place historically, opened the disciples' eyes to perceive what really did happen in the institution of the Eucharist and what really happens in each Eucharist celebrated since.

1. The paschal lamb. Each aspect of this mysterious report of
the passover meal (probably assembled from various elements)
was to be explicated by the Christian celebration with a view
toward the fulfillment of the passover meal. First, an "unblemished, male, young (year-old) lamb" was required as a sacrifice:
only the best is good enough, it can carry no blemish. Then,
the meal must be eaten "hastily" while dressed for the road. In
a Christian sense this can only mean eating while prepared to
depart from the mortal world to God, eating while prepared
to pass through the wilderness of death into the promised land
with God, rather than eating in comfort and carefree expectation of continuing the status quo into an earthly future. The
Christian Lamb is, after all, the Risen One who takes us up
into a "life hidden with Christ in God" (Col 3:3) into a sharing
of his Resurrection. Finally, the Lamb's blood is to be smeared
on our doorposts so that God's judgment might pass over us.
Only Christ's blood, if it is discovered on us, can save us from
the just judgment, for he has passed through the judging of
sins and as Savior has become our Judge.

2. The Eucharist. Paul reports what "was delivered" to him:
Jesus' prayer of thanksgiving over the bread: "This is my body
for you. Do this in remembrance of me." Likewise with the
cup, which "is the New Covenant in my blood". To this Paul
adds: each eucharistic meal is a "proclamation of the death of
the Lord". The Old Testament ceremony now receives its final, unfathomably profound meaning: "Body for you, covenant
in blood" speaks of a sacrifice of extreme love, extreme to the
point that the One sacrificing himself becomes food and drink
for those to whom he gives himself. Not only that, but it also
means transferring authority over this sacrifice to the recipient:
"Do this", not merely "receive this". The same thing will recur
on Easter when the Risen One will say: "Those whose sins you

forgive", instead of simply saying: "Receive forgiveness from me and my Father." What already pushes our imagination to the limit—that the God-man gives himself as food for eternal life to us, his murderers—is now to be surpassed: we are to carry out ourselves what has been done for us, we are to present the Son's sacrifice to the Father.

3. The footwashing. This "shows his love for them to the end" (Jn 13:1). This is an act of love that Peter understandably perceives as completely unacceptable, as turning the world upside down. Yet precisely this inversion is the most upright thing possible. One must first let it happen to himself, precisely as the Lord did it—in his incomparable love's humbling—before he can take it as "an example" (13:14) for himself and practice this self-abasement with the brethren. This is the Gospel's tangible demonstration of the subsequent passage's description of the mystery of the Eucharist: Christians should, like Christ himself, become edible food and potable drink for each other.

[ABC] Good Friday

Isaiah 52:13–53:12; Hebrews 4:14–16; 5:7–9; John 18:1–19:42

THE GREAT READINGS OF TODAY'S LITURGY encircle the central mystery of the Cross, which no human comprehension can exhaustively grasp. Yet all three approximations have one thing in common: that the inexhaustible marvel of love took place "for us". The Servant of God in the first reading suffered the outrage perpetrated upon him for us, for his people. The High Priest of the second reading offered himself to God in fear and tears that he might become the source of salvation for us. And the King of the Jews, as John's Passion account depicts him, "fulfilled" for us all that the Scriptures required, so that in the end he might, for the salvation of the world, found his Church in the outflow from his pierced side.

1. The Servant of Yahweh. That friends of God interceded to plead for their fellow men, especially for the chosen people, was a recurring motif in the history of Israel: Abraham interceded for the sinful city of Sodom; Moses spent forty days and nights before God's face doing penance for Israel's sin and begging God not to destroy it; prophets like Jeremiah and Ezekiel suffered greatly for their people. Yet no one suffered so deeply as the mysterious, nameless Servant of the first reading, the despised and all-forsaken "Man of sorrows", whom people thought struck down by God, who nonetheless "was crushed for our sins", and who "gave his life as an offering for sin". And this sacrifice is effective: "Through his wounds we are healed." This is a preview of the Crucified One, for the Servant cannot possibly be Israel atoning for its own sin. No, this is the Servant who is fully submissive to God, the One in whom God, and God alone, "finds favor"—for who else "would have given a second thought to his fate"? For centuries this Servant of God remained unknown and unregarded by Israel—until he found a name in the crucified servant of the Father.

2. The High Priest. In the Old Covenant the high priest dared enter the Holy of Holies once a year and sprinkle it with the sacrificial blood of an animal. Now, in the second reading, a much more sublime High Priest enters the true Holy of Holies (the Father's heaven) "with his own blood" (Heb 9:12), as both priest and sacrifice. For us he was led into human temptation, for us he begged God with "screams and tears" in human weakness, for us the Son who is eternally yielded to the Father "learned" the obedience of suffering on earth and thus became the "source of eternal salvation" for us. As the Son of God he had to accomplish that in order to achieve effectively the depth of obedient servanthood and obediently sacrificial service.

3. The King. In John's account of the Passion Jesus strides royally through his suffering. He voluntarily lets himself be taken away, sovereignly tells Annas that he had always spoken openly, acknowledges his kingship to Pilate, a kingship that consists in testifying to the truth, namely, in testifying with his blood that the Father has loved the world to the end. Pilate presents him as a guiltless king to the people, who shout "away with him!" "Shall I crucify your king?" Pilate asks, and, as he remands Jesus for execution, orders the inscription, "The King of the Jews", to be drawn up—and this unalterably and in the three world-languages of the day. The Cross is the royal throne from which Jesus "draws to himself" all men, from which he founds his Church by committing his Mother to the beloved disciple, who will introduce her into the fellowship of the Apostles. It is the royal throne from which he completes the founding of his Church by endowing her in his dying with his living Holy Spirit, which he will breathe on his disciples at Easter (Jn 20:22).

FROM DIFFERENT SIDES all three ways lead toward the "flaming mystery of the Cross" (*fulget crucis mysterium*), before which man can only fall down in worship, adoring the supreme revelation of God's love.

[ABC] Easter Vigil

Genesis 22:1–18; Exodus 14:15–15:1;
Matthew 28:1–10

1. With Jesus' death the word of God ends. In the weariness of Mary, pierced by every possible sword of suffering, the Church mutely holds vigil at the grave. All living faith, all living hope is deposited with God. No premature Alleluia sounds. The watching and waiting Church takes the time to recall the long path through all stages of salvation history that God has followed with his people since the creation of the world: *seven events* unfold before the Church's spiritual eyes. She sees salvation even in the most difficult of all events: in Abraham's sacrifice, in the narrow escape across the divided sea, in the homecoming from exile. And she understands that they were nothing but occurrences of grace. The sacrifice of Isaac ultimately confirmed both Abraham's obedience and God's promise; apparent submersion in the sea proved to be Israel's salvation and the burial of its enemies; exile itself was Israel's lengthy purification and return to God.

2. Thus, in the second reading, the Church recognizes that her own death in *baptism* is a dying with Jesus, a dying into eternal salvation in him, a dying into resurrection with him toward God, into a new sinless and deathless life. No mere ceremony can accomplish this miracle; only a genuine "co-crucifixion" with Christ of the old, sinful man, a co-crucifixion that permits a co-dying and co-burial to take place, can accomplish this. This is essentially a gift given by God to the person baptized, a gift that is also a lifelong challenge to make the gift come true in the Christian's existence. The two belong inseparably together if the gift given in Christ is to prevail in the

Christian's life: he must become what he is, he must unfold what he has. Thus the shift from Good Friday to Easter must be two things at once: joy at the most sublime gift and determination to keep one's baptismal promises. It is fitting to renew these promises while celebrating the Easter Vigil.

3. Only now can the holy women hear *the angel's message.* He invites the women to come closer and view the empty place where Jesus lay. "He is not here." No longer visible, tangible, confirmable in time and place—all this must be renounced. In all of world history no one has left so "empty a place" behind as did this person who was buried here only yesterday. He who entered history with such emphasis is no longer comprehensible within history. "He is risen, as he said", he has ripped open a hole in history that can never be filled in again. Thorough guarding of the grave could not prevent this opening and the more men try to fill it, to plug it up, the wider it gapes. Instead of this emptiness the women are given the joy of their message to the disciples, a joy that is further intensified when the Lord himself appears to them and renews the mission: "They should go to Galilee, where they will see me." There, where everything had begun, in the ordinariness of a secular calling, new life would begin. In the unpretentious begins the incomprehensibly unique.

[ABC] Easter Sunday

Acts 10:34–43; Colossians 3:1–4;
John 20:1–18

1. Church of men, Church of women. In the Gospel Mary Magdalen, the first person to see the open grave, rouses the two most important disciples: Peter (ecclesial office) and John (ecclesial love). Both disciples run there "together" yet not together, for, unburdened by the cares borne by Office, Love runs faster. Yet Love yields to Office when it comes to examining the tomb, and Peter thus becomes the first to view the cloth that had covered Jesus' head and establish that no theft had occurred. That is enough to permit Love to enter, who "sees and believes"—not precisely in the Resurrection, but in the correctness of all that has happened with Jesus. This is as far as the two symbolic representatives of the Church go—things have happened properly, faith in Jesus is justified despite all the opaqueness of the situation.

It is the woman for whom this first turns into genuine belief in the Resurrection. She does not "go home" but perseveres at the place where the dead One disappeared, searching for him. The empty place becomes luminous, measured off by the two angels at the head and foot. But this luminous emptiness is not enough for the Church's love—the forgiven woman here seems to represent the Woman herself, Mary the Mother: she has to have her one true Love. This she receives in Jesus' call, "Mary!" With that everything is more than complete—the sought-after corpse is the eternally Living One. But she dare not hold him, for he is on his way to the Father, and earth ought not hold him back. Instead it must consent. As it was with his Incarnation, so now with his return to the Father. This Yes turns into the happiness of the mission to the brethren; giving is more blessed than holding on. The Church is Woman at her most profound depths, as woman she embraces both ecclesial office and ecclesial love, which belong together. "The woman will encompass the man" (Jer 31:22).

2. *The office proclaims.* In the first reading Peter preaches about all of Jesus' activity. He can do this in a triumphal and lofty

manner only from the perspective of the Resurrection event. The Resurrection casts the decisive light on all that preceded it—equipped with the Holy Spirit and the power of God through baptism Jesus became the benefactor and Savior of all, and the Passion seems almost a prelude for the central act: the witness of the Resurrection. Witness is indeed essential, for the appearance of the Glorified One is no spectacle for "the entire nation", rather, it commissions the "predetermined witnesses" to "proclaim" the event "to the people". This opens up into a dual message: for the believers the Lord is "forgiveness of sins", for everyone he is "the one set apart by God as judge". The first Pope's sermon is the epitome of the good news and a summary of official teaching.

3. The Apostle explains. In the second reading Paul draws conclusions for Christian living. Christ's death and Resurrection, both of which took place for us, have involved us existentially: "You have died", "you have been raised up in company with Christ." Since everything coheres in him (Col 1:17), his movement accomplishes everything. Yet just as Christ's being was shaped by his obedience to the Father, so too our being is inseparable from our duty. For us, to be is to have our life hidden with Christ in God, snatched away from the world and thus not capable of display. Only if "Christ, our life, appears", can our hidden truth accompany him into the light. But since our being is also our duty and thus collects the freedom granted us, our efforts must be oriented toward heavenly things. Even when we have mundane things to carry out, we dare not become stuck on them, rather, our intention must aim at what already is our deepest truth, for it is ours now and does not first become so after death. In the gift of Easter lie the demands of Easter and even this is pure gift.

[A] Second Sunday of Easter

Acts 2:42–47; 1 Peter 1:3–9;
John 20:19–31

1. Confession and faith. The Gospel has two focal points: coming from the netherworld Jesus appears to the disciples and offers them heaven's great absolution for the world's sins, which he both bore and confessed on the Cross. Easter is the feast in which the Church is given authority to forgive every repented sin. To that end she receives the Holy Spirit from Jesus. Confession is not penance, rather, it is to be personally endowed with the forgiveness mediated through the Church, forgiveness that makes us as pure as "newborn infants" (1 Pet 2:2). But this must take place in a faith that permits God to work on oneself, not out of a defiance that insists on psychologically perceiving the effects. That is why the story of "doubting Thomas" follows. On behalf of all Christian generations to come he hears the words, "blessed are those who see not and yet believe" (Jn 20:29). What God is doing in us is much too large to fit in the small container of our experience.

2. Not seeing and yet rejoicing. Hence, in the second reading, Peter expresses remarkable praise for those who love the Lord without having seen him, specifically for those who love him in "indescribable and gloriously heavenly joy" rather than out of a burdensome faith. This indescribable and glorious joy streams forth from faith's devotion with no hint of a wish on the part of the Christian to reflect its glory back on himself. This is a faith that is supported by "living hope based on the Resurrection of Jesus Christ", a faith that is made stronger precisely for having endured earthly testing; a faith that reaches its "goal" when it follows the suffering and resurrected Lord. If one wishes to call the "indescribable joy" found in this faith a form of "experience", then it is an experience of the sort that has no desire to hold on to any of the joy for present enjoyment, but instead hastens on toward its "goal" by a lasting letting-go. We are not the ones who grasp Christ and anchor ourselves to him, rather, Christ has caught up with us and grasped us (cf. Phil 3:12).

3. In fellowship. This "experience" of a faith hurrying toward its goal of hope makes Christ essential in the Church's community. The first reading says exactly that. Thomas' doubt set him apart from the disciples' fellowship; Jesus reintegrated him into this community. It is a fellowship of "common prayer", common meals, and even common goods. At its deepest level this community's faith in Jesus Christ was held together by the commonly celebrated Eucharist, for it is here that the believers finally comprehend that this community is not something they have constructed by themselves on a purely human level, rather that it is an institution of the Lord. Only in him and through him do they together constitute the Church, in which each individual's faith is strengthened by the faith of all the others, like many strands twisted together to make one rope.

[A] Third Sunday of Easter

Acts 2:14, 22–28 (22–33); 1 Peter 1:17–21;
Luke 24:13–35

1. The exposition of Scripture. In the wondrous story of the disciples on their way to Emmaus we observe the Church's Resurrection-faith grow under Jesus' exegesis of himself. As the two disciples walk with a stranger, they speak of Jesus as merely a prophet (v. 19). Since this prophet has been executed and the reports from the women were not enough to lift their depression, Jesus takes up the Scriptures, which they ought to know. The question at hand is that of the Messiah himself, not a prophet. All three parts of the Scriptures—the law, the prophets, and the other books (which the Jews called "the Writings") form concentric circles around the Messiah's death and Resurrection. Everything prophetically related in the Scriptures points to the fact that suffering and death are not God's last word about mankind, rather, that the archetypal and ultimate Man, the Messiah, would bring all images into fulfilled truth in his person. Jesus had already told the Sadducees that God is a God of the living and not of the dead; in Jesus he proves himself to be "the Resurrection and the Life" (Jn 11:25). It is no exaggeration or *ex post facto*, artificial interpretation of the Old Covenant to bring this basic idea to light as the fundamental meaning of all the Scriptures up to that point —as Jesus does here and as the Church will continue to do. As if to verify this self-exegesis, the eucharistic blessing of the Bread (the true manna) and the disappearance of Jesus as he entrusts his Word and his Sacrament to the Church form the conclusion to the story.

2. The first reading reveals *the completed teaching* of the Church overwhelmed by the Spirit. Peter expounds it to the assembled peoples, and, to demonstrate the necessity of the Resurrection, he takes up a particularly impressive text from David's Psalms (Ps 16:8–11). In it the person praying expresses the "certain hope" that God would not abandon his body to the netherworld and to decay. It is incontrovertible that David himself has died; thus his confidence points ahead to the fulfillment of God's promise of life in the descendant promised to David. This Old Testament hope has now finally been fulfilled in the

descent of the Holy Spirit upon the Church (v. 33): "If the Spirit of him who raised Jesus from the dead dwells in you, then he who raised Christ from the dead will bring your mortal bodies to life also, through his Spirit dwelling in you" (Rom 8:11).

3. The second reading reaches yet farther afield, *to before the creation of the world.* After all, why has God created this vulnerable world that is subject to death? Unbelievers understandably see human life only as something "futile", senseless. Yet if Christian faith lets us know that God's saving plan was established already from the beginning of his creation; that creation made sense only because it rested on the precious blood of Christ, the Lamb without spot or blemish, chosen before the creation of the world. If this faith also insists that everything finds its meaning through the self-sacrifice of God's Son for the entire wretched creation, then not merely the Old Testament, but all of world history, indeed, the entire creation, follows a trajectory toward the event of redemption that transforms every sense of "senselessness" into faith and hope in God.

[A] Fourth Sunday of Easter

Acts 2:14, 36–41; 1 Peter 2:20–25;
John 10:1–10

1. In this part of the *Gospel of the Good Shepherd* one must pay attention to the central emphases: Jesus is the sole Shepherd of his sheep, hence they know him and follow him if he calls them (from among the larger throng in the sheepfold) and leads them to a rich pasture. He is the legitimate Shepherd, who does not climb over the fence to steal and slaughter like a thief or robber, rather, he enters by the proper gate, which, in another metaphor, he himself is. His sheep are recognizable by the fact that they all have an instinctive sense for the true Shepherd ("they will not follow a stranger, because they do not recognize his voice"), a sensitivity acquired from the unique tone of God's Word, a tone they encounter in Jesus. This Word sounds completely different from the clanging of purely human world views, religions, and ideologies, and Jesus knows that his claim is not comparable to any other. "I am the way, . . . no one comes to the Father except through me" (Jn 14:6); therefore all other ways and doors are false paths. He who claims all truth for himself must voice a divine intolerance for all paths invented by men, none of which leads to the eternally satisfying pasture, to the Father's house. Most people, who cannot see into the hearts of others, can and ought to be tolerant, for they are neither *the* shepherd nor *the* door. Instead of eclectically selecting any old path among many they should seek a feel for the genuine sound of the divine call and beg God for that feel. Of course the intolerance of Jesus' "I-am-words" has irritated the world ever since Christ, for the world contrasts the supposed arrogance of these words with its own doctrine of many paths and thereby of many truths. Yet God's truth is indivisible—precisely when it demonstrates itself to be absolute love. The Good Shepherd will give his life for his sheep; there is no higher, not even a comparable, truth.

2. The second reading connects the *word of the Cross* with the *word of the Shepherd* and thereby confirms what has just been said. By meekly enduring all manner of humiliation, by bearing our sins in his own body on the Cross, by not rising up in wrath against the suffering the world imposed on him, by obediently leaving everything to his Father (the "justly judging judge"), he has "healed" us and endowed us with the instinct

that permits us to hear his example as the genuine call of God. Through the most astonishing word that ever rang out in the world, the "word of the Cross" (1 Cor 1:18), we former "lost sheep" can orient ourselves to the true Shepherd and let him have oversight of our souls.

3. There is *certainty* in Jesus' call. It is unmistakable. Thus, in the first reading, Peter can challenge Israel to recognize the Messiah it crucified as the true Messiah. And the voice of the Church, carried by the Holy Spirit, "cuts to the heart". It is that striking because these listeners are targeted and touched by the prophetic voice of God. Just as the Good Shepherd's word calls and leads his own out from the crowd of other sheep, so the first Pope calls the intended ones "out of this corrupt generation", and does so with a level of success bestowed by God: "About three thousand people were baptized that day."

[A] Fifth Sunday of Easter

Acts 6:1–7; 1 Peter 2:4–9;
John 14:1–12

1. Jesus' departure and return. Now the Gospel readings begin to point to the Ascension and Pentecost. First, however, Jesus admonishes the disciples not to let themselves become confused: "Have faith in me!" Trust that I am doing what is best for you. Then he speaks with utter delicacy of his departure: I am going away, to prepare a place for you, and I shall come again to take you back with me, "that where I am, you may also be". That would be with the Father. The disciples are afraid of the great distance and ask how to find their way to the place.

Jesus' answer is exuberant: he himself is the way and there is no other. But he is much more than that: he is also the goal, for the Father to whom the way leads is in him, visible precisely for anyone who truly sees Jesus for who he is. He is surprised that, after such a long period of proximity, one of his disciples has not yet realized this. In Jesus, who is the Word of God, God the Father speaks to the world. Indeed, the Father does his deeds in him—the miracles, which really should bring anyone to believe that the Father is in the Son as the Son is in the Father. Yet now the earthly form of Jesus must disappear toward the Father, so that no one will confuse this form with God. Jesus will return in a form that cannot be misunderstood: he will return transparent with the glory of the Father. Prior to that, however, he will not leave his own as "orphans". Together with the Father he will live with them in a hidden way (Jn 14:23), yet in a way that permits him to reveal himself to them, and the Holy Spirit of God will give them the insight "that I am in my Father and you are in me and I in you" (v. 20). At the end comes the almost incomprehensible promise to the Church: if she believes in Jesus, she will do greater works than he has done. This refers not to outstanding miracles, but to the fact that there is reserved for the Church an effect on the world that Jesus himself did not wish to have. His task was action, failure, death. In failure and under persecution the Church will smash through all barriers erected against her.

2. The spiritual house. After Jesus' departure and the sending of the Holy Spirit upon the Church, God's living temple is constructed in the midst of humanity (in the second reading) and those who make up the "living stones" of this temple are at the same time the priests who officiate and worship within it, who are even called "royal" priests. Just as the temple at Jerusalem with its material sacrifices was the center of the old worship, so this new temple with its "spiritual sacrifices" is the center of redeemed humanity, constructed on the "chosen, living stone" Jesus Christ. Thus it necessarily shares in his destiny: to be both the cornerstone laid down by God and, in the sight of men, "the rock upon which one stumbles". The Church cannot escape this double destiny: to be a "sign that will be contradicted", set in place to be "the fall and the rise of many" (Lk 2:34).

3. Spiritual and worldly service. The first reading, which tells how the first deacons were set apart for service to the physical needs of the Church so that the Apostles "might concentrate on prayer and the ministry of the word", reveals the dimensions of the spiritual house erected on Christ. Just as the Son was true man sent to minister to men's needs, sicknesses, and spiritual problems even as he remained in contact with the Father in prayer and proclaimed the Father's Word constantly, so the various charisms and offices in the Church are distributed without sacrificing their unity. Reapplied to the Gospel this means that Christ returns to the Father without ceasing to be with his own in the world. He knows them ("they are in the world" [Jn 17:11]) and does not forget them in his prayer; the Spirit he sends them is the divine Spirit yet at the same time the spirit of sending, which guides and inspires the Church's mission.

[A] Sixth Sunday of Easter

Acts 8:5–8, 14–17; 1 Peter 3:15–18;
John 14:15–21

1. Baptism and Confirmation. The first reading might put us off a bit, since we learn from it that people were baptized in Samaria because they had accepted faith in God's Word, but that they did not receive the Holy Spirit with their baptism. Only when the Apostles came from Jerusalem did they receive the Holy Spirit through laying on of hands. Certainly this story does not deny that the Holy Spirit normally is given with baptism, but the story makes clear that Baptism and Confirmation are two different articulations of a single process and that the Church can count them as two sacraments. (Note also the theory of many of the Church Fathers that even heretics could grant valid baptism but could not thereby convey the Holy Spirit; today we no longer share this viewpoint.) Moreover, through Peter and John unity between the newly baptized in Samaria and the Church as a whole was established: for the Jews Samaria was a heretical land.

2. The Spirit of truth. In the Gospel, the Jesus who is leaving behind visible appearance promises "the Spirit of truth" to those who remain in his love. Jesus had called himself "the truth" insofar as the Father's being is perfectly and finally explicated in him, in his life, death, and Resurrection. Only Jesus' human destiny could verify the unheard-of assertion that "God is love" (1 Jn 4:8, 16) and love alone, that all the other characteristics of God are forms and aspects of love. Until the "Spirit of truth" was sent down upon them the disciples could not grasp this truth, a truth that Christ is and lives in front of them. "On that day you will know", Jesus tells them, the unity of love between Father and Son and the unity between Christ and loving man. The Spirit is this unity and creates this unity. The Spirit requires only that men embraced by God's love themselves live entirely for love, for they could be taken up by the Spirit into divine love in no other way. Grace always contains the demand that one receive it and correspond to it.

3. Giving account. What the second reading requires of the Christian—that he "be ready to reply to anyone who asks him about the hope that fills him"—is nothing more than the consequence of what was said in the Gospel. The Christian must indicate by his life that the Spirit of truth inspires him in everything. This takes place not through haughty assertions that one possesses the truth, rather, our reply to those who search us out should be "gentle and respectful". Gentle because we are not proprietors of the truth that has been given to us; respectful, because we must show the necessary respect for the other person's viewpoint and search for truth. And above all, the accounting of our faith that we are to give will not consist in disputatiousness and pertinacity. Instead it should consist of two things: "good conduct" which will silence the stranger's "libel", and in "suffering" for the sake of truth, because thereby we are more and more conformed to the truth we profess. Jesus, who was innocent (which we are not), died for the unrighteous. By imitating him we give the best witness for him. And this witness can ultimately cost us the "flesh", that is, earthly life;[1] precisely therein, together with the witness of Jesus, we are "brought to life in the Spirit".

[A] Ascension

Acts 1:1–11; Ephesians 1:17–23;
Matthew 28:16–20

1. Ascension and mission. The first reading really contains the Gospel. The forty days of the Resurrected One's appearances were a mysterious transition between Jesus' earthly life and death and his exaltation to the Father. Already from the be-

---

[1] Von Balthasar is playing on the fact that the Greek word from which the English "martyr" is derived simply means witness—TRANS.

ginning of his life he was the Spirit-conceived and Spirit-filled One: the selection of the Twelve took place expressly in the Holy Spirit (Acts 1:2). Now he is the One who is completely pneumatically transfigured, the "second Adam from heaven" (1 Cor 15:47), who, on his way to the Father, will become the "lifegiving Spirit" (v. 45) for the Church. While his disciples, who have not yet received the Spirit, are concerned about the "kingdom for Israel" and the time of its coming, Jesus is concerned solely with the "Kingdom of God" (Acts 1:4), which the disciples are to proclaim, in the Holy Spirit, "to the ends of the earth" (Acts 1:9). The disciples' concentration on the arrival of the kingdom for Israel is swept away both by prayerful expectation of the Spirit and their mission to the whole world in the Spirit as "*my* witnesses". This inseparable combination—imploring God to send his Spirit and witnessing—will constitute the essence of the Church. As they gaze after the One who has disappeared, the angels steer them into the double task they have been given.

2. Power over everything and the Church. The second reading depicts the boundless power that God the Father has given the Son who has been taken up to heaven. Raising the dead, exaltation to the right hand of God, and endowment with power over every created force make up one and the same movement. And this is not merely within this world's passing age, but applies to the "future" world transfigured in God. One might think that such an unlimited grant of power to Christ would reduce the Church to a mere part, perhaps an insignificant part, of the realm Christ rules. If he rules over earthly powers, over politics, economics, culture, and religion, then the Church seems to be one among many great things, and a not particularly outstanding one at that. Yet, astonishingly, a distinction is made between the power of the Exalted One over the universe and his position as head of the Church, which is his body. It is not the universe that is his body (there is no "cosmic Christ"), rather the Church alone is his body. It is in the Church, through his sacraments, his Eucharist, his Word, his Spirit, and his mission, that he lives in the manner clarified by the image of body and soul. From this one can already glimpse the fact that the Church dare not exist closed off for herself, but must live openly for the world, which will be drawn into the fullness of Christ and of God through the Church.

3. Boundless authority for mission. Finally, this is confirmed by the Gospel, the radiant conclusion of Matthew. The Lord who appears here and is worshiped is already the Exalted One to whom "all power in heaven and on earth has been given". "Given" because he is the Son who receives everything from the Father, who, however, hands it over unconditionally. This fourfold "everything" encompasses every conceivable dimension and includes in itself the general "catholic" mission of the Church. "All power" is needed in order to give the comprehensive instruction: "to all nations". But the mission statement reads: to teach men to follow "all" that Jesus has said and done. Any sort of selectiveness in life and doctrine is thereby forbidden. This seemingly overwhelming mission is possible because the Lord is with those he sends "always, until the end of the age", thereby guaranteeing the completion of the mission.

[A] Seventh Sunday of Easter

Acts 1:12–14; 1 Peter 4:13–16;
John 17:1–11

1. Jesus' entreaty for the Spirit. In the light of the days leading up to Pentecost, we can view today's Gospel, which contains the beginning of the great prayer of Jesus at his departure from the world, as a prayer to the Father for the sending of the Holy Spirit. It is spoken just as he is making the transition from the world to the Father: "I am in the world no more, I come to you" (v. 11). Already "authority over all mankind has been given him" but at first Jesus could make known the name of the Father, and thereby eternal life, only to a few. Because Jesus is departing, they must be prayed for, and he does so in order that they truly understand what it means to be one with him as he is one with the Father. This understanding is possible only through the sending of the Spirit, and this, in turn, is possible only if Jesus has "finished" everything and breathed the Holy Spirit into his Church. Of course the prayer of Jesus was prayed before his Passion, but it retains its eternal validity since he is always an "advocate with the Father" for us (1 Jn 2:1). His advocacy includes the question of the Holy Spirit, whom he has promised to send to his own from the Father (Jn 15:26).

2. *The Church prays for the Spirit.* In the first reading the Church does what Jesus commanded her to do. Jesus' disciples, together with Mary, the women, and the brothers of Jesus, "persisted with one accord in prayer" for the promised Spirit. We dare not neglect these precise instructions from Jesus, as if we thought that someone who has been baptized and is not aware of having committed any serious sin automatically possesses the Holy Spirit. As *Holy* Spirit he can enter only someone who is "poor in spirit" (Mt 5:3), that is, someone who has emptied and opened up his own spirit to make room for the Spirit of God. The assembled community's prayer requests this poverty in order to make room for the riches of the Spirit. How exquisite that Mary, the perfectly poor vessel of the Holy Spirit, remains among those praying and fills out any incom-

plete or wavering prayer with her perfect prayer. Through her, supplication for heaven's gift is perfected, and that supplication will be infallibly heard.

3. The loving Church prays for the best. Peter's letter (second reading) adds a footnote. He repeats one of the Lord's Beatitudes: "Blessed are you if you are insulted for Jesus' name", and he adds immediately, "for the Spirit of glory, the Spirit of God, rests upon you." It is as if suffering humiliation for Christ's sake itself is a prayer for the Spirit that will immediately be heard, a prayer that indeed is answered in the suffering itself, so that one can endure it in the Spirit of God rather than in dejection or rebellion. What is shameful from an earthly perspective should not be perceived by the Christian as something to be "ashamed" of, rather, he should know that precisely therein he glorifies God. The Acts of the Apostles will confirm this at many points, as will the story of the saints throughout Church history. It is perhaps the persecuted and humiliated Church that can most purely pray for God's Spirit. She needs what she prays for and she has what she prays for.

[ABC] Pentecost

Acts 2:1–11; 1 Corinthians 12:3–7, 12–13; John 20:19–23

1. The *Pentecost event* described by the Acts of the Apostles (in the first reading) will remain incomprehensible to us unless we constantly keep in mind that the Holy Spirit who descends upon the Church is the Spirit of Jesus Christ as well as of God the Father. In other words, the Holy Spirit is the Spirit of the reciprocity of their love that reaches the point of complete interpenetration, a love that simultaneously bears its fruit, namely, the third Person in God. In the created order we have a distant analogy in the fact that married love between a man and a woman bears fruit in a child; every child is physical proof of consummated love, he is the "one body" formed by his parents.

The windstorm and fire with which God fills the Church and, with individual tongue-like flames, each of her members, is the proof of divine fruitfulness that God the Father and the Son give her. In the Spirit of divine fruitfulness she can from now on be fruitful, as was immediately demonstrated in the miraculous way all the peoples understood her language. This is the exact reversal of the *hubris* that led to the construction of the Tower of Babel, a haughty attempt of the human spirit to constitute a single international unity that would fly in the face of God's unity. (Look, they all have a single language, and this is only the beginning of what they might do! [Gen 11:6].) Now the single language of the Church, in which "God's mighty acts" are announced, becomes intelligible to all the nations through God's power. It has to dawn on everyone that this is not one language among many but towers alone above all the others, as God's Word and truth surpasses all the religious discoveries of mankind.

2. The second reading explains this explicitly. *The variety of graces*, powers, and services that are distributed by the triune God derive *from his unity* and point back to this unity. This is not a matter of the many human cultures that the progress of world history seeks—unsuccessfully, if one wishes to retain the peculiarities of each—to bring into an artificial unity. It is a unity of God the Father in the Son and in the Spirit, a unity that unfolds an already established inner fullness that permits each person equipped with a spiritual gift to serve the

purpose of that unity's completeness. This is illustrated by the metaphor of a body, which has many parts only because of its inner vitality. The body referred to here is both a spiritual body constituted by the Spirit and a corporal body belonging to the Incarnate Son. Both of these are inseparable: "For in one Spirit we were all baptized into one body." So also in the Church, inner spiritual life and external structure are inseparable.

3. Finally, the Gospel reveals the *source of this unity:* the Son of God became man not at his own whim but was borne through the Holy Spirit into the womb of the Virgin. From the outset he is both true man born of Mary and the bearer of the Spirit in his actions all the way to the Cross. There, where he obediently completed his entire mission, in death he breathes out his spirit, a spirit over which he has divine control as the One raised from the dead by the Father. Here he breathes the spirit of his unity with the Father into the Church in the quiet of a supper behind locked doors, a stillness that was the quiet forgiveness of personal sins. At Pentecost he will breathe out his unity in a windstorm and fire visible to all, public for the world and the Church. The Church possesses both dimensions: she works both in secret and in the public eye.

[A] Trinity Sunday

Exodus 34:4–6, 8–9; 2 Corinthians 13:11–13;
John 3:16–18

1. "Rich in kindness and fidelity." As the first reading shows, the Old Covenant knows nothing of God's inner mystery, of his triunity. But, as Moses illustrates here, it has an incomparably profound sense of God's inner freedom, mightiness, and abundant vitality, which is expressed in all of the qualities of God that are praised in this passage: he is "merciful, gracious, slow to anger, rich in kindness and fidelity". One can ask him to be so gracious as to go along with a man, to forgive him his sin and guilt. There is no hint here of the slightest trace of a magical grip on God's realm; we find only the reception of that which God is in himself, independent of mankind. He does not need a covenant with Israel in order to maintain these qualities. Rather, Israel surrenders itself to the God whose characteristics these are: "Let us be your own."

2. Trinity as a greeting. Jesus announced the inner mystery of God by distinguishing himself from the Father and yet proclaiming himself as having come from God, and also by distinguishing the Holy Spirit from himself and from the Father with utmost clarity, even though the Spirit is the linking of their mutual love. God's inner vitality, which is independent of the world, was known already to the Old Covenant. Through the Incarnation of the Son it not only became known to the world but the world came to share in it, not by being absorbed into God but by being permitted to enter into the eternal circuit of love in God. Of the many New Testament expressions praising God's threefold life, the second reading offers one of the clearest, one that originates in the "grace of Jesus Christ, the Lord". Total revelation of the Trinity begins with his grace, which consists in his having announced the "love of God" the Father to us with his entire existence, precisely in his Passion and death. Yet this would be too lofty and incomprehensible for us were we not also given "the fellowship of the Holy Spirit", that is, participation in this Spirit, through which we are introduced into the "depths of God", which he alone knows (1 Cor 2:10–12).

3. But only with the Gospel do we gain a faint glimpse of the *extent of divine love.* We would never have guessed that the eternal Father, who has already poured out and exhausted all his love in the Son he has begotten, nonetheless loves the created world so much that he could surrender his "much beloved Son" (Mt 3:17; 17:5) to the darkness of God-forsakenness and the utter torture of the Cross. This apparent senselessness acquires meaning only if the Son's sacrifice is simultaneously seen as his greatest glory: in the Son's having "loved to the end" (Jn 13:1), he manifests all of the Father's love; precisely in this sacrifice the two loves prove to be one—in the Holy Spirit. This love alone is, at the same time, the truth—"grace and truth" are one (Jn 1:14)—so that whoever does not let love take over excludes himself from the truth and thereby hands himself over to judgment. If the triune love is the sole absolute, he who rejects it condemns himself.

[A] Corpus Christi

Deuteronomy 8:2–3, 14–16; 1 Corinthians 10:16–17; John 6:51–58

1. The manna. Jesus' conversation with the Jews about the Eucharist explicitly takes its point of departure from the miracle of the manna that God gave to their forefathers. But in the first reading the miraculous food (water from the rock, manna from heaven) was only given to the people because they were nearly dead of hunger and thirst and their only remaining hope for sustenance was God. The first reading says expressly: "God wanted to test you (to test whether you put all your trust in him) by humbling you (by showing you your weakness)" before he gave you food and drink. Feeding the people with manna is thus understood as proof that "Man does not live by bread alone, but by every word that comes forth from the mouth of God." This physical food in the wilderness can only be understood as the Word of God and as a response to man's need. Only in the wilderness, in the "parched and waterless land", where man can no longer find any sustenance at all and is completely dependent on God, do the bread from heaven and the Word of God become identical.

2. "I am the living bread." The duality-in-unity of God's Word and God's bread is completed in the Gospel through a much greater miracle, in Jesus Christ, who claims that he himself is this unity. This unity-distinction of God's Word remains totally incomprehensible to the disciples, even after the miracle of the multiplication of the loaves that has preceded. Jesus can pass on God's Word, but how can his flesh and blood be the same as this Word? And how can they be so much the same that whoever does not eat his flesh and drink his blood has no expectation of eternal life? Jesus not only invites men to this meal, he pushes and forces them to it. Only he who enjoys him as food has the Word of God and thereby has God himself in him—at this point all comparison with the manna of the forefathers falls away, for, after all, they "died", they did not achieve eternal life, something one can only attain at the meal that is offered here. In light of this revelation, the harshest of Jesus' revelations, a complete separation takes place: most of his followers say no and abandon him from this point, while Peter gives a blind Yes, because he can no longer see any other path than Jesus (Jn 6:66–69). It is good to recall here the situation in the wilderness: God leads into a dead end, into a situation in which no hope of rescue remains except blind trust in God. Jesus gives no explanation of how this miracle is possible; instead he confronts us with the statement: "My flesh is real food and my blood is real drink." Whoever does not accept this, has "no life in him". When receiving the Eucharist each person must remember that he is falling into the arms of God like someone dying of hunger in the wilderness of this life.

3. "Therefore we, many though we are, are one body." In the second reading the Apostle draws the conclusion consequent on what has been blindly accepted as true. Because the body of Christ is a single loaf for many, we together make a single loaf, and this loaf is none other than the body of Christ. There is more involved here than a common meal that strengthens an existing sympathy for each other. Rather, in an incomprehensible way this one physical body that has now taken on eucharistic form has the power to in*corpor*ate us into itself. Again the fact is placed before us, without any explanation. This has nothing to do with magic and charms, but it does have to do with the "foolishness" of divine love, which can discover things that surpass all human ability to explicate it. Yet precisely because God indeed is love, the improbable must be true.

[A] Sacred Heart of Jesus

Deuteronomy 7:6–11; 1 John 4:7–16;
Matthew 11:25–30

ONE MIGHT THINK that after the culmination of the entire Church year in Trinity Sunday additional feasts would only be let-downs. In that case we would overlook the fact that the threefold mystery of God only reveals itself to us through Jesus' complete sacrifice. Both the feast of Corpus Christi and the feast of the Sacred Heart of Jesus finally concretize the manner in which the triune God reveals himself to us. The Father gives the Son in the Eucharist effected by the Holy Spirit; pierced, the Son's heart gives access to the Father's heart, and from the wound flows the Spirit of both for the world.

1. The Gospel says that *Jesus is "humble of heart"*, but within a great trinitarian context: the mutual knowledge of Father and Son is accessible only to those to whom the Son reveals it, and he reveals it to the "childlike", or, in Jesus' sense, to the "humble", that is, to those who already share something of the Son's attitude. This attitude is not something he has had only since he became man, rather, he possesses it as "Son", that is, from eternity. His attitude toward the Father, whom, as the source of divinity, he calls "greater" than himself, his attitude of perfect readiness, is merely a response to the Father's attitude. For the Father withholds nothing from his Son, rather, he gives and reveals to the Son everything that God is and has, down to the ultimate. It is almost as if the original "wounded side" from which the last drop flows is the Father's own wound of love, out of which flows the last drop of everything that he has. If the Incarnate Son invites those who are heavily burdened to himself in order to relieve their load, he is the perfect image of the Father in the world: their Spirit is one and the same.

2. The first reading, from the Old Covenant, which knows not the mystery of the triunity of God, already shows awareness, from the covenant God made with Israel, that *one finds a mystery of inexhaustible love in God.* Any rational basis for choosing Israel is pushed to the side so that love remains the sole motive for God's stooping to choose. Of course the passage mentions that he thereby remains faithful to his oath to their fathers, but that only places the loving choice further back in the time of their fathers, when God basically had even less reason for such exceptional favor to a few men, the patriarchs. It was in light of this bottomless love of God that Israel found the capacity to formulate the "first commandment", the people's response of unconditional love for God.

3. In view of the triune God's *proven love* manifested in Jesus Christ, in the second reading John can simply call God the "Love". John, after all, is the favored witness, the one who, standing under the Cross, saw Jesus' heart pierced and who confirms it in a solemn threefold manner. In his letter he repeats once more the event that gives rise to his assertion that God is love: "We have seen and we testify", he says, as an eyewitness who can say together with the congregation: "We have come to know and believe in the love God has for us." At the feast of the Sacred Heart of Jesus we celebrate the last and decisive proof that the trinitarian God is nothing other than love, and we do so in an absolute and incomprehensible sense that far surpasses us.

[A] Eighth Sunday in Ordinary Time

Isaiah 49:14–15; 1 Corinthians 4:1–5;
Matthew 6:24–34

1. The two lords. This Gospel seems so hard to understand, for who can avoid being concerned about tomorrow, unless he wants to starve to death? Who doesn't have to worry about these things, at least as far as those who are dependent on him are concerned? Moreover, if God feeds the birds and clothes the flowers, why does he let so many men starve or vegetate in indescribable wretchedness? When such questions involuntarily arise we must consider that the entire passage has to do with "two lords", two lords who in the last analysis are irreconcilable and of whom we must choose one to be the lord we serve. The one is God from whom all good things come, who, in the parable of the talents, hands over his goods for us to manage, so that he might receive them back again increased by interest. The other lord is comfortable living as the highest value, for an ultimate good always takes on the rank of divinity. Thus emerges the fact that man cannot have two ultimate goods, two final goals, at the same time. He must choose. He must arrange them according to priority, so that he is clear about which good to choose when times are hard.

2. "The Lord has forsaken me." Zion's cry in the first reading is the cry of hundreds of thousands of wretched people today. But it was also Jesus' cry on the Cross as darkness closed upon his spirit. He felt abandoned by God because he wanted to feel and endure our real forsakenness, not the forsakenness of earthly shortages but the abandonment of our aversion from God, of our sin. God answers out of the highest form of loving care, care that exceeds even that of a mother for her child. Jesus knew of this before he entered the darkness of our sins: "The hour has arrived in which each of you will be scattered to his own home and you will leave me alone. But I am not alone, because the Father is with me" (Jn 16:32). The Father is with him all the more when he is on the Cross, but he cannot know it. God is with all the poor, oppressed, and starving more than with the rich and satiated; he is with Lazarus more than with the rich reveler, with Job more than with Job's friends, but following the Crucified One requires that, for the world's salvation, all the poor scream their need out of a sense of forsakenness.

3. Leave everything to God. Paul sketches the essential attitude in the second reading: "I do not even pass judgment on myself." Nor do I judge the situation God has placed me in—whether I be recognized as the steward of the mysteries of God or whether I am hauled before a court. I do not even pass judgment on whether I am guilty before God or not. Even if I am aware of no guilt in myself (like Job), I do not consider myself righteous, for "my judge is the Lord." In other words, "seek first God's Kingdom and his righteousness" and not material, not even spiritual, comfort. Paul worked for his living; the servants in the parable are supposed to strive to increase the goods that the Lord has entrusted to them. To be lazy is not the same as to "leave everything to God." Yet the good servants work not in order to better their standard of living, but to increase their Lord's goods. Above all, they do not work for the sake of a premature expectation of reward. The reward lies buried in the "leave everything", for then "all these things will be given you besides".

[A] Ninth Sunday in Ordinary Time

Deuteronomy 11:18, 26–28; Romans 3:21–25, 28;
Matthew 7:21–27

1. Hearing and doing. The unity of these two is the climax of this Gospel: "Everyone who listens to these words of mine and acts on them will be like a wise man. . . ." Thus there are two snags: merely hearing without acting, in which case the whole house will be swept away by the stormtide and, despite all cries of "Lord, Lord!", the gates of heaven will remain closed. Or mere action, without first having heard, in which case one is acting according to his own reasoning and not according to what God has laid out. Whoever is not ready first to listen to Jesus' words with Mary will receive a scolding for his activism like Martha. There can be no Christian action without preceding (always preceding) contemplation. He who has not listened to Jesus as he speaks of the Father in heaven cannot pray a proper Our Father.

The first reading also presents precisely this teaching. Israel will receive blessings if it "listens to the Lord's commandments . . . and obeys them" (vv. 27, 28, 32). Moreover, it is a matter of "all the laws" (v. 22). One cannot do a bit of listening, for example, to "blessed are the poor", and then run away thinking he knows everything and set about fixing himself up with an abbreviated and distorted theology of Christian action.

2. What must be heard? Paul tells us in the second reading, since he is speaking from the perspective of the perfected Word of God, from the perspective of the Cross, Easter, and Pentecost. This complete and indivisible Word must be listened to if we really want to understand what God says to us. He tells us that we must, above all, accept his free grace, the grace that Jesus' redemptive work has earned for us with the blood he shed. There is no way to evade this if one is to be righteous before God. God alone prepares the way that we can and must travel to him. Paul can even say that the law itself points us to the pre-eminence of the free grace of God (v. 21). To this the Gospel adds that no charism, regardless how marvelous, can replace or guarantee obedience to the word of Christ— not prophecy, or deliverance from demons, or repeated miracle-working. Paul confirms this emphatically: "Even if I have the most sublime gift of speaking in tongues, possess the highest knowledge of mysteries, give all I have to the poor, even suffer martyrdom, it would all be in vain unless I have love of God and neighbor", which is the only response to his Word that God expects (cf. 1 Cor 13:1–3). It is the response to his love, which, in its revelation, encompasses all that God has done for us in Christ.

3. The cloudburst and the rock. Whoever hears but does not act builds on sand, that is, on himself or on something comparably perishable. Whoever does what he hears from God builds on a rock, that is, on God, whom the Psalms continually refer to as the Rock. As an invisible foundation, it is the rock that constantly keeps the house from collapsing. In the New Covenant the incarnate Word of God, Jesus Christ, is also called the Rock: *petra autem erat Christus* (1 Cor 10:4), and we know that he gives the same name to Peter, the cornerstone of his Church, who became the cornerstone through his confession of faith (Mt 16:18) and who was made a stronger stone through his activity of feeding Christ's flock and dying for it. God–Christ–Peter: all have the same characteristic, namely, being a Rock that can withstand the torrential storm. And, as Jesus repeatedly predicted, the storm will come, to test the soundness of the building. One can even say that persecution not only tests the Christian, but also permits his tenacity to increase (1 Pet 1:6–7).

[A] Tenth Sunday in Ordinary Time

Hosea 6:3–6; Romans 4:18–25;
Matthew 9:9–13

1. Unconditional faith. In the Gospel Matthew hears a challenge from a stranger: Follow me! He drops everything and follows. He makes no inquiry as to who the man is, takes no time to consider things, does not ask for time to think about it or to take care of important business. All we have is a call and a response. And the response is a final response, since Matthew (Levi) never again left the group of twelve disciples. This is pure faith, like Abraham's faith, which Paul celebrates in the second reading. Although Abraham's body was "as good as dead", like the womb of his wife, he unhesitatingly believed God's promise that he would become the father of many nations, since he "was firmly convinced that God had the power to do what he promised" (v. 21). The call of God and of Christ does not coerce men, rather, it gives them both the freedom and the strength to follow out of their own motivation. The call carries a tone that contains both at once: this One who is speaking will motivate me to make the best decision possible and, since he needs me, will grant me the best possible life. All of this is found in the call itself, and the response does not follow only after extended consideration of the nature of the call, rather, the response follows immediately upon the call. In Abraham's case something else is noted: this obedience of faith "was credited to him as righteousness". The obedient one does not do the calculating, rather, God in his sovereignty does the accounting.

2. Mercy, not sacrifice. Jesus' phrase, "It is mercy I desire, not sacrifice", in the Gospel, is a quotation from Hosea and is found at the end of the first reading. Both God's requirement given through the prophet and Jesus' call in the Gospel are pure mercy, yet in the Old Covenant Israel's sight is so obscured that it treats God's grace like a natural phenomenon and offers the ritual burnt offerings in a merely customary manner. That God weighs in with blows of judgment simply creates space for his requirement: love, not ritual; instead of burnt offerings, the realization of what God is truly like. On Jesus' lips the words of the prophet interpret his entire challenge to the world: his call is pure mercy toward sinners, and sinners can sense this, since his is the call of a healing physician. Those who think they are healthy need no physician and thus miss the healing words. To be sure, they offer something ("the tithe of all I possess" [Lk 18:12]), but that costs them no pain and their budget remains untouched. Their budget no more needs healing than they do. In contrast, the tax collector, who was considered a sinner, as a "sick man" can hear the call as a call of mercy.

3. Table fellowship. It is odd that the outcry of one sets many other "tax collectors and sinners" on the way to Jesus, the one who verifies the word of mercy they have just heard by incorporating them into the table fellowship initially intended only for Matthew. In the Scriptures, fellowship at table always has a religious aspect: a communal relationship among people that is grounded in God. All of Jesus' meals take on this character: table fellowship as an expression of God's healing mercy, given voice in Jesus as physician and steadily approaching the meal in which the physician distributes himself as the most sublime medicine of all.

[A] Eleventh Sunday in Ordinary Time

Exodus 19:2–6; Romans 5:6–11;
Matthew 9:36–10:8

1. The choosing of the Twelve. The crowd of people that presses upon Jesus with unspoken expectation arouses in him no fear of inadequacy for the task. Instead it calls forth a profound inner compassion (the Greek word used here expresses the depth of his feeling). Now several motifs come into play at once. The first is not expressly stated in the Gospel but clearly emerges from the other readings: he will have to face the crowd alone as he carries out his overwhelming task: through his death, as Paul says, we "are reconciled with God" (Rom 5:10). Yet his activity does not remain isolated: as man, which he is, he must have coworkers and, if they are really to be such, they must share something of his mission's manner and power. And now comes the characteristic parallelism: just as he received his mission from the Father, so he will ask his Father for these coworkers. His prayer is undoubtedly directed primarily to the Father, and the Father hears it and gives Jesus himself the authority to call disciples and equip them with the authority they will need. Yet this authority depends on Jesus' personal and total obedience, obedience all the way to the Cross. He can acquire genuine coworkers only on the strength of the totality of his obedience.

2. *The primacy of Jesus' involvement.* Both readings show how God's action is prior to the involvement of God's coworkers. In Exodus it is God alone who freed Israel from Egypt on eagle's wings. The formation of the nation was his doing alone. Only after this has been done can Moses proclaim to the people that it is God who "has chosen Israel from among all nations to be his own special possession" and who wants to make Israel "a kingdom of priests and a holy people". Only from this point onward will God work with Israel in world history. Although the "entire earth" indeed belongs to God and he would thereby have power enough to act alone, he has nonetheless invested his world-historical activity in a nation. Paul says this even more clearly in the second reading: "Jesus died for us while we were God's enemies", something beyond comprehension, for, although it would be astounding enough if someone were to die for a righteous person, here someone dies for hostile sinners. Only on the basis of this incomprehensible act are

we associated with him, as "reconciled" and "saved" and do we become his "friends" (Jn 15:13–14), indeed, his "coworkers" (1 Cor 3:9; 3 Jn 8). It is pointless to ask why, if he has done everything himself, he needs coworkers, since we are completely incorporated into his Cross and his Resurrection, his chief accomplishment.

3. Mission. Even the sending in the Gospel testifies to the fact that he bestows some of his own power of mission upon his disciples. Like him they can and must proclaim the imminence of the Kingdom of heaven, they can and must also heal the sick, even raise the dead and drive out demons. The Acts of the Apostles tells of many instances in which they did this physically and literally. Yet is not every sacred confession and absolution a healing of the sick, indeed, is it not often a raising from the dead and an exorcism of demons? Jesus' own unique mission is entrusted to the Church as a whole, including the laity in their own role. That is how the Father, the "Lord of the harvest", heard and granted the Son's prayer.

[A] Twelfth Sunday in Ordinary Time

Jeremiah 20:10–13; Romans 5:12–15;
Matthew 10:26–33

1. "Fear not" occurs three times in the Gospel reading; in one instance we are told what to fear. On the other hand, anything that takes place as part of Jesus' mission is no cause for fear. Mainly, the disciples ought to proclaim openly "from the rooftops" what the Lord taught them privately, for it is destined to become known to the whole world and nothing can keep it from becoming known. Of course the person proclaiming it is at risk; he is like a sheep among wolves: he must reckon with martyrdom as the reward for his preaching. Yet even in martyrdom he need not fear, for the enemy cannot harm his soul. Only one is worth fearing, he who can plunge body and soul into hell; but that cannot happen so long as he remains faithful to his mission. Third, the Christian carrying out his apostolate should not fear, for the Father's hand protects him far better than he realizes: he who cares about the most insignificant of animals, about a single hair, will care all the more about his children. Jesus speaks of "your Father". The larger context makes clear that a man is safe as long as and to the extent that he carries out his Christian mission, regardless how daring his actions may seem.

2. The threat. In the first reading Jeremiah expresses the utter limits of being threatened. In whispers people are discussing how to denounce him to the authorities. The worst revenge they could take would be to catch him in a careless expression and then hand him over. His closest acquaintances are among the opposition, so he really is surrounded by "terror on all sides". This can happen on occasion to a Christian, in which case he must remind himself of Jesus' threefold "fear not". The prophet knows he is safe in the midst of terror: the Lord stands by him "like a mighty champion". He has "entrusted his cause" to the Lord and that is enough to ensure that he, the "poor", "defenseless" one will be rescued from the grip of evildoers. His security is expressed, in typical Old Testament fashion, in negative terms: his enemies will "blunder" and "get nowhere", they shall be "put to utter shame". In the New Covenant, however, the terror extends all the way to the Cross; the hymn of victory that Jeremiah strikes up at the end of the first reading is Easter and Ascension.

3. Confidence. Paul gains his unheard of confidence from Easter and Ascension. On the one side are arrayed not merely a few personal enemies, but the entire world, which has fallen away from God in sin and death. In light of this, Paul's song of victory takes on cosmic dimensions. Through Jesus' redemptive act, grace has finally won the upper hand against sin and its consequences, which means that hope has triumphed over fear. Paul, too, will learn first-hand what Jeremiah's sense of forsakenness is like (2 Cor 1:8–9; 2 Tim 4:9–16). Yet, like the prophet he adds: "But the Lord stood by me and gave me strength. . . . He will rescue me from every evil threat" (2 Tim 4:17–18). He knows more than that: his sufferings are absorbed into the Redeemer's and in his Redeemer's suffering Paul's sufferings acquire salvific significance for the community.

[A] Thirteenth Sunday in Ordinary Time

2 Kings 4:8–11, 14–16; Romans 6:3–4, 8–11;
Matthew 10:37–42

THE GOSPEL HAS TWO PARTS: (1) daring to lose all of one's own and to gain oneself in Christ (vv. 37–39, cf. the second reading); (2) daring to accept the slightest thing offered by God in order to receive God in it (vv. 40–42, cf. the first reading).

1. Daring to lose all of one's own. In Christ God gives man everything; hence the requirement to set aside all of one's own in order to make room for this "one and all". Jesus' awareness of being this "one and all" is amazing: "Such a one is not worthy of me." And the requirement expressly includes the path of the Cross: whoever is not ready to accompany Jesus on it has not dared everything. For precisely here is where the concluding maxim with its talk of "losing one's life" is taken seriously. This does not have to do merely with some natural law of life ("let it die to grow") but takes place expressly "for my sake", which basically means a dying and loss of such finality that it has no room for a hidden anticipation of getting back what has been lost.

2. Dying in order to live for God. In the second reading Paul shows that this dying and burial with Jesus includes hope of a resurrected life for God with Christ, a hope, however, that excludes any self-seeking calculation of regaining the loss. Only the "old man" could do that sort of calculation; whereas in dying in Christ we become new men and death (to which belongs any sort of egotistical thinking) has no more hold over us. Christ died "to sin" not only by robbing sin of its power over the world once and for all, but also by taking away sin's power over men. He lives "for God" in absolute devotion to God for the sake of God's saving will for the world. As those who have died to sin, we are required likewise "to live for God in Christ Jesus", that is, to put ourselves at the disposal of God's saving work in the world in the same attitude as Jesus. In this disposability modeled on the attitude of the Lord we gain life through the loss of our calculating egoism.

3. Receiving "one of these little ones". In being ready to receive God's messenger, whether he is a "prophet", a "holy man" or a "mere" "disciple" of Christ (and who is not one of these "little ones"?), one receives a share in God's grace. Both the receiver and the received should know this. The one received radiates something of his charism of mission wherever he is given opportunity to do so. We have a marvelous example of this in the first reading: the woman of Shunem, who hosts the prophet Elisha and even sets aside a room for his regular use, receives from him what she dared not hope for: despite her husband's advanced age she receives a son. The fruitfulness of the prophetic mission expresses itself in an Old Testament sense in this physical fruitfulness of the receiving woman. In the New Covenant the gift can be an even greater spiritual fruitfulness.

[A] Fourteenth Sunday in Ordinary Time

Zechariah 9:9–10; Romans 8:9, 11–13;
Matthew 11:25–30

THE GOSPEL CONTAINS THREE ASSERTIONS: (1) The revelation of the Father is given to "minors"; (2) it takes place only through the Son, through Christ, who reveals it to whomever he wishes; (3) by pointing to his own meekness he addresses this revelation of the Father and Son to all who are burdened.

1. Revelation to minors. Everything originates from the Father; Jesus, the Revealer, thanks the Father that he can reveal. And it was already the Father's plan that Jesus not reach the "wise and learned", who think they already know everything and know better. Instead he was to reach those who are still "dependents", that is, those inexperienced in the theology of the Scriptures. These are the same as the "poor in spirit" and the "sick" who seek a physician, like the weary and shepherdless sheep. These poor have spirits that are open rather than crammed full of thousands of theories. Though they may be scorned by the learned, these are the ones God has chosen in advance to receive his revelation. In an even more profound way it will become clear that the Son, both as mediator of the Father's mind and based on his own frame of mind (humility and lowliness), can only be understood by the "minors" he addresses.

2. A single Revealer. Precisely because he and he alone knows the mind of the Father, he can speak the lordly words: "All things have been handed over to me by my Father." The result is that only the Son knows the Father and only the Father knows the Son in finality. This declaration lifts the veil of the trinitarian mystery, and the subsequent handing on of the mind of the Son to men points toward the Holy Spirit, who places the mind of both, of the Father and the Son in our hearts, as the second reading explicitly emphasizes. By granting us a glimpse of the innermost mutual relations of Father and Son we see something decisive: the Son does not merely carry out the Father's commands, rather, he reveals the Father and himself only to those whom he has selected for this purpose. Who these are is made clear by the concluding sentence.

3. The burdened find rest. All who are worn out and burdened by anything are invited; to them alone is rest promised. (The unburdened don't need rest.) Now note the contrast: those who come to Jesus carry "heavy burdens" but Jesus' "yoke is easy" and his "burden is light". Yet his burden, the Cross, is the heaviest there is. Nor can one say that the Cross is heavy only for him, not for those who help carry it. The solution lies in Jesus' attitude, for he refers to himself as "gentle" and "humble of heart". In other words he does not sob under the burden loaded on him; he does not complain, does not compare and measure his own strength. "Learn from me" and you will realize that your heavy burden in the end really is "light". It is no accident that the Messiah appears in the first reading as a humble man riding on an equally humble beast of burden. Nor is it coincidence that we are commanded in the second reading to have the "Spirit of God" (the Father) and the "Spirit of Christ" in us and to let ourselves be shaped by this Spirit. The fleshly man moans under his burden, but "we are not indebted to the flesh, brethren, that we should live according to the flesh", sobbing our way toward death. Instead we are able to live according to the divine Spirit dwelling in us, the Spirit of the love between Father and Son, and we can rejoice that Jesus lets us carry a bit of his yoke, a bit of his Cross. That is how, in the Spirit, we share in God's repose.

[A] Fifteenth Sunday in Ordinary Time

Isaiah 55:10–11; Romans 8:18–23;
Matthew 13:1–23

1. The Parable of the Sower was supposed to be comprehended. In the Gospel reading Jesus tells a parable to the crowd (while he is sitting in a boat): only a fourth part of the scattered seed comes up, but this portion produces a bountiful harvest. The disciples ask: "Why do you speak in parables?" Jesus' lengthy answer points out that at least an initial understanding of divine things must be present in listeners' hearts if the "Kingdom word" is to bear fruit in them. "To anyone who has [this starting point], more will be given" (v. 12). Basically one can speak of God only in images; anyone whose heart is hardened or unwilling to understand because of superficiality or worldly preoccupations (v. 22) cannot penetrate to the kernel, to the divine reality intended in these metaphors. In such cases, the seed dries up and the evil one steals away even the kernel (v. 19).

By the grace of God this starting point for comprehension is found in the disciples; what is portrayed in the reading as Jesus' exposition is essentially the understanding that the Holy Spirit develops in the heart of the Church.

2. The blessedness of comprehension. Yet this ecclesial understanding comes after Easter. For now the disciples inquire about the significance of speaking in parables; only after the Holy Spirit comes will he teach them how to visualize their way from the symbol to reality. And those capable of this insight will always remain a minority in this world. In the second reading Paul tells us that the entire creation was made subject to "futility", or "nothingness", that it is in labor but gives birth to nothing, and that "Even we, despite the first fruits of the Spirit in our hearts, moan as we await our revelation." As Christians we are among those whose hearts harbor a hint of comprehension, yet how much effort is required even of us to find truth in the parable! And how much must we beware lest stony soil prevent God's seed from taking root even in us, who really ought to see and hear.

3. The infallibility of the Word. Yet the end of the parable brings an unconditional promise that, in good soil, the seed produces hundredfold, sixtyfold, thirtyfold. In other words, overall the harvest is a good one. God will get a good return even in the poor ground of this world: in his eyes a saint outweighs a hundred apathetic or disbelieving people. The first reading gives a virtual triumphant proclamation of this. The grace of God is like rain that makes the earth germinate and sprout, giving the sower seed and edible bread. So too "the Word that goes forth from my mouth shall not return to me void, but shall do my will." And it will produce not merely a portion of what God's plan intended, but rather "achieves every end for which I sent it". A Christian cannot listen to God's cry of triumph without thinking about the Son's Cross: if his life's work seems to have been shattered by the hardheartedness of his listeners, so was his Cross representative of the rain that breaks up the parched earth.

[A] Sixteenth Sunday in Ordinary Time

Wisdom 12:13, 16–19; Romans 8:26–27;
Matthew 13:24–43

1. The Kingdom of God wins out. In the Gospel reading Jesus announces the Kingdom of God in three more parables. This time he says explicitly that he has chosen this form of speaking in order to proclaim what has been hidden from the beginning of the world (v. 35). There is no other way on earth to talk about heaven.

The three images he offers all reveal something of the paradox of the Kingdom growing in a world so unready for the divine. In the first image the seed of God grows in the midst of weeds sown not by God but by his enemy. God lets them grow in order not to endanger the seed prematurely. The second parable says something almost opposite: the Jews celebrate the Feast of Unleavened Bread (together with the Passover), that is, to them yeast seems to be corrupting. Yet now the Christian *pascha* is to penetrate the dough and slowly set everything into ferment. Finally, the Kingdom of God is like the most minute seedgrain but in the end outgrows all other vegetation. Only the first parable is explained—referring again to the Holy Spirit in the Church; the second and third parables are so transparent that they need no gloss.

2. Thus it is the Holy Spirit who interprets where natural human comprehension falls short. This is what the second reading says explicitly. Even though Christian, a man often asks in perplexity how he can properly turn to God and away from the earth with its fields overgrown with weeds. He senses that his prayer is an impure mixture of wheat and noxious weeds[2] that he dare not present to God. "Then the Spirit himself intercedes for us"; he knows how the request has to sound before God and he expresses that prayer in the depths of our hearts. Therefore, when our prayer reaches the Father, he hears not only his own Spirit but the inseparable unity of our hearts with him, and out of this unity the Father listens only to that portion that is right. We are present. We pray in the Spirit, but simultaneously with our own spirits and intellects (cf. 1 Cor 14:15). It is not the case that the Spirit is the wheat and we are merely weeds.

3. The separation and forbearance. In the Gospel of the weeds in wheat an inexorable separation takes place in the end. The weeds are gathered and burned while the wheat is brought into God's granary. This separation process is needed because nothing impure can enter the Father's Kingdom. Are there men who are nothing but weeds and impurity? That decision must be left to God. But in the first reading, from the Book of Wisdom, we learn that God exercises perfect justice in his "unlimited might", yet precisely this might permits him to govern with "leniency", "protection", and "kindness". He shows his leniency to his people in order that "those who are just might be kind". And not only that, but "you gave your sons good ground for hope that you would permit repentance for their sins."

---

[2] Von Balthasar refers here to poison rye grass (darnel, *Lolium temulentum*), a member of the rye grass family that is poisonous to livestock. In premodern times, the grains of darnel could not easily be separated from grains of wheat during the winnowing process—TRANS.

[A] Seventeenth Sunday in Ordinary Time

1 Kings 3:5, 7–12; Romans 8:28–30;
Matthew 13:44–52

1. Investing everything. In the Gospel Jesus once more tells three parables that are intended to give a clear view of the Kingdom of heaven. The first two resemble each other in what they say and in what is required by what they say: earthly prudence alone requires that the farmer and the merchant sell everything in order to acquire something much more valuable: the treasure found in the field and the precious pearl. To do so is largely shrewdness rather than any sort of wager. Whoever understands the value of what Jesus offers will not hesitate to get rid of everything of his own, to become poor in spirit and in pure faith, in order to obtain what has been offered. "Blessed are the poor in spirit [that is, those whose attitude toward everything is one of renunciation], for theirs is the Kingdom of heaven." Yet not everyone finds the treasure and the pearl, not everyone is ready for full investment. Thus, as last Sunday, we have a third parable that draws a conclusion of eschatological judgment from a decision made within time—the net is brought to shore and the useless fish are thrown away. This means that God's offer of a unique chance is backed up by a stern warning not to miss it. At stake is the loss or gain of the whole meaning of human existence. Just as the farmer and the merchant are shrewd enough not to hesitate for a moment, so the Christian who has grasped what is at stake will take action immediately.

2. "Have you understood all this?" They say they do, perhaps only by reason of their complete post-Easter insight. For at Easter Jesus had explained to them the entire meaning of the Scriptures, of "everything written about me in the law of Moses and in the prophets and psalms" (Lk 24:44). They understand the Old "parable" in the light of the New. Thus at the end of his talk in parables Jesus can compare himself with "a head of a household who brings from his storeroom both the new and the old" for the "disciples of the Kingdom of heaven". Far from being outdated, the old takes on a new polish, an exalted meaning, in the light of the new.

3. New and old. Both the first and second readings suitably symbolize the old and the new. God wishes to grant a favor to the new and inexperienced King Solomon, and Solomon asks for "an understanding heart" in order to "distinguish right from wrong" in his role as ruler. He makes the right request, he invests everything to acquire the treasure of the field and the precious pearl. That pleases God, Solomon receives the priceless treasure and, in the bargain, everything else.

One can transfer this "old" undiminished into the "new", although the goods now offered are far more lavish. Those "who love God", who have decided for God out of their innermost thirst, are told that their free decision has been eternally embraced and sheltered by God's decision. If they truly love, they are shaped like Christ, and nothing can force them off the path leading from predestination to election, to justification, and eternal glorification. Far from being a deterministic cycle (cf. James 3:6) this is the self-completing circle of love.

[A] Eighteenth Sunday in Ordinary Time

Isaiah 55:1–3; Romans 8:35, 37–39;
Matthew 14:13–21

THE CONTEXT FOR THE GOSPEL of the multiplication of the loaves is significant. John the Baptist has been beheaded; Jesus is also probably in danger (Lk 13:31ff.), and he pulls back. The crowd follows him, compassion conquers him again: he teaches them and heals. Then the disciples come up with the thought that the people should be dismissed so that they can buy food for their evening meal. Jesus tries to withdraw again: "Give them something to eat." Since they cannot, he must return to action yet again. God's revelations in Christ are tied to the needs of mankind.

1. Too little, too much. The theme wends its way through the Gospels: from the first public revelation at Cana onward we find that men have too little and God gives them too much. No more wine and then, likewise, later, an abundance. Five loaves of bread and, after thousands have been fed, twelve baskets of uneaten food that must be placed in the disciples' care. This material paradox is, of course, only a "symbol". It is a metaphor with a spiritual meaning: the Almighty is meek and humble of heart, the Revealer rejected by all has been given charge of judgment over the world. This is not merely a matter of the contrast between man's poverty and God's wealth, rather, it has to do with a much deeper paradox: that God becomes poor in order to enrich us all (2 Cor 8:9), that he, the persecuted One, pours out his incomprehensible wealth on us precisely in this situation of poverty.

2. Gratis. There can be no other relationship between God and man than the one described in the first reading, and it surpasses any relationship that a human mind can take in at first glance. "You who have no money, come. . . . Come, without paying and without cost, drink wine and milk." Only where this free giving and receiving takes place does a man get what he bargained for; as long as he calculates and his balance is somehow totaled up, he will come out short: "Why pay your money for what does not feed you and your hard-earned wages for what fails to satisfy?" asks the first reading. This simply means that only the gratis nature of love and grace can satisfy the soul's abysmal hunger. This, however, also means that some inclination toward this gratis nature must either be present in the soul or be produced in it by the free gift itself. No one could satiate himself with God's priceless love if he calculatingly receives it and hoards it for himself. All calculation must be dismissed if a man is to enter into the "eternal covenant" God offers him.

3. Finally. What follows upon such an entry is shown by Paul's exuberant song of triumph in the second reading. Through God's utter sacrifice of all that he has, he becomes the source from which the covenant is made an "eternal" one. And he who truly agrees to this flood of givenness enters into the eternalness that is found beyond all sort of earthly threat and trial. "Nothing can separate us"—not because we have the strength to "conquer" everything, but because all the strength needed for that comes from the "love of God" that "is in Christ Jesus, our Lord".

[A] Nineteenth Sunday in Ordinary Time

1 Kings 19:8–9, 11–13; Romans 9:1–5;
Matthew 14:22–33

1. God as ghost. The Gospel drama in which Jesus walks on
the nocturnal, stormy lake opens with Jesus praying "in solitude on the mountain" and ends with genuine worship by the
disciples: "They did him homage, saying, 'Truly you are the
Son of God.'" His majestic strides over the waves, the even
clearer superiority over the forces of nature exhibited when he
permits Peter to climb out of the boat and come to him, and
his eye-opening sovereignty over wind and waves all reveal to
the disciples far better than his teaching and miraculous healings how loftily he exceeds their poor humanity without prov-
ing that he is, as they thought, a ghost. Or, a better way to
put it might be: he is a poor man like them, as his Passion
will overwhelmingly demonstrate, but he is a poor man voluntarily, which reveals his origin in God. He can remain true
to his task of unveiling his divinity in order to strengthen his
disciples' faith but this same task requires that he conceal that
divinity for the most part and forgo help from the "legion of
angels" his Father would send should he request it (Mt 26:53).
Forgoing angelic help and undergoing the suffering that follows both demonstrate his divinity in a more profound way
than the great miracles.

These are forms of training in faith: In the face of an apparent specter the disciples have to learn to believe in the reality of Jesus based solely on his words, "It is I." When Peter
climbs out of the boat he reverts to fear and begins to sink. He
then has to endure a scolding for his lack of faith. Instead of
thinking about his ability and inability he should have marched
steadily toward the "Son of God" out of the faith he was given.

2. The whispering God. In the first reading Elijah receives training in this same faith by means of a mysterious symbolism. He has been promised an encounter with God's majesty as it passes by. And he has to learn that the great forces of nature which once proclaimed God's presence on Sinai, the same sort of powerful storm experienced by the disciples on the lake, the earthquake that the Psalms depict as a sign of his proximity, the fire that once revealed God in a bramble bush are, at most, premonitions of God in earthly metaphors—they are not his actual presence. Only when the "tiny, whispering sound" comes does Elijah know that he must bury his face in his cloak. This inexpressible gentleness is something of a hint of the Incarnation of the Son: God wishes to be as gentle as Jesus will be: "He will not cry out or shout, no one will hear his voice in the street, a bruised reed he will not break, and a smoldering wick he will not quench" (Is 42:2–3).

3. Not without the brethren. In the second reading Paul laments that Israel has not carried Elijah's faith to the ultimate, to the Incarnation of the Son of God. Like all those blessed by God, Israel has received the "sonship" (Rom 9:4) that finds completion in the fact that Christ "who is over all" (v. 5) took flesh from Israel. The Jews should have recognized the ultimate Sonship in Jesus' meekness and gentleness, instead of waiting for someone to take up the earthly position of power they hoped for from their Messiah. If it could bring "his brethren and kinsmen according to the flesh" to faith and salvation, Paul would like to be cursed into separation from Christ. This audacious wish is part of the fullness of Christian faith, which has learned love for every sort of weakness out of its encounter with the softspoken God. In imitation of Christ, a Christian does not want to be saved apart from his brothers.

[A] Twentieth Sunday in Ordinary Time

Isaiah 56:1, 6–7; Romans 11:13–15, 29–32;
Matthew 15:21–28

1. The Gentile believes. The Gospel about the Canaanite woman sounds unusually harsh. At first Jesus appears not to want to acknowledge that he hears her imploring request; then he says that his mission has to do only with Israel. His third statement underlines the second: the bread he offers belongs to the children, not to the dogs. Now comes the marvelous phrase from the woman: "You are right, Lord" (she sees his point and concedes it), but the dogs at least receive the crumbs that fall from the family's table. This the Lord cannot resist, any more than he can resist the Gentile centurion of Capernaum: this humble, trusting faith in the Lord conquers his heart and her request is granted. In Capernaum it was "Lord, don't trouble yourself; I am not worthy", here it is a willingness to occupy the lowest position, under the table. In each case there was faith: "Such great faith I have not found in Israel" (Mt 8:10).

2. It is easy to overlook the fact that the earthly mission of Jesus really has to do with Israel: *he is the Messiah of the chosen people*, Israel, around which the Gentile nations are to flock after it has been made whole and come to true faith. This the first reading says clearly. Jesus cannot make an end run around his messianic mission; he can act only by fulfilling it. This mission is accomplished on the Cross, where, rejected by Israel, he suffers not only for Israel but for all sinners. Yet in the Gospel today Jesus finds perfect trust outside of Israel. Giving the right response to God forces him to take account of Israel's mission as a light to all nations (explicitly stated in the first reading) in his work as Messiah already before the Cross.

3. Imprisoned in disobedience. If today one refuses to see Israel's role in God's plan of salvation, then he will not understand this universal plan of salvation. Paul expounds it for us in the second reading, although even in the explaining it remains mysterious enough, since it is God's plan. The Gentiles would appear to have grounds for being jealous of Israel—why should it be favored? Yet now that the Messiah has been rejected by Israel and the Gentiles realize that Jesus also died for them, the Jews might become jealous. Precisely this jealousy makes Israel attentive to the fact that divine salvation has gone forth, and Paul thinks that this may permit "at least a few to realize" that salvation really did flow from the Messiah they rejected. Moreover, the covenant that God offered to Israel is irrevocable. As is said elsewhere: "Even if we are faithless he is faithful, for he cannot deny himself" (2 Tim 2:13). If sinful Gentiles are permitted to experience God's merciful love undeservedly, then sinful Israel, when it finally realizes that it is sinful and that its righteousness of law cannot help, "will also find mercy" (v. 31). Mercy is the final word. As in the Gospel, it is the most profound characteristic of God, a characteristic that can be grasped by us sinners only if we know that we do not deserve it, that God's love is something completely freely given. Hence the concluding word regarding God's plan of salvation for human history: "God has imprisoned all in disobedience" —Jews, Gentiles, and Christians—"that he might have mercy on all."

[A] Twenty-first Sunday in Ordinary Time

Isaiah 22:19–23; Romans 11:33–36;
Matthew 16:13–20

1. The rock. In the Gospel two metaphors dominate Jesus' response to Simon Peter's confession of faith: the images of a rock and of keys. Both originate in the Old Testament, are continued in the New Testament and, as the Gospel shows, ultimately are applied to the institution founded by Jesus. First we consider the metaphor of the rock. In the Psalms God is repeatedly called the rock, meaning the foundation that one can depend on unconditionally: "My help comes from God, he alone is my rock" (Ps 62:3). His divine Word is the perfectly trustworthy Word, even when it becomes man and thereby becomes the Savior of the people: "And the rock was Christ" (1 Cor 10:4). Without abandoning this quality Jesus permits Simon Peter to share in it: "You are the rock, and on this rock I will build my Church." The Church will also participate in this quality of unconditional trustworthiness: "The gates of hell shall not prevail against her." This quality can only be transferred through perfect faith, which is had by the grace of the heavenly Father, not by Peter's fine human insight. Faith in God and in Christ can only become rockhard faith in a rocky fortress through God and Christ himself. Such faith is a foundation upon which Christ, not man, builds his Church.

2. The key. Actually the second quality is found already in the quality of being a rockhard foundation. This second quality is the authority symbolized by the transfer of keys to a trusted servant of the king and the people. In those days keys were very large; thus in the first reading the servant can have the "key of the House of David" placed on his shoulders, almost like a cross, certainly as a burdensome responsibility. It is authoritative power: "When he opens, no one shall shut; when he shuts, no one shall open" (Is 22:22). In the New Covenant it is Jesus "who has the key of David, who opens and no one can close, who closes and no one can open" (Rev 3:7). This is the chief key to eternal life; to it belongs also the "keys to death and the netherworld" (Rev 1:18). And now Christ gives the man, Peter, upon whom the Church is to be built a share in this power of the keys that penetrates to the other world: what he binds or looses on earth shall be bound or loosed in heaven. Let us note carefully that in the Old Covenant, with Christ, and with Peter it is always a specific person who receives these keys. This is no impersonal office, no presidency, for example, to which someone else can be named as a replacement for the incumbent. As instituted by Christ it involves a very specific person as recipient of the keys. No skeleton key exists whereby someone else might also open and close. This applies to all who share in the priestly office derived from the Apostles: only the appointed pastor of a congregation (and his priestly assistants) can have the keys, which he may not lend to or share with anyone, though he can delegate "offices" and assignments. Instead of the pastor being built on the rock of the congregation, it is the congregation, a part of the Church, that is built on the rock of Peter in which all priestly offices have a share.

3. The best possible. Now the song of praise for God in the second reading can sound forth as a conclusion: how rich, indeed how inscrutable are God's plans, including those relating to the Church. "Who has been his counselor?" How could his Church have been better instituted, better adapted to the modern, present-day world? Again and again today this Church established on the rock of Peter and on his power of the keys proves to be the best possible one.

[A] Twenty-second Sunday in Ordinary Time

Jeremiah 20:7–9; Romans 12:1–2;
Matthew 16:21–27

1. The plan. When, in the Gospel reading, Jesus conclusively presents his intended mission, not only the world but even the Church (initially) takes offense at the Cross. The Church consists of people, all of whom wish to escape suffering as much and as long as possible. All religions outside of Christianity respond in some way to this plan—how can a man flee suffering? Through Stoicism, through rescue from the "cycle of rebirths", by sinking into meditation? In contrast, Christ became man in order to suffer, to suffer more than any other person ever has suffered. Whoever hinders him is his opponent. And instead of hearing Christ say, "Rejoice that I suffer for you", the one who would hinder him hears, "Take up your own cross out of love for me and on behalf of your brother, for whose salvation we must suffer. There is no way of salvation except me. Your salvation does not consist in eliminating your 'I' but in sacrificing your 'I' for others, which cannot take place without pain and the cross."

That the cross is found precisely in consistent obedience to God is evident in the first reading:

2. The same for the servant as the Lord. Jeremiah can scarcely bear to proclaim God's word without diluting or truncating it. He is asked to confront the people with their injustices, indeed, he has to "scream" in their ears: "violence and outrage" (words that frequently recur in this prophet). For his pains he receives nothing but scorn. As he proclaims God's message he can see the destruction of the nation coming but no one will believe him. He feels as if even God has duped him: his mission is an utter failure. One can understand why he would like to evade it, think no more of it, say no more about it! But precisely then it becomes unbearable—now the unproclaimed message blazes in his heart. A Christian too must speak and thereby expose himself to people's mockery: the mocking voice of one's surroundings, of public opinion, of newspapers and the mass media. The temptation to say nothing more, to let the world run its course, is immense. The world is heading toward its destruction anyway, what point is there in telling the world anything? But such silence would then burn inwardly just as powerfully as it did in the prophet's heart: the message has to have an outlet. Standing up to the hail of contempt and mockery is in the end nothing other than following Christ: "The slave is not greater than his master" (Jn 15:20). On the Cross itself Jesus was mocked and slandered as never before. He thereby took upon himself the world's rejection, conquering and overcoming it inwardly.

3. A sacrifice suited to the Logos. In the second reading Paul summarizes in simple words the lifelong task of Christians: in light of God's mercy they should offer themselves bodily as a living and holy sacrifice, which constitutes true worship suited to Christ the Word. Devoting one's entire life to the cause of God and Christ transforms one's entire existence into a single liturgical celebration. This is celebrated bodily, facing the world, but without conforming to the world. Christian existence, if lived according to the Logos—in imitation of Christ, is thereby both a sermon to the world and a sacrifice for the world, since Christians have their share in Christ's self-sacrifice for the world. Of course, as Paul says, this requires of each person a constant self-examination to see whether he is saying Yes to the scandal of the Cross, whether he is willing to present the truth of Christ to the surrounding world.

[A] Twenty-third Sunday in Ordinary Time

Ezekiel 33:7–9; Romans 13:8–10;
Matthew 18:15–20

1. Christian order. The texts for this Sunday's celebration are absolutely decisive for the form God wants for the Church. In the center stands loving mutual admonition. This is an obligation resting on every Christian, for we are members of a single body and the entire organism cannot afford to be indifferent when a single member injures itself and thereby damages the life of the whole. Of course, the Gospel makes it clear that admonition (and such correction as may be necessary) dare take place only as a sign of divine self-revelation and of the ecclesial order established by Christ. At the same time, the person disciplined must show humility that points away from himself toward the objective grace of God and its requirement. In the second reading Paul locates that requirement entirely within Christian love, which brings together all the individual commandments and thereby fulfills the law, God's guidance. The person sinning may perhaps respond with his conception of love; in that case one has to show him that his conception is too narrow and one-sided to be God's intended fulfillment of all the commandments.

2. The Church's limits. Yet the person remains free. Even the best admonition, whether it takes place personally and confidentially or more officially through an appointed representative of the Church, can run up against a boundary set by a clear and resounding No. At this point the first reading becomes significant: if the admonisher has done his task and the offender still refuses to turn from his false path, then he has met his obligation and, as the reading says, has preserved his life. The obligation is laid down with utter earnestness, but God does not promise that it will meet with success. Thus in the entire New Testament God indicates only a single boundary line beyond which the sinner or fallen one can no longer consider himself a member of God's Church. The Church does not direct him to leave her communion, rather, he excommunicates himself. The Church has to recognize what has happened and must confirm it, in order to ensure that the person involved understands what has happened. This was already true of the Old Covenant, as the first reading shows, and it must thus be all the more characteristic of the New Covenant, where membership in the ecclesial fellowship of Christ is more personal, filled with greater responsibility, and more colorful.

3. Jesus' promise. From Jesus' two final comments we see how ecclesial, common prayer can really count on a heavenly hearing. Both promises are magnificent: whatever two ask for out of shared and loving expectancy toward God will be granted. Wherever two or three are assembled in Jesus' name he is in their midst. In the time of Jesus there was a rabbinic maxim: "If two sit side-by-side with the words of the Torah between them, then the Shekinah [God's presence in the world] abides in their midst." Here prayer has replaced sitting; the new, living Law, Jesus Christ, takes the place of the law; instead of God's Shekinah we have his incarnate eucharistic Presence. We must try to bring all those who migrate to the margins and fall over the edge back into the mystery of this ecclesial center.

[A] Twenty-fourth Sunday in Ordinary Time

Sirach 27:30–28:7 (27:33–28:9); Romans 14:7–9;
Matthew 18:21–35

1. Forgive us our debts. Few parables in the Gospel have the
overpowering force of this one—not even the slightest objection can be raised against it. Almost no other parable confronts us so dramatically with the extent of our sinful love-
lessness: we demand incessantly from our fellow men what we
think they owe us, without giving a moment's thought to the
immensity of the debt God has forgiven us. Distractedly we
pray the petition of the Lord's Prayer: "Forgive us our debts,
as we also . . .", but we fail to consider how unwilling we are
to renounce a bit of our earthly justice, even though God has
waived passing heavenly judgment on us.

The reading from the Old Covenant recognizes all of this
in minute detail: "A man refuses mercy to his fellow men yet
seeks to be granted pardon by the Lord." Even to the Old Testament sage this was an utter impossibility. Thus he appeals
not to general humanistic sensitivities but explicitly to God's
covenant, to God's offer of both grace and forgiveness of sins
to Israel: "Think of the covenant of the Most High and forgive
faults."

2. Free to forgive. The second reading deepens this foundation christologically. We who sit in judgment over right and
wrong do not even belong to ourselves. In all of our existence
we are those who owe ourselves to the forgiving goodness of
the One who has already on our behalf taken away our debt.
When Paul says, "None of us lives for himself", it means two
things: no one owes his existence to himself; as someone who
exists he owes himself to God. More than that, he owes him-

self more profoundly to the One who has already paid his debt and he remains his debtor in the deepest sense. This by no means makes him into a servant or slave of the friend, rather, just the opposite: the King releases into freedom the servant whose debts he forgave. If we owe ourselves entirely to Christ, then we owe ourselves to divine love that has loved us "to the end" (Jn 13:1). To owe ourselves to love means to be permitted to love and to be able to love. For man that is precisely the most sublime freedom.

3. Self-judgment. "Wrath and anger are hateful things, yet the sinner hugs them tight", Sirach says. Now the Gospel speaks of the king's anger as he throws the "wretched servant" into prison, that is, hands him over to the very justice he had insisted on for himself. What is this wrath of God? It is the effect that a loveless person produces from God's infinite love. Or, to put it another way, it is the effect that God's love produces in a loveless person. A loveless person who closes the door to divine mercy out of a narrowly egotistical understanding of debt-forgiveness clearly condemns himself. God's love judges no one; the verdict, as John says, consists in man's refusal to accept God's love (Jn 3:18–20, 12:47–48). James summarizes this in a short statement: "Judgment is merciless to the one who has not shown mercy, while mercy triumphs over judgment" (James 2:13). And the Lord himself says, "The measure with which you measure will in turn be measured out to you" (Lk 6:38).

[A] Twenty-fifth Sunday in Ordinary Time

Isaiah 55:6–9; Philippians 1:20–24, 27;
Matthew 20:1–16

1. Beyond justice. In the parable of the workers in the vineyard
it is important to pay attention to the point being made: that,
out of his sovereign generosity God very well can and constantly
does exceed the bounds of distributive justice. Sovereignty is
emphasized here: "Am I not free to do what I wish with that
which belongs to me?" But generosity is also emphasized: "Or
are you envious because I am generous?" One certainly could
apply the parable to the Jews and Gentiles: the Jews have
worked from early morning onward, the Gentiles came at the
last minute. But in fact each receives his wage according to
God's free and bountiful generosity, for the entire covenant
with Israel was, after all, an expression of God's sovereign and
lavishly generous action. Yet the parable has meaning for every
age and every nation that wishes to grasp Jesus' basic theme.
God has always exceeded the level of simple distributive justice
and therefore, in Christ, he requires that people do the same:
"For I say to you, unless your righteousness [justice][3] exceeds
that of the scribes and Pharisees, you will not enter into the
Kingdom of heaven" (Mt 5:20).

---

[3] The biblical words for justice can with equal validity be translated as righteousness, and the distinction made in English between the two does not exist in the
same way in German. In this meditation *Gerechtigkeit* has normally been translated
as "justice". The same word, *Gerechtigkeit*, is von Balthasar's choice in translating
Mt 5:20 at the end of the paragraph; in keeping with the standard translation of this
verse in English we have rendered it as "righteousness". The reader should realize
that von Balthasar is deliberately connecting biblical ideas that the English language
tends to distance slightly from each other. Cf. pp. 339 and 359—TRANS.

2. *God's love-justice.* This does not mean that God's love and mercy are unjust. Justice is just as much a characteristic of God as love and mercy are. That is why the Sermon on the Mount insists that Jesus did not come to abrogate the law but to fulfill it, and that none of the commandments of the law, insofar as it comes from God, can be abrogated (Mt 5:17–19). Any interpretation of the Sermon on the Mount that overlooks this, precisely when dealing with the application of love of enemies and defenselessness in the social order, is mistaken. This world's order, both public and private, is not abolished, it is simply surpassed by the actions of Christ and of his followers. The first reading expresses in drastic language the way in which God's thoughts surpass human conceptions of what is right and proper: God's ways exceed human thinking to the same degree as heaven surpasses the earth. Divine thinking and doing are labeled mercy and forgiveness, yet, as grace, they contain in themselves a demand for conversion, a demand that is entirely just when viewed from the perspective of grace.

3. *The Church in imitation.* In the second reading Paul gives us a remarkable confirmation of the assertions we have just made. What constitutes for him the better way to imitate God's generosity? Although men wish for long lives, he would rather die in order to be with Christ. Yet despite this wishful longing he recognizes that the will of God just might consist in his remaining alive and fruitful on earth for the sake of the community. Paul does not choose, rather, he lets God choose what is better for him. Contrary to what many think, this "better" is not made up of a steady increase in good works and apostolic effort, rather, solely in carrying out the will of God, whose plans surpass the Apostle's wishes and longings like heaven surpasses earth. So too the thoughts of the vineyard owner exceed those of the long- and short-term workers, yet they are in each case

the best, and therefore the most grace-filled, thoughts for each person.

[A] Twenty-sixth Sunday in Ordinary Time

Ezekiel 18:25–28; Philippians 2:1–11;
Matthew 21:28–32

1. Saying and doing. If one hears it in the light of the entire Gospel reading, with its concluding statement about publicans and sinners addressed to an audience of chief priests and elders, Jesus' parable of the two sons, one promising but not delivering obedience, the other initially refusing but eventually offering obedience, carries two meanings. The first is: a late conversion is better than the self-righteous delusion that one needs no conversion. Jesus has come to call and to heal the sick, not those who think themselves healthy (Mt 9:12–13). The second teaching distinguishes sharply between talk and action. It contrasts a person who piously promises God he will do something and thereby deceives himself into thinking he has already done enough with one who actually does something, often with an outward demeanor that would not lead anyone to expect any such action from him. We have here echoes of the "Lord, Lord" cries at the end of the Sermon on the Mount, and of the house built on sand rather than rock. Both Gospel themes are made most clear in the other readings.

2. Late conversion. The first reading, from Ezekiel, takes account of late conversion. Paths in life often are confused. One loses himself in the fields of sin, far from God. Perhaps, like the second son in the Gospel, he gives God a resounding No. But to be able to reject God's command he must first have heard it, and, since the command keeps echoing, the sinner's carrying-on ceases to be fun. His bad conscience pursues him and spoils his pleasure in sinning. Like Israel, the sinner grouses at this spoil-sport God: "The Lord's way is not fair!" (Ezek 18:25), yet he knows that God cannot be wrong. That is how it must have been with the prostitute who converted at Jesus' feet in the Pharisee's house (Lk 7). The event of a conversion, even if a late one like that of the thief on the cross, is so significant for God that he silently sweeps away all twistedness and corruption and opens an entirely new lifetime account for the one who has turned toward him. In the end, at the judgment, the data of such a life are not simply added up and totaled, rather, one entire column is simply erased and a new one begun immediately following. That is how the tax collectors and prostitutes are able to enter the Kingdom of heaven ahead of the Pharisees.

3. Deeds count. The second reading shows how deeds, not words, count. The dominant example is Jesus Christ himself, who emptied himself, took the form of a slave, and was obedient to God even to death on the Cross. Here we hear only about his actions, not a word about his teaching, even though, of course, every word he spoke was spoken in obedience to the Father. Paul's great exhortation to the Church has one purpose: that all might have an attitude that corresponds to an existence in Christ. Since Christ did not spare himself, but rather died on the Cross for all his brothers and sisters, each Christian should not immediately think of himself but should instead "regard others as more important" than himself. This is possible only if he has the humility of Christ, which takes the last seat and does nothing out of "selfishness or vainglory". The first son's Yes was that sort of vainglory: he wanted to appear to be the model child. In so doing he automatically elevates himself above others, which is why he equally automatically becomes a false member of the community of Christ.

[A] Twenty-seventh Sunday in Ordinary Time

Isaiah 5:1–7; Philippians 4:6–9;
Matthew 21:33–43

1. The rejection of God's messenger. The parable of the "evil vineyard tenants" undoubtedly was given with a view toward Israel's actions in the story of God's salvation: The servants sent by the owner of the vineyard to collect his share of the harvest certainly are the prophets. Their demands on God's behalf are scorned and they are murdered by the selfish tenants. Yet the parable would not be part of the New Testament if it had nothing to do with the Church. As the concluding words say, the Church is the nation entrusted with the Kingdom taken from Israel so that God can finally receive the anticipated harvest. We must ask whether the Church as we know her has really given God that harvest. He receives it from the servants sent to the Church, especially from the saints with missions (whether canonized or not). But the question for us is: How has the Church received them and how does she continue to receive them? Badly, for the most part, often not at all. Many of them, including popes, bishops, and priests, endure martyrdom within the Church herself: rejection, suspicion, scorn, and contempt. Even when canonized after their deaths their images are often falsified to satisfy people's desires: Augustine becomes the leader in persecuting heretics; Francis, a nature-fanatic, Ignatius, a sly schemer. What Jesus said remains true after all the centuries: "A prophet is never without honor except in his native place and among his own kin and in his own house" (Mk 6:4). Each member of the Church must ask himself whether God's disappointment at the results from the vineyard he himself has planted—"I hoped for sweet grapes, but it produced only wild grapes" (first reading)—does not apply to him personally, to someone who usually criticizes the Church as a whole.

2. The disappointment of God. Yes, the disappointment of God! Disappointment at the synagogue and at the Church, who has always tended to run from him, today perhaps more than ever, since, in matters of faith, liturgy, and morality she thinks she knows better than God and his old-fashioned revelation. Instead of serving God in praise and adoration she is always running after foreign gods: the Mass as the congregation's self-fulfillment (if the performance was satisfactory people applaud), prayer as psychic hygiene, dogma as psychological archetype, etc. She provides fuel to keep Paul's concern burning: "I am afraid that, as the serpent deceived Eve by his cunning, your thoughts may be corrupted from a sincere commitment to Christ" (2 Cor 11:3). Just as "a remnant" of the synagogue remains loyal and wholesome (Rom 11:5), so this "holy remnant"—and certainly much more—Mary, the saints, and the Church of the truly faithful, will last forever.

3. The remnant. In the second reading Paul, who considered himself part of this remnant, describes the attitude that should characterize it. Even if the unfaithful Church is dominated by a constant restlessness, by addiction to the world's newest, most profitable, and most marketable, the faithful remnant is dominated by "the peace of God that surpasses all understanding", despite persecution, indeed precisely in the midst of persecution. If Paul promises the congregation that "the peace of God will be with you", then one will recognize the true Christian by this peace as it rules over him, even as he mourns the state Christianity is in and even though he is one of those who hunger and thirst, who are pronounced blessed.

[A] Twenty-eighth Sunday in Ordinary Time

Isaiah 25:6–10; Philippians 4:12–14, 19–20;
Matthew 22:1–14

1. The call of the King. God the Father is the king in the Gospel. He prepares a wedding dinner for his son. In the first reading this meal is portrayed as a feast of joy in the messianic end-time, because not only Israel but all the nations are invited to it. The veil of sadness that has covered the Gentiles is now lifted, indeed, all grounds for mourning, even death, have vanished. The Old Testament picture has no shadow. In contrast, the New Testament image is covered with many shadows. Let us first ask what sort of meal God the Father prepares for his Son. It is a wedding meal; the Book of Revelation calls it the Wedding of the Lamb (Rev 19:7; 21:9ff.). The Lamb is the Son who, by means of his perfect sacrifice, brings about the marital union with the Church-Bride not only as Bridegroom but also as Eucharist. In the eucharistic Feast it is God the Father who gives the supper: *"My* dinner is ready", he has his servants announce, "Come to the wedding." In solemn prayer the Church thanks the Father for his supreme and most exuberant gift: his Son as bread and wine. This thanksgiving arises from the Church, who becomes a bride by means of the meal. The Father gives his last and best; he has nothing better. Therefore, he who scorns this most precious gift can expect nothing more. He judges himself, he falls into ruin.

2. Forms of scorning the invitation include both scorning the invitation to the wedding and accepting it but participating unworthily. Matthew combines these two ways of making God's supreme gift worthless. The first form is indifference: those invited care nothing for the grace offered them—they have better things to do, their earthly business is more pressing. But since God has entered into a covenant with man, he cannot tolerate this sort of contempt for his offer. Just as Jeremiah had to announce the end of Jerusalem, so too the Evangelist announces the final end of the holy city: it will be reduced to rubble by the Romans. The second form of unworthiness, contrasting with the indifference of the invited guests, is that of the man who strolls into the Eucharistic Celebration as if entering a pub. Why should he get dressed up? The King should be happy that I come at all, that I still communicate, that I bother myself enough to leave my pew to stuff a bit of bread in my mouth. This man has to account for his behavior: Don't you have at least the faintest inkling that you are at the highest Feast of the Ruler of the cosmos? "But he was reduced to silence." Perhaps only after being tossed out it will occur to him what he has missed out on because of his lackadaisical behavior.

3. Understanding the spirit of the call. God bestows things on us without measure. But he does this to the end that we will learn to give ourselves without calculating, without stinginess. In the second reading Paul rejoices that his congregation has learned to give. The whole meaning of the Eucharist becomes complete in this giving of what the King has given. Of course we can never thank God enough for what he has given, but the best thanks, the thanksgiving that makes him happiest, is that we absorb something of the spirit of self-giving sacrifice, understand it, and implement it.

[A] Twenty-ninth Sunday in Ordinary Time

Isaiah 45:1, 4–6; 1 Thessalonians 1:1–5;
Matthew 22:15–21

1. Jesus evades the trap. The question asked of Jesus in the Gospel—whether one ought to pay taxes to Caesar—is an attempt to trap Jesus. In the framework within which the questioners' minds are moving, escape seems impossible. By saying "Yes" he contradicts the holy people's direct relationship with God and disavows their striving for political freedom. By saying "No" he places himself on the side of the Zealots who have developed a political theology of liberation for themselves; openly or secretly he becomes an agitator against Roman rule. On the political level occupied by the questioners, he can find no third possibility, no back door exit. But Jesus does not permit himself to enter this level. He recognizes its legitimacy only by climbing over it and thereby relativizing it. As a "fleshly people" the Jews have gotten themselves stuck on this level even though they would not have had to. Christians will follow Jesus' uprising and sense their responsibility for the world's politics from a higher stance. The second reading, in which Paul proclaims God's Word to the Thessalonians with power (but not political power) and the Holy Spirit, is the upbeat for a completely different sort of theology of liberation.

2. Desacralizing the emperor. Asking to see a silver coin, which bears the emperor's portrait and inscription, Jesus gives an initial answer: "Then give to Caesar what is Caesar's." In the ancient world a ruler's power extended as far as his money. This is a limited power, subordinate to God's power. Here the first reading becomes significant: God has given King Cyrus a mission that is both political and religious—to let the exiled Israelites return home. Yet the opposite can also occur: God gives the prophet Jeremiah the mission of telling King Jehoiakim he should submit to the king of Babylon instead of engaging in political "theology" against him. Jesus' answer seems to be a political answer, yet he speaks from a higher level, as the subsequent clause reveals.

3. We owe everything to God. "Give God what belongs to God." Everything belongs to God, because man is created according to God's image, not Caesar's, and because God is Ruler over all earthly kings. Kings think they are sacral powers and claim divine attributes; Jesus demystifies this sacrality. God alone is Lord and earthly rulers at most receive a divine stewardship under which they are to ensure political order by God's commission. For realizing this Christians will pay a bloody price. Yet Jesus does not pursue the question of the legitimate or exaggerated claims of worldly authorities. The only thing that really matters to him is that God receive all that is owed him, which is indeed everything, whether natural or supernatural. Where worldly power rises in rebellion against this "everything", a rebellion that goes far beyond political matters, Jesus and those who stand with him will resist that rebellion. He recognizes Pilate's power to crucify him, but only as a power granted to Pilate: thus, although Pilate has no notion of this, it is consonant with the Father's will.

[A] Thirtieth Sunday in Ordinary Time

Exodus 22:20–27; 1 Thessalonians 1:5–10;
Matthew 22:34–40

1. Priority in the law. The Jews, who had 615 laws to follow, divided them into major and minor commandments. The ques-

tion asked of Jesus about the "greater" commandment was really about the "greatest". The Jews basically must have known
that the command to love God had priority, and they also
knew that love of neighbor was emphatically laid down in the
law. Yet, since any sense of direction has fallen victim to the
maze of countless commandments, Jesus restores the priori-
ties here in no uncertain terms: Love of God before anything
else, as the response of the entire person to God's total self-
giving covenant: love him with your mind, yes, but on a deeper
level, with your heart, and, incorporating both, with "all your
soul". Because he himself is both God and man, he can join
love of God and love of neighbor inseparably. But he does not
stop there. In what is probably the most striking part of his
answer to the question, he makes all the other laws and the
prophets' explications of them dependent on this double commandment as the norm and standard for all morality. Drawing
on men's preunderstanding but giving it order and clarity, Jesus
here erects the fundamental structure for all Christian ethics.
No exceptional standard can be valid without love of neighbor,
nor can love of neighbor take precedence over love of God.

2. Ecclesial implementation. When one turns to Paul (second
reading), one finds "faith in God" as "turning to God from
idols" at the center of his opening address to the Thessalonian
church. By following the example of Paul, who more than any
other Apostle emphasized the inseparability of love of God and
love of neighbor, this congregation has become a direct moral
example "for all believers". In his "canticle of love" (1 Cor 13)
Paul depicts this inseparability so well that one sees it in every
sentence: the love of God and of Christ takes effect in one's
behavior toward others; just as God loves us in Christ, so a
Christian's love must be patient, generous, selfless, enduring
everything and putting up with everything. This love is Chris-

tian in a double sense: because Christ reveals the Father's love to us and because we can structure our entire moral behavior according to Christ's example. No ethic is simpler and more transparent than the Christian ethic.

3. Love of neighbor as thanksgiving to God. Now it is the Old Testament that brings home to us the importance of love of neighbor, by recalling not only that Israel kept the first commandment, to love God, but also that Israel owes its entire existence to God's love, the love that brought Israel out of Egypt. When they were strangers in Egypt God showed the Israelites the sort of love one gives to one's own. With this memory refreshed, Israel is now supposed to deal equally lovingly and protectively with the stranger, the poor, widows, and orphans. This early text from Israel's "book of the covenant" helps us anticipate the concluding text of the New Covenant: "If you have done this to the least of these my brothers, you have done it to me." The first love God bestowed on me by giving me the grace to be created by him and to be his child obligates me to reveal this divine love to the least of my brothers in deeds as well as in words.

[A] Thirty-first Sunday in Ordinary Time

Malachi 1:14–2:2, 8–10; 1 Thessalonians 2:7–9, 13; Matthew 23:1–12

1. Priesthood as an office of service. All of the texts today have to do with the role of the clergy in the people of God. First, in the Gospel, Christ attacks the false and ruinous example of the scribes and Pharisees who teach the law of God but do not obey it, who load men down with heavy burdens that the leaders themselves do not shoulder, and who are constantly trying to ensure that they will be given precedence and respect. The Church of Christ, in contrast, is a people made up of brothers, a communion in God, who alone is Father and Master, and in Christ, who alone is the teacher. When Jesus establishes his Church on Peter and the other Apostles and grants them forms of authority that do not belong to everyone, he does so in order that they might serve the brethren. This is something Jesus continually brought home to them and exemplified by his own actions (Lk 22:26–27). In its innermost essence the office he institutes is an office of service, a "service at table". One might say that members of the clergy are more aware of this today than in earlier times; therefore the criticism leveled at them—that they try to use their office to lord over people —often arises from an un-Christian democratism. Yet today there are indeed some who elbow their way into the priesthood out of the same lust for domination that was laid at the feet of the Pharisees. It is as if they think they receive an exalted position by being made priests, which corresponds neither to the Gospel nor to the consciousness of the majority of the clergy today.

2. God's accusations. In the first reading we find a false clericalism being scolded, not during the time of Jesus but 450 years before Christ. What God accuses the priests of here is not irrelevant today. Here too the basis established is that "we all have the same Father" and thus are all brothers. Because this has been forgotten, three valid charges can be leveled at the cleric. First, he "has not taken it to heart to give glory to my name". Instead of giving priority to God's glory, he has proclaimed a this-worldly psychological and sociological ethic that the people relish. Second, through this sort of "teaching", he causes "many to falter": they no longer understand the religion of the covenant and distance themselves from it or simply turn away from God. The later Psalms clearly reveal this situation. Third, in teaching people he has played favorites: certain people are preferred; he works closely with select cliques, among whom he carries out group dynamics and such, while others are left to themselves. God's warnings about such methods are stern: these priests "profane the covenant"; God hurls his "curse" at them.

3. The genuine priest. In contrast, in the second reading, Paul gives us an ideal portrait of how a priest should conduct himself in a Christian office: he loves the congregation entrusted to him like a mother loves a child. He relates to its members not as an official but as a person; like Christ, he permits the members to participate in his life. He should not become a material burden to the congregation; therefore he works. And he experiences his greatest joy when people genuinely perceive him as a servant, when they understand his preaching as pure transmission of the Word of God, "as it truly is", not as the word of a man, not even a saintly man. He has no interest in gaining influence over the congregation—all he strives for is that God's Word might be "at work in you who believe". He will encounter false accusations of lust for domination and arrogance. But he knows that such accusations are part of priestly service. "When ridiculed, we bless; . . . we have become like the world's rubbish, the scum of all" (1 Cor 4:12–13).

[A] Thirty-second Sunday in Ordinary Time

Wisdom 6:12–17; 1 Thessalonians 4:12–18;
Matthew 25:1–13

As the Church year draws to a close we turn our attention to the consummation of history and the return of Christ.

1. In light of the other life. The important concern is to keep faith vigilant in us. In the first reading Paul arouses faith in those who mourn for their dead as if "they have no hope". Rather than annihilation or migration of the soul he holds out to such people the possibility of participation in Christ's Resurrection, which has refuted death's apparent finality. This resurrection of the dead is so certain and urgent that, in his view, it takes place before the living are transported to heaven. In any case, the sequence is less important than the certainty that all who belong to Christ "will be with the Lord unceasingly", and that therefore it is essential that one be ready and vigilant for the day and hour of Christ's return, as the entire New Testament tirelessly insists.

2. Wisdom as watching. For the Christian wisdom consists precisely in this constant watchfulness. In the first reading we see that man need not search far for this wisdom, or prudence, for Wisdom sits at his door and he merely needs to let her enter. But for her sake he needs to "keep vigil", remain sleepless (Wis 6:15). By being vigilant he remains "free of care", free of anxiety about his fate after death. Throughout the Book of Wisdom, God's gift of Wisdom, or prudence, is always a consoling, encouraging vehicle of God's goodness. She promises that "the just will live for ever" (5:15) and will attain "incorruptibility" and an "eternal reign" with God (6:18, 21). The "hope" of the just "is full of immortality" (3:4).

3. The parable about readiness. This leads to the basic point of
the Gospel about the wise and foolish virgins. To watch and
wait in hope is prudent, even if night has fallen. Not to be
prepared for the Hour is foolish. At the hour of death one
must have the oil of preparedness at hand for there will be no
time to go fetch oil, no time somehow to acquire this readiness
somewhere. The Gospel readily admits that the hours of night
and uncertainty can be long, that there can be moments during life when even the wise "doze off", yet the Song of Songs
tells us "I slumber but my heart keeps vigil" (5:2). Readiness
for God can be lively at any moment, even in the midst of
secular business. That the five wise virgins cannot share their
oil with the other five has nothing to do with the mystery of
the communion of saints, in which each saint is ready to share
everything with another. Here we are dealing with the attain-
ment of sanctity itself, which is indivisible: the Bridegroom can
do nothing with partial sanctities, since only complete sanctity
can be communicated. Only the perfectly holy Son of God
could bear the sins of the world. The image of those who arrive too late and pound away at the door only to be turned
away as strangers does not point to God's hardheartedness and
unwillingness to forgive sinners. All it says is that our tepid-
ity and indifference can run up against a genuine "too late".
The Gospel holds out this possibility so that we can grasp the
seriousness of the concluding warning: "Therefore, keep your
eyes open, for you know not the day nor the hour."

[A] Thirty-third Sunday in Ordinary Time

*Proverbs 31:10–13, 19–20, 30–31; 1 Thessalonians 5:1–6;
Matthew 25:14–30*

1. The talents. The Gospel has to do with man giving account
before God. The Creator has "entrusted his possessions" to
the creatures; the Savior has entrusted his possessions to the
redeemed, each "according to his abilities", in other words,
in a very personalized fashion. "Talents" are valuable sums of
money; we talk about intellectual talents that are given equally
personally to individuals: we have received them in trust and
are supposed to work with them not only for ourselves ("self-
realization") but for God. For we owe ourselves, together with
all we have, to God. In the parable the owner disappears; we
servants remain behind with all his assets, and something in
the very nature of a talent means that it has to produce something. The lazy servant has eyes only for the lord's strictness,
not his kind generosity, and tangles himself up in contradictions: "You harvest where you have not planted; so out of fear I
went off and buried your money in the ground." If he had really
viewed the talent entrusted to him as a measure of sternness,
he should have worked all the harder; but his ostensible fear
let him forget that the nature of the goods entrusted to him is
to produce more. God gives living things to the living, living
things that need to grow; to bury them as if they were dead
things makes no sense, because in that case we could not even
return to God the living thing he gave us. In contrast, to the
servants who return to him both the fruitful things and their
fruits, he grants them in trust an incalculable, eternal fruitfulness.

2. Work during the day. Paul warns us in the second reading
against procrastinating with our efforts, because the day at

which we must give flawless account is unknown to us. We are not living in darkness, during which sleep is permitted, rather, we are "children of the day", of the time for work. The "others", who would rather sleep, are trying to surround themselves with a world in which "peace and security" dominate, which would then permit leisure and sleep. But our temporal life, whether public or private, is not so constituted. Precisely when one is cradled by security sudden ruin comes like "labor pains come upon a pregnant woman". Peace does not arise of its own accord, rather, to the degree that it can be achieved on earth, one must struggle for peace with "sober" effort in bright daylight. Anyone who strives in a Christian sense is always ready to render account; the day of the Lord cannot take him "by surprise like a thief".

3. The example of the woman. In the Old Covenant the model for such effort is the industrious woman. For a Christian this depiction of an exemplary worker will immediately recall Mary. "Her husband's heart trusts her"; Christ can entrust his entire treasure to her and "he has an unfailing prize." From her Yes, from her readiness for everything—her readiness for the Incarnation, for abandonment, for the Cross, for being guided into the Church—from all that she is and does Christ can construct the best that God intended for his creation and salvation. In the midst of many sinners who do not deliver on their promises, she is the faultless one, the Church without spot or wrinkle. "Give her a reward for her labors!" And even from heaven it is apparent that she has been given the "great task" of the parable: "She reaches out her hands to the poor, and extends her arms to the needy."

[A] Christic King

Ezekiel 34:11–12, 15–17; 1 Corinthians 15:20–26, 28;
Matthew 25:31–46

1. "I was hungry and you gave me food." The Church year closes
with the great description of the Christ's Last Judgment. He
appears as "King" of mankind, sitting on the "Throne of his
glory". Two motifs are found throughout the immense paint-
ing: the first and central theme is that everything we do or do
not do to the least of his brothers is done or not done to him.
The second theme is found right there: if the first theme is
the absolute criterion, then those who undergo judgment must
be completely separated into right and left, eternal reward and
eternal punishment. Thus the second motif depends on the first
one, which provides the decisive teaching given by the entire
tableau: the judging, glorious King knows his solidarity with
the least of his brothers—who are simply very stately and imposing. Christ makes common cause with the hungry and the
thirsty, with aliens and the homeless, with the unclothed, the
sick, and the imprisoned. Only in such solidarity is he King,
as the One who has sovereignly climbed down to the lowest
and most shameful human situations and become acquainted
with them. Each person, whose life will someday be examined
by the Judge, should ponder this constantly: in the most mis-
erable of our fellow men we have already met our Judge. As
men we are all members of a single body, sharing with each
other solidarity in our being, something we must be aware of
and behave properly toward. You ought to "share your bread
with the hungry, give shelter to the homeless, clothe the naked
you see, and not turn your back on your own flesh" (Is 58:7).

2. "He must reign until God has put all enemies under his feet."
The second reading's eschatological imagery portrays not only

the Son's sole rule, which takes effect throughout all world history, but beyond that gives hope that the subjection of all "enemies", "all sovereignty, authority, and power", will succeed. Thus when the Son hands over to the Father the work he has completed, in order that "God may be all in all", it will not include any rebelliousness against God.

3. Still, we cannot simply exclude the theme of separation. *"I will seek out the animals that are lost"*, are God's words as shepherd of mankind in the first reading. He will also exert himself on behalf of the injured and the weak, "tending them rightly". Yet this setting things right is not the same as a general amnesty. Instead God "does right by one animal in regard to another", or, as a later verse reads: "I will judge between the fat and the lean sheep, because with flank and shoulder you push all the weak sheep with your horns until you have driven them out" (Ezek 34:20–21). The love with which God pastures his sheep cannot do without justice, yet the Old Testament never says that God practices justice without love.

YEAR B

[B] First Sunday of Advent

Isaiah 63:16–17, 19, 64:2–7; 1 Corinthians 1:3–9;
Mark 13:33–37

1. Watch! The Church year begins with the Gospel call for vigilance, since the time of the Lord's coming is uncertain. Christmas has a firm date, but the Lord's coming into our life and death, into the life and consummation of the Church does not. We carry "full responsibility" for God's goods on earth; each of us has an assigned task. Special vigilance is required of the gatekeeper, who must keep on keeping watch even after the Lord's coming, just as those at work in the house must keep on working. And this gatekeeping task can be understood as the mission of the Church and the mission of each Christian. All Christians are addressed by the single challenge: "I tell all of you: Be on guard!" We cannot shirk our assigned work, for it is a question of the Lord's assents, not ours. No matter what we are doing, whether spiritual or secular, we are doing for him, not for ourselves. We are building his Kingdom, not our own.

2. With God's help. The second reading says that the Lord has equipped us perfectly for this work, by means of the charisms ("gifts of grace") that God has given us for the interim during which we await the "revelation of our Lord Jesus Christ". We do not wait idly, rather, we wait by employing the gift that was given us for action. The gift is a freely given "richness of everything in him"; the assets for "knowledge", "witnessing", and "speech" must yield their anticipated return. Nor does

God look idly down on our work—he actively works with us by "fortifying" us when we are uncertain or tired. We will not lack for aid from him if we only keep at the work assigned us. But do we do that? Is our busy time employed to build up what God has given us to do or must we not rather join the prophet in the first reading in a lament, an outcry that has to be sounded precisely at the beginning of the Church year?

3. The face of the world. "Why do you let us wander, O Lord, from your ways and harden our hearts so that we fear you not?" This is a crying out to God, not a decrying of God, for God has not failed us, indeed, God is "our Redeemer named forever". We are the ones who have been unfaithful from time immemorial. We have become so wrapped up in our worldly concerns that "no one calls upon your name anymore", "no one rouses himself to cling to you." Thus no one can blame God for "delivering us up" to the "power", to the logic, of "our guilt". We are not unaware of our own guilt: "All our good deeds" and all our marvelous and threatening progress "are like polluted rags"; the supposed flowering of our culture is like "withered leaves carried away by the wind". All that is left to those who still know about God and his faithfulness is an outcry: "O that you would rend the heavens and come down!" Despite all our ingratitude, do not forget that we are still "the work of your hands", the clay that you, the "potter", can still reshape.

[B] Second Sunday of Advent

Isaiah 40:1–5, 9–11; 2 Peter 3:8–14;
Mark 1:1–8

1. In the Gospel *the Baptist* makes his appearance: he refers to himself as, and he is indeed, a "voice in the wilderness".

More than ever this world is wilderness, and "the wilderness grows"—artificially, through the clearing of rain forests, something all cultural and development plans seem powerless to halt; spiritually, as the religious landscape turns into a vast, overgrown prairie where men can scarcely hear the cry "Prepare the way of the Lord." This "voice" echoes in the midst of the swirling cacophony of the mass media, sandwiched between the news items that tumble over each other. And even though the prophet makes his entrance in a strikingly counter-cultural get-up—camel's hair clothing, with grasshoppers and wild honey for food—years of youthful protesters have made us accustomed to this sort of thing. (Although ultimately these youth, except for those bent on genuine criminal lives, do indeed want to play their part in the grand game adults play.) In such a world, a theology can make headlines only if it involves itself in politics or exhorts people to social change. The Baptist would have a much harder time of it today than two millennia ago, when people came out to him, confessed their sins, and were prepared to believe him when he said that someone greater than him would follow, someone for whom one should prepare himself.

2. The first reading provides the full *context for his message*. That content goes beyond tomorrow's or the next day's events: the exiled Israelites will be permitted to return home from Babylonia and rebuild their temple. The message speaks of an imminent future in which "all mortals shall see the glory of the Lord", in which God himself will gather mankind like a shepherd and finally lead them home. This eschatological event is to be proclaimed from a "high mountain" as a message of joy. The chaos of world history, with its cavities and hills—nothing but winding roads!—will in the end prove to be a straight and level path upon which God himself has always been walking.

When viewed from within this world, history seems to have followed a trajectory toward unforeseeable catastrophe; when viewed from its outcome, however, it is a safe and pleasant path home.

3. God's time. The second reading tells us that we lack an overview. We count the days and years, and our calculations always turn out to be false. The day of the Lord's coming has been predicted throughout all centuries and has not yet arrived. That is because God's time is completely different from ours: "A thousand years are as a day." People talk haughtily and mockingly of "delay" and naïve apocalyptic anticipation. But "the Lord does not delay in keeping his promise." He is on his way, constantly, and, like a fisherman, he hauls the giant net of world history to shore. Viewed from within the world, whether the world's end will be catastrophic disturbs neither God's plan nor the Christian's confidence. Christians simply need to strive to be "unblemished" and "to be at peace in his sight" at the homecoming. This peace prepares the way for Advent.

[B] Third Sunday of Advent

*Isaiah 61:1–2, 10–11; 1 Thessalonians 5:16–24;
John 1:6–8, 19–28*

1. Gaudete Sunday: we anticipate God not with fear and trembling but with rejoicing. In the first reading the prophet announces his coming and explains it: the coming of the Lord's messenger will mean healing and liberation to all who are poor, brokenhearted, imprisoned, and captive. This "year of the Lord's favor" applies to all of us, for all of us are imprisoned by ourselves and captivated by ourselves; far from being uninjured, all of us are so fractured and poverty-stricken that we cannot heal ourselves. Yet it is not by means of a strange miracle outside us that God will accomplish healing, rather, God works from within us, just as an organism heals from the inside out. Since God has implanted his Holy Spirit in our hearts, his Spirit can transform us from the inside: "as the earth brings forth its plants, and a garden makes its growth spring up". The God who created us is not distant or estranged from our innermost person, rather, he holds the key to our most hidden depths; only later do we perhaps notice that he has been at work in us for some time.

2. Growth from the inside. Thus we grow into the attitude required of us by the second reading: because we belong to Christ, joy should outweigh everything else in us; because we cannot heal and construct ourselves, we have to pray and thank and make room for the Spirit at work in us. To this end we dare not despise the guidance that comes from God. (How often we ignore it because we already think we know everything!) We have to know how to discern good from evil, and we must ensure actively, not passively, that the Spirit has opportunity to go to work in us. In the process God's peace is applied to every aspect of our existence, three of which are represented here: peace in body, soul, and, beyond them both, spirit. The human spirit is precisely that hidden depth of our self where the Holy Spirit is at work, our innermost being in which a door opens up to God, permitting him to enter his own possession.

3. Distance as nearness. Like the Baptist in the Gospel, a person who is conscious of this can be a witness for God's light while steadfastly denying that he himself is the light. From afar he has not the least thought of saying that he himself is light, at least in the innermost spark where his spirit touches the Spirit of God. The closer one comes to God for the purpose of testifying of him, the more clearly one sees the distance between God and creature. The more one vacates space within himself for God, the more he becomes a simple instrument of God, a "voice crying in the wilderness: Make straight the way of the Lord." The more God treats the Mother of his Son as his residence, the more she senses herself to be the "lowly handmaid". When people ask the Baptist about his authority for baptizing, he makes yet another distinction: I baptize with water, he of whom I testify will grant true Spirit-baptism; even though Jesus will elevate him above all the other prophets, he feels he is unworthy to unlace his sandals. "You may call me friend; I confess I am a servant" (Augustine).

[B] Fourth Sunday of Advent

2 Samuel 7:1–5, 8–12, 14, 16; Romans 16:25–27;
Luke 1:26–38

1. The house of David. Living in his palace, King David has a bad conscience because, compared to him, God has to live in a mere tent (first reading). Therefore he decides to do what most kings of nations do: build God an imposing dwelling-place. But God intervenes, with words of both criticism and promise. David is forgetting that God built up his entire kingdom from the moment when he made the young shepherd into a king by anointing him. And God has stood by him through all his victories. Yet this grace extends even farther: the house God has begun to build will be brought to conclusion in David's descendants and ultimately in the great Heir in whom the house will find perfection. God lives not only in palaces but in men who believe and love. They are his temples and churches and they will never fall into ruins. David's house will continue in his Son and will last forevermore. This is fulfilled in the Gospel.

2. The virgin, betrothed to the man from the house of David, is chosen by God to be his incomparable temple. God's Son, brought by the Spirit to her womb, will make his home in her, and her entire existence will serve his development into a complete man. Here too God's work does not first begin with the moment of annunciation, rather, with the first moment of Mary's existence. With her Immaculate Conception God begins to work on his temple; only because he makes her capable of saying an unconditional Yes to him can he move into her house and assure her, like David, that this house will last forever in her Son. "He will rule over the house of Jacob and his reign will be without end." Mary's son is far more than the son of David: "Something greater than Solomon is here" (Mt 12:42); David himself calls him Lord (Mt 22:45). Yet even if Jesus Christ is going to construct the ultimate temple of God "out of living stones" (1 Pet 2:5) set on top of himself as the "cornerstone", he will never forget that he owes himself to the holy house of his mother just as much as he is a descendant of David through Joseph. Her motherhood is so imperishable that, from the Cross, he can name her the Mother of his Church. The Church certainly originates in his flesh and blood, but her "Mystical Body", as Jesus' own body, cannot fail to have the same Mother—she to whom he himself owes his existence. And he gives to those within the Church who share in Mary's fruitfulness a share in her motherhood (Methodius, *The Banquet*, III, 8).

3. The temple that God is building for himself will be complete only when "all the Gentiles have been brought to the obedience of faith". That is how the letter to the Romans ends. The Christians who already believe are the means of the last phase of construction, for instead of shutting themselves up in their Church they remain open for the "mystery made manifest" to them by God. This final construction also proceeds upon the basis of the "prophetic writings", which speak of David and of the Virgin. Far from being confined to the Church, they show that the "Gospel" addresses the world as a whole. The temple built by God always points beyond itself to a greater edifice planned by God, an edifice that will only be finished when "Christ has put all his enemies under his feet" and "hands over the Kingdom to God the Father, after he has destroyed every (other) sovereignty and every authority and power" (1 Cor 15: 25, 24).

[B] The Christmas Masses

(See Year A, pp. 21–28.)

[B] Holy Family

Genesis 15:1–6, 21:1–3; Hebrews 11:8, 11–12, 17–19;
Luke 2:22–40

1. Abraham's faith. It is significant that the entire liturgy for this feast is dominated by the theme of faith. In both readings the family, which is rooted in both the Old and New Covenants, results from God's renewed activity: Abraham's body is reproductively dead, Sarah is infertile, Abraham has

[For this feast, von Balthasar offers reflections on additional readings which are options given in the German Lectionary—ED.]

already made his chief household servant his heir. Then God alters destiny. Both parents become fruitful, and the son of the promise, Isaac, is to be a pure gift of God. This episode stands as though an inscription that applies to all marriages in Israel: the fruitfulness of all marriages points toward the Messiah and always bears something of God's supernatural gift. A child is God's gift and ultimately belongs to him and serves his purposes; a family dare not close itself off, rather, just as God originally opened it up, it must remain open and at God's disposal.

2. Abraham's sacrifice. Such openness is widened to the point of humanly unbearable incomprehensibility when God tests Abraham by asking him to return the son of the promise. God has attached his promises to this son's potency, to his potential descendants—numberless "as the stars of heaven". The people of Israel always retold this episode as one of the most important in their history. God intervenes in the very family he had miraculously founded, and he shatters it. From man's perspective God has obviously contradicted himself, but because it is God who is contradicting himself, Abraham obeys and prepares himself to give back to God the most precious gift he gave him. The second reading gives Sarah a role as well. The family that owes its existence to God now becomes not merely an open family but indeed a bleeding one.

3. The sword in Mary's soul. The event that founded the people of Israel finds its final fulfillment in the Holy Family, which the Gospel depicts for us in the temple. God does not make Joseph, the last patriarch, physically fruitful but he reaches the highest level of human fruitfulness by stepping aside to let God's unique generative potency hold sway. Joseph's personal offering is buried in a scarcely noticeable liturgical act—the two doves, the offering of a poor man. And the mother's sacrifice, her total surrender to God, is covered by the veil of the prescribed purification ritual. Then comes the prophecy that defines the inner shape of this family. On the one hand, the towering significance of the Child being presented reveals that this family will open up to spread far beyond its earthly limits. On the other hand, the sword that will pierce the mother's soul means that she will be included in the Child's greater destiny. Not only must she let go of her child and thereby offer him up, but she herself will be drawn into the offering when her child's time of sacrifice arrives. Thus the old family of flesh and blood will find completion in the new spiritual family in which Mary, penetrated by the sword, once more becomes the Mother of many.

The Holy Family is no idyll in Nazareth. It is located between the sacrifice on Mount Moriah and the sacrifice on Golgotha.

[B] January 1:
Mary, Mother of God

(See Year A, p. 30.)

[B] Second Sunday after Christmas

(See Year A, p. 32.)

[B] Epiphany of the Lord

(See Year A, p. 34.)

[B] Baptism of the Lord

Isaiah 55:1–11; 1 John 5:1–9;
Mark 1:7–11

THE THEME UNITING THE TEXTS for today's celebration is not so much the act of baptism as it is the connection between water and healing salvation. Water is the symbol of freely given grace that cleanses and refreshes.

1. Water and Spirit. In the Gospel's depiction of the baptism of the Lord heaven opens above his obedient participation in water baptism at the end of the Old Covenant, the Spirit hovers over the One baptized, and the Father proclaims him his beloved Son. He is the archetype of all those who will receive Christian baptism after him: all shall receive the Spirit from above and be born anew as children of God. Earthly water is not something that can be dispensed with, for it has been incorporated into the threefold action of the baptism of Jesus. What formerly was a symbol is now part of a sacrament and, indeed, an irreplaceable part for anyone who must be "born again from water and the Spirit" (Jn 3:5) in order to share in divine life. This is so because the Son become man is submerged into salvation history and incorporates its old symbols (the saving trip through the Flood [1 Pet 3:20–22], the submerging of the people in the abyss of the sea [1 Cor 10:1–2], and John's baptism) into the new, trinitarian, saving action.

2. Water without cost. In the first reading, water becomes an anticipatory image of grace bestowed from on high, without which the earth—and also the thirsty heart of man—would

[For this feast, von Balthasar offers reflections on additional readings which are options given in the German Lectionary—ED.]

remain arid. "All you who are thirsty, come to the water, buy without money!" Anything that must be purchased with money "nourishes not" and "satisfies not"—there can be no commercial exchange with God, rather, one must simply receive his gifts, which are compared with "rain" falling from heaven that is essential to the growth that makes bread possible on earth (Is 55:10). Only what is watered by God can, by means of the rain he sends, return proper fruit to him: in God's Word we are able to speak to him, in his Spirit we can be born again to him.

3. Water and blood. Yet "Spirit and water" does not suffice for the second reading. It adds blood as a third element, that blood which, together with water, flowed from the lacerated side of Christ. The One the Father designates at baptism as his beloved and chosen Son is the One destined for the Cross, the One who will fulfill the complete will of the triune God there. And now "these three, the Spirit, the water, and the blood" have become a single "testimony for his Son". Each person baptized must realize that he owes the fact that he is a child of God to this unity of the water and blood of Christ. Whoever enters upon Christ's life by baptism will somehow end up where his life ended up, in order, "together with the Spirit" (Jn 15:26–27), to testify of faith in Christ.

[B] Second Sunday in Ordinary Time

1 Samuel 3:3–10, 19; 1 Corinthians 6:13–15, 17–20;
John 1:35–42

1. The first vocations. The scene found in the Gospel follows upon the story of the baptism of Jesus. He now begins his

apostolic life. But it is not he who immediately issues a call for
followers, rather, the Baptist, the Old Covenant drawing to a
close, sends his disciples to him. One is called Andrew, the
unnamed other one must certainly be John, the writer of the
Gospel. Discipleship here simply means followership, walking
behind Jesus without knowing anything more than that one has
been sent. Before long, however, Jesus turns around and looks
at the two of them walking toward him. "What are you looking for?" They cannot put it into words, so they ask a question
in return: "Master, where do you live?" Tell us where you are
at home, so we can get to know you better. "Come and see!"
He issues an invitation to accompany him, unaccompanied by
any instruction. Only the one who accompanies will see. And
the account confirms that this is what happened: "They went
with him and saw and stayed." "Abiding", or "staying" is the
word John uses for Jesus' ultimate being, the word of faith and
of love. Even the third disciple, Simon, is not called but is
brought to him, almost forced to come. Jesus takes a look at
him: I know you—"You are Simon, the son of John." But I
need you for a different purpose—you shall be called Cephas,
Rock, Peter. In the very first chapter of the Gospel of John
everything is definitive and absolute; we find only challenges,
not invitations. Jesus not only requires everything of this man,
he requires him as the foundation stone for everything he is
going to build. In the last chapter of the book Peter will be
the foundation stone to such a degree that he will also have
to undergird ecclesial love: "Simon, do you love me more than
these?"

2. A story of a calling. The first reading tells the story of the
calling of the first prophet, the boy Samuel. God calls him
out of his sleep. He hears the call but does not know who
has called him. "At that time Samuel was not familiar with the

Lord." Thus at both the first and second call he goes to Eli the priest, until Eli realizes at the third call that the Lord himself was calling the boy. Eli gives Samuel appropriate instructions: "If he calls you again, say: 'Speak, Lord, for your servant is listening.'" In a New Testament sense this points to ecclesial, priestly mediation. Young people do indeed hear a call, but are unsure and unable to interpret and explicate it properly. The Church, the priest, who can distinguish a genuine from a merely imagined call, enters the picture. Like Eli in the Old Covenant, the priest must be able to discern whether it is really God who is calling and if it is, train people to listen to the word perfectly, like a servant.

3. The second reading makes it clear that one who truly hears and applies what he learns to his life "*no longer belongs to himself*". He has been purchased and, like a slave, belongs body and soul to his Lord. Here the emphasis is placed on the body, which has been taken from the one called, for, as Paul says, the one called is now a member in the holy body of Christ. Anyone who sins in his own body soils the body of Christ. The dispossession that takes place in these stories of vocation is total, not partial: the whole man enters God's service bodily, to accompany, see, stay.

[B] Third Sunday in Ordinary Time

Jonah 3:1–5, 10; 1 Corinthians 7:29–31;
Mark 1:14–20

THESE THREE TEXTS ALL EMPHASIZE the urgency of conversion, for there is no time for anything else.

1. Jonah's preaching. The first reading has astounded many: Jonah was supposed to call the city of Ninevah to conversion: "In forty days Ninevah will be destroyed." Conversion follows but destruction does not. It is clear that God wanted to achieve conversion and had no interest in destruction. Since conversion took place there was no need for destruction to follow. But the threat of destruction was no mere scare tactic. He really meant it and the Ninevites rightly took him seriously in this regard. Perhaps they also understood the positive side: that God always wants the good, never destruction; that only where conversion is brushed aside must he wipe out evil for the sake of good. The irony of the book of Jonah is that the prophet becomes annoyed at Yahweh's inconsistency: How can a God threaten ruin and then not carry it out?

2. In the second reading Paul draws sweeping conclusions from the *shortness of time*. It has less to do with "expectancy" than with the nature of earthly time. In and of itself time is so pressing that one cannot settle into it with unconcerned comfort. All levels of the Church must realize this, for in this passage the Apostle is not speaking only of lay people. He applies a negative coefficient to all activities and modes of behavior: weep with dry eyes, marry as though one has no spouse, buy as if one owns nothing, etc. Because of the urgency of the time and the disintegrating shape of the world, all the goods that we have and need to use in this world must be owned and employed with enough indifference that one could do without them at any point. Time is loaned to us only on the condition that it can be canceled at a moment's notice.

3. The Gospel shows the conclusions stemming from Jesus' declaration that time is "fulfilled". With the fulfillment of time the Kingdom of God stands *at the threshold of earthly time*, and

it thus makes sense to devote oneself and one's entire existence to this infallibly dawning reality. This is not something
one does on his own initiative, rather, he is called to it and
equipped for it by God. In this passage Jesus calls four disciples away from their worldly activities (and they obey the
call without grumbling) so that they can be equipped for their
occupation in the Kingdom of God. They are to be fishers of
men, since, after all, they know how to fish. These are models
of callings, but they are not really exceptional. Christians who
remain within their worldly occupations are called to serve the
Kingdom that Jesus proclaims; to answer this call they need
precisely the sort of indifference that Paul speaks of in the second reading. Just as the sons of Zebedee left their father and
the family's paid employees behind in order to follow Jesus,
so the Christian who remains in the world has to let go of
much that seems indispensable to him, if he is serious about
following Jesus. "No one who puts a hand to the plow and
looks back at what was left behind is fit for the Kingdom of
God" (Lk 9:62).

[B] Fourth Sunday in Ordinary Time

Deuteronomy 18:15–20; 1 Corinthians 7:32–35;
Mark 1:21–28

1. In the Gospel, when Jesus drives out a demonic spirit his
teaching is recognized as a "*completely new teaching*", namely,
teaching presented "with authority". This completely new
teaching "frightens" people. They see the proof of newness in
the deliverance from the demon, but this can at most only be a
confirmation of his authority, not the doctrine itself. The decisive point is found at the opening of the Gospel: Jesus teaches

in the synagogue "and the people were spellbound by his teaching". His "divine authority" was apparent in the teaching itself, distinguishing it from the teaching of "the scribes". The new doctrine demands a radicality in obedience to God that is completely different from the legalistic strictness required by the scribes. This radicality by no means requires a flight from the world of the sort practiced by the Qumran community, rather, in the midst of the world and its work and drudgery it calls to a life lived undividedly, solely for God and according to his command. This command, which Jesus expounds to men, is both infinitely simple and infinitely demanding. He constantly repeated it: love God above all else and love your neighbor as yourself. All of the law and the prophets depends on this (cf. Mt 7:12). This is the perfection attainable by man; a perfection in which he can and should be like his heavenly Father (cf. Mt 5:48). In this there is no division, only an integrated whole.

2. In the second reading Paul focuses on the *same radicalism*. Ostensibly he distinguishes two categories of men: those who remain unmarried in order to "busy themselves with the Lord's affairs", and those who marry and thus wish "to busy themselves with things of this world and with pleasing their wives". But, as his "household rules" indicate (for example, Col 3; 1 Tim 2–5; cf. 1 Pet 3), none of this is intended to counsel men not to marry or not to practice a secular occupation. Instead he wants to make some observations about the normal characteristics of worldly-minded people. He may perhaps indicate a slight preference for being unmarried ("It would be fine with me if everyone were as I am." [1 Cor 7:7]), but he immediately adds: "But each one has his own particular gift from God", by which it is entirely possible for him to serve God and love his neighbor "undividedly", even in the midst of marriage and the world. In many instances one wonders whether it is easier

to live undividedly under the "evangelical counsels" (celibacy, voluntary poverty etc.) than in a healthy Christian marriage. The pastoral letters oppose those who "forbid marriage"—for, to the contrary, "everything created by God is good" (1 Tim 4:3–4).

3. Moses had already anticipated this ultimate teaching whose simplicity encompasses everything. In the first reading he looked ahead to the prophet of whom God says: "I will put my words into his mouth." "The Lord will raise him up" in fulfillment of all that was begun in the Old Covenant. As a result one needs to listen to whatever he says.

[B] Fifth Sunday in Ordinary Time

Job 7:1–4, 6–7; 1 Corinthians 9:16–19, 22–23;
Mark 1:29–39

1. "This is what I have come to do." From this Gospel one realizes that the work Jesus did on earth was an overwhelming task. He was to "reclaim the lost sheep of Israel", a mission that, given the spiritual and political structure of the country, was simply impossible to carry out, yet a mission to which he devotes every bit of energy he possesses. As he heals Peter's mother-in-law "the whole town gathers outside the door", and he dispenses his kindnesses to them. He rises before dawn so that he can finally pray in solitude, but is tracked down and told: "Everyone is looking for you." It is the same message as the night before. He does not excuse himself by insisting that he wants to pray now, rather he moves on into the new work "in the neighboring villages, so that I can preach there too, for this is what I have come to do". And the villages are only the beginning: "He went throughout all Galilee." A true messenger of Christian faith can model himself on Jesus' tireless effort: even if the total task that lies ahead of him is, from a human perspective, unattainable, nonetheless he will accomplish as much of it as his strength permits, and the remainder will be added either through suffering or at least through an obedient attitude. There is no excuse for him not to do all that lies within his power.

2. *"Made a slave for all."* In the second reading Paul follows the Lord's example as closely as possible. God has assigned him the task of proclaiming the Gospel; it is therefore his duty, not his own free choice. To show God his free obedience he can forgo the reward he has earned, but nothing releases him from the strict obligation to devote himself in every possible way to the task he has been given. He thus arrives not as the great lord who possesses truth, but as the slave who serves everyone. In the verses omitted here he says that he would be a slave to the Jews, would translate himself into the Jewish mentality, in order to speak to them of the Messiah, and that he would become a slave of the Gentiles in order to proclaim to them the Savior of the world. Finally, as the lectionary passage resumes, he is willing to become a slave of the weak, even though he knows he is strong, in order to win as many as possible of the less enlightened, the ever hesitant and wavering, for Christ. No one is left out: "I have made myself all things to all men." And he does this not out of a certainty that he already participates in the fulfilled promises of the Gospel, rather, in the hope that he himself will share in that which he proclaims to others.

3. *"Military service"* is what the patient Job calls man's life on earth in the first reading. Man is no lord, but a "slave who longs for the shade", no employer (the employer is God) but

a "hired hand". This is a general characterization of human, mortal, life. Christ and his Apostles do not contradict this description of human life. The "restlessness" that Job speaks of simply becomes the unrestrainable zeal to work for God and his Kingdom, whether through external activity or involvement in prayer. For prayer itself is a Christian's involvement on behalf of the world, and it is as fruitful, indeed, more fruitful, than mere external busyness.

[B] Sixth Sunday in Ordinary Time

Leviticus 13:1–2, 43–46; 1 Corinthians 10:31–11:1;
Mark 1:40–45

1. "I do will it; be made clean." Jesus' encounter with the leper who asked for healing reveals how completely new his message was in comparison with the Old Testament and rabbinical traditions. A leper was not merely excluded from society as required by the quite understandable hygienic prescriptions of the Pentateuch, but the rabbinic rules explained that the illness was caused by severe transgression of the law and forbade any sort of approach to the victim of leprosy. If a leper approached other people he was to be stoned. Jesus permits the leper to approach and then does something unthinkable for a Jew: he touches him. For Jesus is the healing Savior sent from God, and he not only concerns himself with those who are spiritually diseased (the spiritually healthy need no physician [Mt 9:12]) but also indicates by his touch that he has no fear of contagion, indeed, he deliberately takes upon himself the disease of men: their sins. Matthew describes Jesus' actions by quoting the words about the Servant of God: "He took away our infirmities and bore our diseases" (Mt 8:17; Is 53:4). But the events related in the Gospel reading are not dominated by serenity. The Greek text describes Jesus' anger ("he hissed at him") over the man's misery, which is counter to God's will. To satisfy the requirements of the law, he sends the cured man to the priest for certification of the healing. "Proof for them" means two things: so that they will realize that I can heal the sick, but also so that they will understand that I am fulfilling, not abolishing, the law. The fact that the man does not respect his command to be silent about his cure is a disobedience that significantly hinders Jesus' work: he can no longer "enter a town openly", for he does not wish to be viewed as a medicine man.

2. "Unclean! unclean!" The first reading recalls the law's rules about skin diseases. For the afflicted person these are extremely strict measures that not only require his exclusion from society and forbid him to groom himself but also insist that he call out "Unclean! Unclean!" to warn anyone approaching him. This is really what someone in the Church who has committed a serious sin ought to do: as long as his sinfulness continues, as long as he endangers others with his contagion, he ought not hypocritically hide his *de facto* separation from the "communion of saints". As the unclean person, he is the one who ought to fall at Jesus' feet as soon as possible and say: "If you will, you can cure me."

3. "Imitate me as I imitate Christ." In the second reading the Apostle Paul seeks as much as possible to be like his Lord. He cannot do what Christ uniquely does, namely, take the sins of mankind upon himself ("Was Paul crucified for you?" [1 Cor 1:13]), but he can reach out to accept the physically, and especially the spiritually, diseased and give them healing by virtue of the power of Jesus. Rather than condescension, his "accommodation" of the sick and weak is an attitude of pure service, which can extend as far as a sharing in the vicarious suffering of Jesus for the Church (Col 1:24).

[B] Seventh Sunday in Ordinary Time

Isaiah 43:18–19, 21–22, 24–25; 2 Corinthians 1:18–22; Mark 2:1–12

1. "Authority to forgive sins." The dramatic scene described in the Gospel—the immense crowd, the paralytic lowered through a hole in the roof to arrive in front of Jesus, who forgives his sins, which annoys the scribes, whom Jesus asks: "Is it easier to forgive sins or to heal physically?"—ends with the solemn assurance that the Son of Man has the power to forgive sins on earth, something proven by the healing of this sick man. Naturally, the people are astounded at this healing, which takes on meaning only in conjunction with the forgiveness of sins. Jesus begins by healing the disease that is by far the most serious: man's spiritual paralysis, which he brings upon himself by turning away from God, a disease that he cannot heal by himself, not even by the many psychological methods men discover as a means to forget their guilt or absolve themselves. Only the very God who has been offended has the power and the grace to forgive the injury done to him, and since he has sent his Son into the world to proclaim and accomplish this forgiveness, this One has the power that Jesus ascribes to himself. He has this power because the ultimate price of this grace, the Cross and the acceptance of guilt by a guiltless One, is assured from the outset. Just as the Last Supper is an anticipation of the Cross, so too is Jesus' forgiving of sins during his life on earth. It removes from men the burden that they by themselves are unable to budge, but it also shows, as the first reading proves, how much work the sinner loads onto God, since the entirety of divine love is needed to lift this burden from us.

2. *"You have wearied me with your sins."* With these words God indicts the people through the prophet. While you, you ungrateful people, "grew weary of me", while you were neglecting me, no longer praying to me, bringing me no more sacrifice, no longer believing in my power and kindness, while you were unburdening yourselves of me, you "were burdening me with your sins, and wearing me out with your crimes". How could the God who has poured out all his love on Israel feel anything other than pain at such indifference and aversion? Yet the God of love does not pout. Instead he looks for a new means of reconciliation: "See, I am doing something new!" Out of his divine creative power, God, who is love, wipes out the crimes of the people, not for Israel's sake but "for my own sake". He forgives and starts over again. There is only one condition: the people must realize this and take hold of the gift God offers them.

3. *God's Yes.* In the second, Christian, reading it becomes abundantly clear that God does not say Yes and No simultaneously, rather, he constantly says Yes. For the man who has understood this in faith there can be no other path than to stop saying Yes one minute and No the next and to respond with the pure Yes of "God's faithfulness in Christ". His acceptance into the new people of God, that is, his baptism, has already placed God's Spirit deep in his heart—the Spirit of "yes-saying"—which he now only needs to follow.

[B] Ash Wednesday

(See Year A, p. 51.)

[B] First Sunday of Lent

Genesis 9:8–15; 1 Peter 3:18–22;
Mark 1:12–15

1. "Believe in the gospel!" The gospel, the joyful news whose proclamation Jesus now inaugurates, a message that will be a single message for the entire world, for both this world and what lies beyond this world, begins with his forty-day fast. Instead of undertaking this fast as a self-motivated ascetic practice, he is driven into the wilderness by the Spirit of God. Likewise at the end of the Church's time of fasting [Lent], it is pure obedience to the Father rather than any sort of self-inspired asceticism that moves him to endure the Cross. The enormous, unbounded fruitfulness of Christ's work presupposes awesome renunciation at both beginning and end. For more than a month he lives solely from the Father's word and mission, without any nourishment: "My food is to do the will of him who sent me, and to finish his work" (Jn 4:34). After Jesus, all the saints whose messages bear fruit somehow learn to empty themselves of all that is their own in order to announce the approach of God's Kingdom effectively. As he fasts, the Lord lives between wild beasts and angels, who "waited on him". He lives between bodily danger and supernatural protection, between the extremes of all creation. Emptying himself of the human and ordinary, he becomes aware of the dimensions of the cosmos that he, as Savior of the world, is to bring back to God. Out of this preparation hidden from the world

—renunciation of everything, even of life's necessities—he can step forth and announce: "This is the time of fulfillment."

2. "This is the sign of the covenant." Both readings indicate the extent of the world that is to be saved. The first depicts God's covenant with Noah, which undergirds everything else. It has to do with the promise of an ultimate state of reconciliation between God and the world. The flood of merciless punishment belongs to the never-recurring past. At the conclusion of the storm of wrath the sun breaks through and produces a rainbow which, resting on earth, reaches to the heavens and reminds God of his covenant "with all living things, with all living beings". Neither the covenant with Israel nor the "New Covenant" of Christ abolishes or circumscribes this covenant with Noah.

3. "He went to the spirits in prison." The second reading gives an, admittedly cryptic, answer to the question of the fate of those who died before Christ. Jesus "died for the unrighteous" in order to lead them home to God. Therefore he, the physically dead one who is spiritually alive, went to the "captive spirits" in the netherworld to preach to them, to bring them the message of salvation. For before his death and netherworld journey no one could reach God (Heb 11:40). Before Jesus' Resurrection there was also no baptism that might have protected us from this Old Testament Sheol, the "prison" housing the dead, which was part of the not yet completely redeemed world. But to reach the dead Jesus had to suffer death himself, a death that we recall at the end of the Lenten fast, the death by which he can make good on the promise given in the covenant with Noah: the promise to subject to himself the entire world, including even "the final enemy, Death" (1 Cor 15:26), and its kingdom, in order to lay the cosmos "at the Father's feet".

[B] Second Sunday of Lent

Genesis 22:1–2, 9, 10–13, 15–18; Romans 8:31–34;
Mark 9:2–10

1. "Take your son, your only one, whom you love." The Gospel
of the Transfiguration is preceded by the first reading telling
the story of Abraham's sacrifice. And for good reason, for the
Transfiguration of the Lord was to be the Father's demonstration of what his "beloved Son" truly is, the One whom he
will permit to be "slaughtered" for and by mankind. For the
Jews, Abraham's sacrifice is, with good reason, the climax of
their relationship with God, and they emphasize that it was a
double sacrifice: the sacrifice of a father, who draws his knife,
and the sacrifice of a son, who agrees to his own slaughter. It is
often said that Abraham is merely a type or anticipation, since
he did not actually have to go through with the slaughter. But
perhaps he did complete the act in his intention, in his attitude,
in his heart, when he took hold of the knife. In any case, it is
the extreme form of what God can require in imitation of his
own intention from a man who is in a covenant relationship
with him. The horror of it consists not in the command to
kill the son of one's own body—this was part of surrounding
religions and, illicitly, in Israel itself—rather, the horror lies
in the fact that this son was miraculously given by God and
destined to imitate and accomplish the divine promises. In his
command God contradicts himself. Yet though the command
may be incomprehensibly contradictory to man, he must obey
because God is God.

2. "He did not spare his own Son." The second reading resolves
the apparent paradox by showing that God reveals himself as
love in essence, a love that does not contradict itself if it sends

the Son of God into real death and thereby fulfills the promise to "give everything", namely, to bestow eternal life. Here the extreme is not the one-sided obedience of man in the face of an incomprehensible command of God, rather it is the way the Son's obedient willingness to enter death for the sake of everyone is united with the Father's willingness to sacrifice to the point of not holding back his Son in order to give us everything. In this, God is not only with us, as in the Old Testament's "Emmanuel", but is ultimately "for us", his chosen ones. In this he has not merely given us something great, but has given us everything he is and has. Now God is so completely on our side that any (juridical) indictment against us loses all its force. No one can accuse us before God's judgment seat, because the Son God sacrificed is such an irrefutable advocate that he silences any human charge against us.

3. Transfiguration. In this perspective the true meaning of the trinitarian light of love radiating from the Son on the mountain in the Gospel can be understood. In no way is this a light produced through absorption in oneself (as in certain Far Eastern forms of meditation), rather it is the radiant truth of the three-in-one light of perfect surrender: it shows what the Father has really given up to "slaughter" for the world, what the new Isaac permits to be done to himself out of obedient love toward the Father, what the "overshadowing" luminous cloud veils into divine mystery. "Fear" and chatter on the part of the men necessarily follow, but they are commanded to avoid abusing by empty talk what they have witnessed. It will interpret itself in the death and Resurrection of the Lord.

[B] Third Sunday of Lent

Exodus 20:1–17; 1 Corinthians 1:22–25;
John 2:13–25

1. "Destroy this temple." The story of the cleansing of the temple is told in the middle of Lent so that we can give thought to what constitutes true worship and what a true house of God is. Two main accents shape the Gospel: Jesus' relentless attack as he drives all commerce from his Father's house of prayer, and the proof he offers when asked about the authority by which he acts: the true temple of his body, destroyed by men, will be restored within three days. Until this happens, as long as death and Resurrection lie in the future, the old temple must exclusively serve the purpose of prayer. The God of the Old Covenant could tolerate no strange gods, especially not the god mammon, alongside himself.

Each of the two other readings expounds the Gospel: the first reading explains the first accent, and the second reading explains the second.

2. "For I am a jealous God." The great self-revelation of the God of the Covenant in the first reading has two parts (and an insertion): in the first part, having proven his vitality and power in leading the people out of Egypt, God introduces himself as the sole God (Dt 6:4). Therefore all worship must be reserved for him alone and every form of idol worship must be judged worthy of punishment. In the second part he requires the people to live in a manner consistent with a covenant with the unique Majesty, doing so on the basis of the "Ten Commandments". All of the commandments are requirements for man living in covenant with God rather than merely natural laws or social norms (they can, of course, be natural laws or social norms in addition to being demanded by the covenant). Inserted between the two parts is the sabbath law, which in this context points above all to the fact that one day is held back from man's days and belongs to God. Resting from work on this day forces men to be constantly aware of God.

3. "The Jews demand signs." The second reading explains the second main motif of the Gospel. The Jews required proof of Jesus' authority: "What sign can you show us authorizing you to do these things?" Jesus both rejects yet grants their demand for a sign as a condition of coming to faith. He gives them the one sign they are permitted to have: "An evil and unfaithful generation seeks a sign, but no sign will be given it except the sign of Jonah the prophet": three days and nights in the belly of the whale, three days and nights in the womb of the earth (Mt 12:38–40). So too in today's Gospel about the destroyed and rebuilt temple. The only sign that God gives is the "one that is foolish" by men's standards, the "weak one", the Cross. Faith is needed to receive this sign, whereas the Jews first want to see before giving themselves to faith. Thus the sign remains a "stumbling block", an irritating annoyance to them, while to those called to belief "Christ, God's power and God's wisdom" is proclaimed in the most sublime and unique sign of Jesus' death and Resurrection.

[B] Fourth Sunday of Lent

2 Chronicles 36:14–17, 19–23; Ephesians 2:4–10; John 3:14–21

1. "Whoever does not believe is condemned already." The Gospel gives us a chance to revise our understanding of divine judgment during this time of repentance. The decisive point is that whoever scorns God's love condemns himself. God is not at all eager to condemn men. He is nothing but love, love that goes as far as the Father sacrificing his Son out of love for the world. There is nothing more for him to give us. The whole question is whether we accept God's love so that it can prove effective and fruitful in us, or whether we cower in our darkness in order to evade the light of this love. In the latter instance, "we hate the light", we hate true love, and we affirm our egoism in any form whatsoever (even purely sensual love is egoism). When that happens, we are "already condemned", but by ourselves, not by God.

2. *"Do the good deeds which God prepared for us in advance."* The New Testament reading once more reveals the "great love" of God for us sinners, since he has raised us up with Christ and given us a place in heaven. We have not fought our way to this place by ourselves, rather, it is given us by God's love and grace. And yet we do not automatically share in this eternal life, rather, we must appropriate God's gift to us through our "good deeds". Still, we need not laboriously discover these: the Scripture says that God "prepared them for us in advance". He shows us through our conscience, through revelation, through the Church, and through other people what he has in mind for us to do. Carrying out these deeds prepared for us in advance may cost us something, but we should sense that the requirement that we see things through is yet another grace offered us by the love of God, which permits us to do the deed itself calmly and with gratitude.

3. The first reading reveals in a new way how *God's judgment* and God's grace operate. Israel is initially reminded here of how long God's patience was extended before Israel's scorn for his

messengers pushed God to the point "that there was no rem-
edy". The only way out was the total destruction of Jerusalem
and exile in Babylon. Yet even then the destiny of the people
has not reached an end—the exile is for a limited time, and
there is the prospect of an earthly rescuer (King Cyrus) who,
as God's instrument, permits the exiles to return home. This
is the Old Covenant, for God's grace has not yet come to an
end, is not yet "consumed". How things ultimately will turn
out for those who scorn the supreme grace of God, which is
offered in Jesus Christ, cannot be figured out from the Old
Testament examples. We have only a blind hope that, in the
end, God will have mercy even on the most obdurate, that his
light will shine down even into the deepest darkness.

[B] Fifth Sunday of Lent

Jeremiah 31:31–34; Hebrews 5:7–9;
John 12:20–33

1. "Whoever clings to his life will lose it." Today's mighty Gospel
strikes the upbeat for the Passion. Gentiles wish to see Jesus:
his mission, which extends beyond Israel to include all "nations", is completed only in death; only from the Cross will
he draw all men to himself, as the conclusion of the passage
proclaims. That is why the grain of wheat must die, for there is
no other way for it to bear rich fruit. Jesus says this of himself,
but he also says it with great emphasis for all who "serve" him
and wish to follow him. Facing this death (freighted as it is
with the sins of the world) he is troubled by fear. In the anxiety of the Mount of Olives he asks whether he dare ask the
Father to spare him; yet he knows that the entire Incarnation
is meaningful only if he endures the "hour" and drinks the

cup. Thus he says, "Father, glorify your name." The Father's voice confirms that the entire plan of salvation, all the way to the Cross and Resurrection, is a single "glorifying" of divine, merciful love that has triumphed over evil (the "prince of this world"). Each word of this Gospel reading is so inseparably woven into all the others that the entirety of God's salvific work comes into view in the light of the approaching Cross.

2. *"Obedience learned through suffering."* In the Gospel John muffles the pointedness of suffering; for him everything, even the darkest, is already an appearance of Love's glory. In the second reading, the letter to the Hebrews lets the harsh tones of the Passion ring out: he who is sinking into the night of suffering offered "loud cries and tears, prayers and supplications" to the God "who was able to save him from death". One can be obedient even under these circumstances, indeed, in the darkest suffering everyone, even Christ, must learn obedience in a new way. Any man who suffers physically or psychologically has experienced this: what he thought he already had made into a habit must be learned all over again from the beginning. Jesus cried out to the Father and the text says that the Father heard him and freed him from fear—yes indeed, but not yet, rather only when he arose from death and hell. Only when the Son has "finished everything" can the light of love that is buried in all suffering shine forth openly. And only when everything has been suffered through to the last and lowliest can the New Covenant referred to in the first reading be considered established.

3. *"I will place my law within them."* God makes a "New Covenant" after the first one he made has been "broken". It was hard, perhaps scarcely possible, to keep the first covenant as long as God's rule was above all a rule of power: "with up-

raised arm" he had led the people out of Egypt, and they had
no inward insight into the essence of God's love. To them the
love required by the covenant seemed like a command, like a
law, and men always long to break laws in order to show that
they are more powerful than the laws. But when the law of
love now penetrates their hearts and they learn to understand
from the inside that God is love because he loved men even to
the point of taking their guilt upon himself, then the covenant
has inwardly become another covenant. Each person understands from within, no one needs to instruct another about it
as one instructs schoolchildren. "All, from least to greatest, shall
know me."

[B] Palm Sunday

(First and second readings as in Year A, p. 62);
Passion from Mark 14:1–15:47

IF A HOMILY IS GIVEN TODAY, one could lift out a few of the
main themes from the Passion according to Mark and deal
with them in the light of the other two readings. The Old
Testament reading concerns the way the Servant of God faced
suffering: he endured, without resisting, knowing that God had
willed it this way and therefore would stand by him. The New
Testament reading depicts the Son of God's voluntary descent
in perfect obedience all the way to death on the Cross. Because
this descent was not merely an example of endurance for our
benefit, but was also the archetype of perfect human obedience, the Easter exaltation that followed is also portrayed, for
without it Jesus' suffering and all the world's suffering would
be meaningless. For the believer who hears the account of the
Passion, it has meaning only as a work of God's love that will

open out into Easter. But he dare not let this knowledge of the outcome sanitize all the realism of the way of the Cross by thinking "everything will turn out okay", rather, he must enter into it as earnestly as possible. This is what God and, in his name, the Church, require.

1. The waste. The Passion account opens with the story of the loving waste of expensive perfume in Bethany, and it does so for good reason. Jesus brushes off all the criticism: the woman has done the right thing—she has anointed him (Messiah means "anointed one") for his death. This is the final act of the loving Church, which retains its validity to the end of the world. Wastefulness is the original Christian attitude, only thereafter does calculating charity for the poor have its place. After his death has become a certainty because of Judas' betrayal, Jesus wastes himself even more boundlessly in his Eucharist. Everyone drinks the shed blood in advance, and this will continue to take place to the end of the world. The entire Passion occurs under the sign of this complete self-wasting of God's love for the world.

2. The general betrayal. The behavior of men in the Passion account is portrayed with a realism bordering on gruesomeness. Any and all sins imaginable are committed against God himself in the person of Jesus. First the disciples fall asleep when they should have watched and prayed—a dozing that will continue throughout Church history. Then the open betrayal for the sake of material gain, a betrayal that takes place with Jesus' full knowledge; nor is betrayal confined to a single disciple, rather, even the one on whom the Church is to be built denies his Lord. Then comes the cowardly flight of all the others. That the betrayal takes place with a kiss will also find its repetitions. And the general flight of those who have been called to follow Jesus is so panicky that one of them leaves behind even his last stitch of clothing. So much for the disciples. Then the chosen people deny their Messiah in open court, handing him over to the Gentiles. They follow this by choosing Barabbas in order to block Jesus' acquittal and insist on his crucifixion. Jews and Gentiles then compete with each other in all manner of mockery, physical humiliation and torture, and scorn for Jesus' saving mission—even at the foot of the Cross.

3. The last cry. The Gospel according to Mark reports only one word of Jesus from the Cross: "Why have you forsaken me?" For now there is no answer to this "Why". No relief is possible at this point. Therefore the life of the world's Savior ends with a "great cry" in which he gives not only human but also divine-human expression to the injustice world history has done to God, to this incomprehensible outrage against him. It is precisely this cry at the point of death that brings the centurion, the first convert, to faith.

[B] Holy Thursday

(See Year A, p. 64.)

[B] Good Friday

(See Year A, p. 66.)

[B] Easter Vigil

(First and second readings as in Year A, p. 69);
Gospel: Mark 16:1–8

THE WOMEN WHO (according to Mark) stood under the Cross
as representatives of the loving Church, continue to play this
role on Easter morning. It is fundamentally astonishing that
they do not let themselves be discouraged either by the fearful events or by the impossibility of what they planned to do
("Who will roll back the stone for us"). Instead they steadily
pursue their devout plan to anoint Jesus' corpse with sweet-
smelling perfumes and thereby to protect it from decay as much
as is humanly possible. We see here elements of a naïve folk-
piety that surefootedly follows its own path over all outer im-
pediments and spiritual objections. And God rewards that piety
by removing the obstacles—the stone has already been removed
—and by having a satisfactory explanation for the astonishing
circumstances the women encounter at the end of their pilgrimage, as they enter the sacredness of the open grave in
their singleminded purposefulness. Their fright is understandable, indeed it is virtually traditional in Holy Scripture wherever someone encounters divine epiphany. The angel's speech
has an unearthly beauty, one could not speak more lovingly yet
to the point. The word of calm at the outset permits the women
to comprehend the subsequent message. Then the angel makes
clear that he knows what they are looking for: this particular
man, "Jesus of Nazareth" who died on the Cross the day before
yesterday. Now comes the simple, almost matter-of-fact statement, "He is risen, he is not here", as if one were saying to a
visitor, "The person you came to see has left the house." There
is something divine in this quiet matter-of-factness, and it has
to do with the logic of the Cross—that the Resurrection must

follow the Cross. "See the place where they laid him", that is, convince yourselves that the person you seek is no longer here. Then comes the instruction to tell the disciples, and, as proof that the message is true, the appeal to Jesus' own words: "You will see him there, as he told you." "In Galilee"—there, where you are at home and where all of this began for you. It is his land, but above all it is yours, and you will find him there, where your daily life takes its course.

[B] Easter Sunday

(See Year A, p. 70.)

[B] Second Sunday of Easter

Acts 4:32–35; 1 John 5:1–6;
John 20:19–31

1. "Peace be with you." The Gospel portrays the Resurrected One's appearances on the evening of Easter and a week later. What he brings back with him upon his return from the Cross, death, and hell is ultimate, perfect peace. A peace "not as the world gives", but a much deeper peace. This takes place in three scenes.

First he wishes for his disciples the peace that he himself *is* ("for he is our peace" [Eph 2:14]). He backs this up by showing them his wounds. It is precisely the deadly work that men have done to him which is the foundation for the peace that emanates from him. Hatred has raged against him but his love had the greater stamina. The focus is not on reconciliation with the disciples who had shamefully denied him and fled; all of that is submerged under the great peace he offers them. Yet his gift goes much farther.

He breathes on them and bestows on them his own spirit of mission, the Spirit that empowers and authorizes them to pass on to other men the peace he has given them: "If you forgive men's sins, . . ." From the outset the gift of Jesus is given in order to be passed on to others. God judges men as he forgives them (confession and contrition are required); so too the Church's forgiving must be a judgment—it must take place in truth and not in ignorance. A possible "refusal of forgiveness" is a matter of love; postponement of forgiveness aims to bring about a more complete readiness to receive forgiveness.

All of this must take place in faith, hence the episode with Thomas. An attitude of believing surrender rather than insistence on seeing and experiencing is the prerequisite for receiving peace, for any reception of a divine gift. One can have no peace as long as he doubts and holds back. He has to fall down and say in faith: "My Lord, and my God!"

2. *"None of them claimed anything as his own."* In the first reading the first Church's unity is the sign that its members are living the peace of Jesus. Demarcations between "mine" and "thine" are the source of strife between men, whether it is a matter of intellectual or material "private property". This peace is completely spiritually, and not sociologically, inspired. Sociologically it would be almost impossible to achieve what is described here: "To each was distributed according to his need."

3. *"Love God and do what he has commanded."* The second reading expands things even more. The peace established by Christ now is given names that are at the same time its conditions:

"love of God" (of the Father, of the Son, of men), "belief in God" (who conquers the restless world). This union of love and faith is the Easter gift of Jesus: making peace between God and the world. In the Church this gift becomes concrete in the sacraments of Baptism (water), Eucharist (blood), and Confirmation (Spirit). Whoever receives them in their inner meaning and lets them take effect receives the peace of Christ and spreads it throughout the world.

[B] Third Sunday of Easter

Acts 3:12–15, 17–19; 1 John 2:1–5;
Luke 24:35–48

1. "Everything must be fulfilled." When Jesus appears to the assembled disciples, the first thing he does is to remove the fear that they are seeing a ghost. He does this by letting his physicality be perceived as tangibly as possible. They are to see—the wounds on his hands and feet; they are to touch—in order to convince themselves of his bodily presence; finally they are to see him eat earthly food—broiled fish. Yet all of this merely introduces his real teaching. He wants them to recognize that what he said during his mortal life about fulfilling the entire Old Covenant (divided according to the Jewish categories: "the Law, the Prophets, and the Psalms") has been fulfilled in his death and Resurrection. This event, he says, is the epitome of all the Scriptures and this epitome, whose core is the "forgiveness of sins", is to be proclaimed to "all nations" by its witnesses, by the Church. Readers of the Old Testament focusing on particular passages might have trouble catching sight of this essence, yet all of Israel's dramatic history with God has no other goal and thus no other meaning than what we find summed up here in Jesus' own testimony. Israel's ongoing, purely earthly, "descent into hell" and "rescue from great ruin" by God (1 Sam 2:6; Dt 32:39; Wis 16:13; Tob 13:2) is a rehearsal for understanding the ultimate death and Resurrection of Jesus for the entire world. Still, he first has to "open the eyes" of the disciples to this.

2. *"You acted out of ignorance."* In his sermon in the temple (first reading) Peter shows that he understood this. He can thus describe in drastic terms the people's crime ("you put to death the Author of life") but then add that the people and even their leaders did this out of ignorance. They had not understood that the prophets taught that the Messiah would suffer—the suffering prophets and their fate were perhaps the strongest prophecy of all. Peter does not pursue the question whether or not the Jews were culpable for this lack of knowledge. As Paul says, "To this day, whenever Moses is read, a veil lies over their hearts." It is a veil that can "be lifted" only if Israel "turns to the Lord" (2 Cor 3:14–16). Therefore Peter challenges the Jews: "Turn around, repent, so that your sins might be wiped away." The two stand side-by-side: Israel's mysterious "ignorance" (Paul talks about blindness, stubbornness) and the call to conversion. There is no hint of the idea that Israel is to be replaced by the Church, but also no hint of a double path of salvation in which Israel would be saved by its (returning) Messiah (Act 3:20ff.) and the Church by Jesus Christ. No—they are to wait for the Messiah *and* turn around.

3. *"We have an advocate with the Father."* In the second reading Jesus' statement to the disciples that forgiveness of sins is accomplished through his death and Resurrection is celebrated as the event that gives comfort and hope to us sinners. Any individual who sins and repents can have a share in the great

absolution given to the world. But repentance, conversion, is required, for the liar who calls himself a Christian but does not keep God's command, persists in pre-Christian ignorance, worse still, he lives in contradiction and therefore not in the "Truth".

[B] Fourth Sunday of Easter

Acts 4:8–12; 1 John 3:1–2;
John 10:11–18

1. "The Good Shepherd gives his life for the sheep." Despite Jesus' realistic word-picture, the parable of the Good Shepherd only fully comes alive in Jesus himself, God's appointed "Shepherd" of men. He names two characteristics of such a shepherd: first the shepherd's commitment to the flock even to the point of death, second, the reciprocal recognition between sheep and shepherd, which is anchored in the innermost mystery of God.

The theme of self-giving to the point of death is found at both the beginning and the end of the Gospel. This devotion contrasts sharply with the flight of the "hired hand", who, when facing danger, has the excuse that the life of a man is more valuable than the life of a dumb animal. This argument loses its force, however, when the shepherd cares so much for his sheep that he prefers them to his own life. That is scarcely conceivable in purely natural terms, but it becomes a central truth in the realm of grace. It only makes sense with the aid of the second theme of the parable: the shepherd knows his sheep and the animals likewise instinctively recognize him. For Jesus this is merely the point of comparison for a completely different recognition: "as the Father knows me and I know the Father". This has nothing to do with instinct but with the most profound mutual recognition, as it is found in absolute trinitarian love. When Jesus applies this utterly sublime trinitarian love-recognition to the inward mutuality between himself and his own, he elevates this knowledge far above that which is hinted at by the parable.

And thus it becomes clear that the first motif of the parable (giving one's life for the sheep) and the second motif (mutual recognition) coincide rather than merely parallel each other. The Father's and Son's knowledge of each other is identical with their mutual and perfect self-giving, and therefore the knowledge exchanged between Jesus and his own is one with the perfect self-giving of Jesus for and to his own, and it implicitly includes the unity of the Christian's knowledge and loving dedication to his Lord. At the end both themes are expressly joined together: the Father (also) loves the Son for his perfect self-giving for the sake of men, a self-giving which is both freely chosen by the Son and commissioned by the Father. This unmitigated surrender to mankind, because it is divine love, is at the same time the power that achieves victory over death ("the power to take up life again").

2. *"No other name under heaven."* In the first reading Peter gives the Lord all glory for the miracle he has effected. He is interrogated and examined regarding the agent of the lame man's healing. His answer: through no one except through the "cornerstone" you "rejected", for in Jesus alone a man can encounter healing, both spiritual and physical. The point is not that, Jesus excepted, all who care for sheep are "hired hands", for the Lord himself installed Peter to pasture his flock—precisely Jesus' flock, not Peter's. Thus everything effective and appropriate ultimately is accomplished by the "chief Shepherd alone" (1 Pet 5:4), even if through the activity of his assistants.

3. "The world does not recognize us." When read in this context, the second reading says that the world cannot comprehend the relationship between Jesus and his own, for example, the relationship between a pope or bishop and Christ, their Lord. Because the world does not recognize Christ, it cannot see the Church in her union with Christ and cannot measure the distance between them. But the reading goes farther: as long as she is a pilgrim on earth the Church herself cannot completely understand this relationship. It is so mysterious that it will reveal itself only in eternal life, where the relationship between the God-man and the Church will be embedded in the trinitarian relationship without being absorbed by it.

[B] Fifth Sunday of Easter

Acts 9:26–31; 1 John 3:18–24;
John 15:1–8

1. "I am the true vine." The parable of the vine conveys a marvelous sense of assurance: that we are somehow rooted, firmly and enduringly; that our birth does not leave us orphaned, isolated, dependent solely on our fragile selves; that we are not merely creatures of an inscrutable Creator who may indeed give us existence and sustain us—for as long as it pleases him; that we do stem from an empowering and fructifying origin out of which we can lead a useful and meaningful existence. Yet the assertion that pervades the entire Gospel is more than this assurance. It is the *requirement*, based on the assurance, that we persist in our origin: "Remain in me, as I remain in you." The requirement is so urgent that a threat lies behind it: whoever does not remain will wither away and be pruned off and burned. This takes place in a natural sense, as the parable of the vine and branches shows, but it also takes place in a personal sense, since God the Father himself is concerned for the union between his Son and his branches and members. This union is the central event of the world and its history, and it is such an intimate union that it tolerates no compromise: the branches are either attached to the vine's trunk or they are separated. We have to take this to heart: "Without me you can do nothing"—no matter how much you think you can accomplish by yourselves.

2. The first reading, which tells of *Paul's implantation into the Church* derives its meaning from the Gospel. The disciples in Jerusalem are fearful, unable to believe that the notorious persecutor could now suddenly become a true branch on the vine. It is Jesus Christ himself, not men, who selects men to be his branches. The future will demonstrate that Paul's integration is a complete one permitting him to bear fruit as a branch of the vine ("I have toiled harder than all of them" [1 Cor 15:10]), even though the Church often remains mistrustful of converts, as Paul's departure from Jerusalem and return to his homeland demonstrate. It will fall to the same man, Barnabas, who here introduces Paul to the Apostles, to fetch Paul back from Tarsus for their joint apostolate (Acts 11:25).

3. *"God is greater than our hearts."* Still, fickle men that we are, we keep asking ourselves, "Am I really a branch rooted in the vine?" Which dominates me: trust in God's grace for me or my well-founded doubts whether I live up to that grace? The second reading answers both sides of the question. Confidence ought to predominate in us, "because we are keeping his commandments", because we seek to keep them. If, as is possible, "our heart [conscience] accuses us", it rightfully, indeed necessarily, has recourse to God's mercy. He, who "is greater than our hearts", knows everything. Together with Peter, who is crushed by his having denied Christ, we can say, "Lord, you know everything, you know that I love you" (Jn 21:17). Peter also shows us that this presupposes a genuine desire to repent, for otherwise we could not convince ourselves that we are speaking "in the Spirit" that "he gave us".

[B] Sixth Sunday of Easter

Acts 10:25–26, 34–35, 44–48; 1 John 4:7–10;
John 15:9–17

1. "Remain in my love." Today's Gospel, the last before Ascension, sounds like a last will and testament: these words are supposed to remain alive in the hearts of believers, permitting Jesus to address us inwardly in heart and conscience long after he no longer lives among us outwardly. These words of farewell are also an irrevocable promise, an assurance that includes, sealed within itself, a requirement. Jesus talks about his great love, love that rests in his death for his friends; but since we are his friends we must carry out his assignments. He promises them that his love will remain in them—a testamentary commitment—if they remain in his love, if they obey his commandment of love exactly as he has obeyed the Father's commandment of love. His farewell promises are so overwhelmingly immense that they simply contain within themselves the demands they make of us. Has he not communicated to us the entire abyss of God's love and chosen us to live within it? What could be more obvious than that we will be satisfied with this totality (for outside of it there is simply nothing)? This shared totality is something for which we can constantly ask the Father: if we remain in the Son, "then the

Father will give you everything". Gift and assignment are inseparable, indeed, the assignment is a pure gift of grace. With that the Gospel already anticipates Pentecost: the gift is God's Spirit, who will work within us to help carry out the assignment, which is love.

2. The Gentiles receive the Spirit. The first reading shows us that the grace of becoming and being a Christian is not dependent on any purely earthly, ecclesial tradition but is always a free gift from God, "who pays no attention to a person's status" and "to whom anyone from any nation who fears him and does right is acceptable". Here we have the story of the Gentile centurion and his household, who are given the Holy Spirit even before baptism. Represented by Peter, the Church then obeys God by recognizing this choice of God and by sacramentally receiving the chosen ones. The freedom of God even in regard to the institution expressly established by Christ as he departed, was brought home to Peter at the end of John's Gospel: "If this is what I want . . . what does it matter to you? Follow me" (Jn 21:22). The Church dare not take upon herself the dimensions of the Kingdom of God, even though she must strive hard to evangelize and gather together all men, for whom Christ died and rose again. Certainly supernatural love can be present outside the Church ("if I want it so"), but it is precisely this love that drives the centurion Cornelius to become a member of the Church, in which, as the second reading shows, the triune God's love is central.

3. "Everyone who loves is begotten of God." We are challenged to love each other because God is love. At the same time, we are reminded that we ought not think we know by our own resources what love is. Love can only be understood and defined by means of what God has done for us: he has given his Son as an atonement offering for our sins. Yet we dare not let the statement that we have no natural means of knowing what love is discourage us from loving each other, for love is revealed to us not merely for the sake of knowing it or talking about it or believing in it but for a real copying of love, a doing of love that is indeed possible: "Dear brothers, let us love one another, for love is of God."

[B] Ascension

Acts 1:1–11; Ephesians 1:17–23;
Mark 16:15–20

1. "To the ends of the earth." All three readings for today's feast revolve around a single mystery: that Jesus' departure to the Father is simultaneously the Church's send-off for her mission to all the world.

The first reading initially destroys the naïve expectation of the disciples that the resurrected Lord would employ his authority on earth to set up the Kingdom of God (they call it the "kingdom of Israel"); this would lead to positions of honor for them (as the sons of Zebedee had once thought [Mt 20:21]). But something better is intended for them: they are to be harnessed to the task of constructing the Kingdom (which means they have to renounce knowledge of deadlines and date-setting). The Holy Spirit will equip them for this task but they will have to exert themselves from "Jerusalem and all Judea and Samaria to the ends of the earth". To open this worldwide space for them and make it accessible, Jesus' visible form disappears. The center of the cosmos is no longer the place where he is visible, the center is now everywhere, which is where the Church will constantly have to go.

2. Two promises. The Gospel supplements the account of the Ascension on two sides: the words of commission have the same breadth ("into the whole world") but the disciples are not primarily promised that they will find faith everywhere they go. God, not their preaching, will bring faith, provided man accepts this grace. Men can (by their own fault, not by the fault of the preacher) reject God's grace and thereby shut themselves off, outside salvation. Next, the disciples are promised special protection and special authority as an indication that they are obedient to the Holy Spirit in their preaching. This will enable them to ascribe their successes to the Lord who sent them rather than to themselves; the same will apply to those who come to faith through their preaching. With this instruction and promise the Lord has told the Church all she needs to know, follow, and hope until the end of time. Thereupon he disappears into heaven.

3. "For the building up of the body of Christ." The second reading adds something important, putting the Ascension into perspective from two new angles. In the first place, we realize that the ascent of Jesus "above the heavens" in no way means that he henceforth abandons the Church to labor alone, rather, he is indeed the One who, from on high, directs the diverse personal missions within his Church. Missions are not something one seeks out for himself. They are granted to a person from on high and, although we refer to them as charisms of the Holy Spirit, they are also ways to imitate Christ and are distributed to each person by Christ himself. In the second place, the differentiations within the Church serve a single purpose: "to lead all to the unity of faith and knowledge" of Christ, indeed, to give the Lord himself his perfected form. This unity is pursued in all sorts of ways and is transmitted by the grace of God. If in heaven a Father of all, a Christ, and a Spirit together advance ecclesial unity, this unity of sacrament ("one baptism") and spiritual attitude ("one faith", "a common hope") must correspond to the divine-triune unity, so that God might be "over all and through all and in all" also in his creation.

[B] Seventh Sunday of Easter

Acts 1:15–17, 20–26; 1 John 4:11–16;
John 17:6, 11–19

1. Prayer during the transition. Jesus' high priestly prayer, the middle portion of which forms the Gospel today, is also prayed as his transition from the world to the Father. For him it is the transition from earthly life to death on the Cross and to Resurrection. For us it can be understood as a transition from Ascension to Pentecost: the Lord has departed to the Father, the Spirit has not yet arrived.

Wherever we live, we live constantly in this transition. Jesus says that he is praying this while "still in the world", although "I am not of the world." And he asks the Father not to take us "out of the world", although we are no more "of the world" than he is. The formula "in the world but not of the world" is thus literally part of this prayer. On behalf of his own, Jesus makes a dual request of the Father: that he "guard them from the evil one", who will test them as long as they "are in the world", and that he "consecrate them by means of truth". This presupposes Jesus' consecration in his Passion ("I consecrate myself for them"), which, however, can also be applied to our consecration by means of the coming of the Holy Spirit. Our justification by the merits of Christ and our sanctification by the sending of the Holy Spirit into our hearts can never be separated from each other. Only when "the love of God is poured out into our hearts by the Holy Spirit" (Rom 5:5) are we "consecrated by means of truth", because, for Jesus, "the truth" is simply the mutual love between Father and Son in the Godhead, which Jesus has revealed. This Love is simply the Holy Spirit.

2. *"He has given us of his Spirit."* The second reading perfectly confirms this. From the love of God the Father, who "has sent the Son as Savior of the world", it follows that we "should love one another". If we ask why the latter follows from the former and how, in any case, it is possible, the answer comes: "He has given us of his Spirit." Through the gift of God's Spirit placed in us we are made capable of mutual love in a form that corresponds to God's love and are made capable of the insight that God's love and our love are not separate from each other but interwoven, so that "we remain in him and he in us."

3. *"Show us which of these two you have chosen."* What does the first reading, which tells the story of how the group of Apostles was supplemented by the addition of Matthias, have to do with what we have considered so far? The manner in which the group was augmented shows us that the infant Church was perfectly aware that ecclesial missions must originate from God and, if the Church herself is to act, she must ask him for such missions. The means employed—casting lots—is a fitting sign that the choice has been left to God. The Church chooses no priests, bishops, and popes without having heartily begged God for them. In this way she shows that her existence is one of transition—in the world but not of the world. She is concerned to maintain a worldly structure, but she waits on God for direction.

[B] Pentecost

Acts 2:1–11; Galatians 5:16–25;
John 15:26–27, 16:12–15

1. The Spirit of truth. The Gospel reveals to us the central task of the Holy Spirit who has been sent to us: "He will lead you into all truth", because he himself is "the Spirit of truth". The truth spoken of here is the truth of God as it has been finally but not exhaustively revealed in Jesus Christ. It consists in the fact that God is love and that God the Father loved the world enough to give his Son. No one, not the disciples, not we, would have ever understood this if the Spirit of God had not been given in order to guide us into the inner attitude and saving activity of God himself (cf. 1 Cor 2). The Holy Spirit originates in the Godhead from the limitless love between Father and Son; the Spirit is this love and testifies to this love, if he is "poured out into our hearts as the love of God" (Rom 5:5). Because the Spirit is the fruit of this mutual love in God, he does not reveal something specific to himself but through all centuries explicates in ever new ways how inscrutable and incomprehensible eternal love is. The Son says that the Spirit introduces what is "mine", and this "mine" is simultaneously that of the Father. However one does not guide someone into love in the same way he introduces a theoretical science, rather, he introduces someone to love by permitting him to participate in love's reality, by teaching him to love within the all-encompassing love of God.

2. The fruit of the Spirit. The second reading illustrates this. It requires that we let ourselves be "led" and "guided" by the

[For this feast, von Balthasar offers reflections on additional readings which are options given in the German Lectionary—Ed.]

Spirit in our day-to-day lives, that is, that we not merely believe truth but do truth. This cannot happen without a struggle against what the Holy Scriptures call the "flesh"—against a life that ignores God to fasten onto nothing but earthly power and pleasures, a life that undermines man's dignity both intellectually and bodily. If we, in contrast, "follow the Spirit", we discover a humanness that unbelieving people will view as a well-balanced humaneness. A person who spreads "love, joy, peace, kindness" around, who gives off "friendliness", and who "is in control of himself", is someone people like to associate with. Only those who look beneath the surface see that all these pleasant characteristics are not mere character traits or acquired etiquette but have deeper, more hidden sources. Yet those who have "crucified their passions and desires" in imitation of Christ do not reveal to others that they live out of the Spirit of God, much less that they follow him. The Spirit is like a hidden spring inside them, from which these pleasant characteristics bubble forth.

3. "Each one heard them speaking in his own language." The first reading tells of the events on the first Pentecost: the Spirit enables these uneducated Galileans to make themselves comprehensible to all men within their various languages and cultures. Through the Spirit of Christ they speak a single language that everyone can understand and affirm. A genuinely lived Christianity would be at the same time a genuine humanism, which everyone would recognize as such and, unless utterly depraved, affirm. The truth of Christ portrayed by the Spirit requires no complex inculturation process. The fruits of the Spirit, as described above, are tasty in anyone's mouth. As she follows her Lord, the Church will indeed be persecuted, but she must constantly watch to see if the persecution results from her failure to present Jesus' truth genuinely in the Spirit.

[B] Trinity Sunday

Deuteronomy 4:32–34, 39–40; Romans 8:14–17;
Matthew 28:16–20

1. "Baptize them in the name of the Father, the Son, and the Holy Spirit." The exalted Lord gives the Church the command to baptize under the sign of God's triunity all the men she can reach. Ecclesial baptism is often described as the impression made by a seal—the baptized person ought to know to whom he belongs and whose life and example he has to follow. The divine Trinity is not merely an opaque mystery (as it is often portrayed to us), it is the way God wishes to make himself known to the world and especially to us Christians. He is our Father who loved us so much that he offered up his Son for us and, more than that, granted us his Spirit, so that we can recognize God as boundless love. Who, Paul asks, can know the depths of God? Only his own Spirit. Yet precisely this Spirit he has put into our hearts, "so that we might understand the things freely given by God" (1 Cor 2:12). If one knows Christian truth it is simply false to say that man is unable to know God. Not only has God made known to us his existence (something that every person who realizes he has not made himself has a hint of), but he has given us a glimpse of his innermost being. This the Church ought to announce to "all peoples".

2. "That we are children of God." The second reading tells us that the Church not only gives believers and the baptized a glimpse into God from the outside, but that she even lets us enter into his inner life as love. The reading begins with the Holy Spirit who has been given to us, the Spirit who, if we accept him, shows us that we are "sons of God" the Father in Jesus Christ. This is according to the Father's eternal plan—we were made for this purpose (Eph 1:4–12). If "all the treasures of wisdom and knowledge are hidden" in Christ (Col 2:3), we then also become the "co-heirs" of all these riches, which are not earthly treasures but treasures of eternal love. They are precisely what man longs for, since he knows that earthly goods, which are subject to rust and being eaten by moths, are so perishable. God's being, unveiled to us as endless, continually new love that never wears out its welcome, is far more than the most demanding human longing could ask for.

3. "Has any God ever ventured anything like this. . . ?" Even in the Old Covenant Israel could not show enough astonishment at the love God bestowed on it, as the first reading tells us. Israel knew that there was nothing in the entire world or among any of the religions that could compare with this love. We are challenged to prove this to ourselves: "Ask from one end of heaven to the other" whether anything comparable to this love can be found. This is all the more true since, by Christ's life, death, and Resurrection, God has completed the covenant he made with Israel and thereby unveiled to us his entire loving glory. The husk that still covered the Old Testament has been pulled off, and we "gaze with unveiled face on the Lord's radiance" (2 Cor 3:18), becoming more thoroughly formed into this glory of love.

[B] Corpus Christi

Exodus 24:3–8; Hebrews 9:11–15;
Mark 14:12–16, 22–26

1. "This is my blood, the blood of the covenant." In the Gospel Jesus sends two disciples ahead to prepare the paschal meal, but there is little left for them to do, since Jesus himself has seen to everything in advance and given the two appropriate instructions. So too he leaves up to us a certain kind of preparation for the eucharistic Feast, but all the essentials have been formed by him; he alone is the center, indeed the sole content of what is celebrated. The congregation need not "form" this center, because the center is always completely unpredictable and overwhelming for them: that Jesus takes a piece of normal bread and distributes it with the words, "Take, this is my body." And the next thing he does is almost more incomprehensible: that he takes the cup of wine and gives it to them to drink with the words, "This is my blood, the blood of the covenant to be poured out for many." He says this while he is still sitting at table with them—in his action he anticipates the shedding of his blood. And by speaking of the "blood of the covenant", he points back to the origin of the covenant at Sinai, the subject of the first reading. Yet at the same time he also shows how much he surpasses this "Old Covenant" in a "New Covenant" (1 Cor 11:25)—the second reading will point up the distance between the beginnings at Sinai and their fulfillment in the Gospel. Both readings show that Jesus completes his Father's work with the institution of the Eucharist, and that he does this in the Holy Spirit, since he offers himself up on the Cross "by the power of the eternal Spirit" (Heb 9:14). Thus Corpus Christi is a profoundly trinitarian feast.

2. *"Moses took the blood . . . and said: this is the blood of the covenant."* The covenant that God offers the people in the first reading was accepted by them "with one voice". It became a reciprocal covenant. As a ritual and official seal of its seriousness, indeed, of its indissolubility, young bulls were slaughtered and Moses, as a mediator between God and the people, sprinkled half of the sacrificial blood on the altar and half on the people,

after the covenant document was read aloud. His explanatory words, "this is the blood of the covenant", remind us of the loyalty-relationship men inaugurate when they make a pact of "blood-brotherhood" by sharing something of their innermost vitality. Yet one final thing is missing from this brotherhood pact at Sinai: the blood being sprinkled in both directions is animal blood. The second reading will remove this foreign element, "the blood of goats and bulls", replacing it with the blood of the One who in his own person is both God and man.

3. "The mediator of a new covenant." The Old Covenant, in itself indissoluble, is completed when the ultimate mediator comes before the Father "with his own blood", atones for all the unfaithfulness of the human partner in the covenant, and, because he is able to offer himself for the world "through the eternal Spirit", "brings about eternal redemption". If Jesus presents us with his eternal offering not merely for reception but also for "doing" ("do this in my remembrance" [1 Cor 11:25]), is there any limit to the awesome reverence with which we must carry out this "doing" of the "eternal redemption"?

[B] Sacred Heart of Jesus

Hosea 11:1, 3–4, 8–9; Ephesians 3:8–12, 14–19;
John 19:31–37

1. "With bands of love." The first reading portrays for us God's love for his "son" Israel. This is a love that expresses itself in all sorts of tenderness. Like parents who lift a small child to their cheek or take him in their arms, who feed the child and later help him take his first steps, so God has acted toward his chosen son. Yet just as parents receive no thanks for their efforts, so God receives nothing but ingratitude from his child. "With human cords" he has "drawn the child to himself, with bands of love", but the cords and bands themselves irritated the son, who wanted to squirm free and be independent—not from human parents, but from God, from Love itself. Now, what will happen to God as a result? He, who wanted to wrap the child in "bands of love", finds himself chained by love because not only does he have love, but he is Love. "For I am God, not a man." Here God bares his heart: he cannot rage with anger and destroy—a course of action that would have been just. He cannot give up on the runaway. Already we have a glimpse of the image of the father in the parable of the Prodigal Son. All God can do is to maintain a lookout, run to meet his son, embrace him, and hold a feast.

2. *"Comprehend the love of Christ, which surpasses all understanding."* The second reading states it plainly: chained by faithfulness to his covenant, even though it is the freest love of all; almost laughable in its clinging to a partner who repeatedly breaks the union (as in Hosea's marriage to a prostitute), God's love remains incomprehensible to man. Yet Paul insists that we must comprehend precisely this incomprehensible love, that we recognize God's folly as his higher wisdom, for "the folly of God is wiser than the wisdom of men"—it is "God's mysterious, hidden wisdom" (1 Cor 1:25; 2:7). Therefore "whoever thinks he is wise must first become a fool in order to become wise" (1 Cor 3:18), and Christians should "be fools on Christ's account" (1 Cor 4:10). The point of all of this is simply the love of God, which places all the other characteristics of God in its train and at its complete disposal. Believers should understand this.

3. "This testimony has been given by an eyewitness." The proof of what we have found in the two readings is found in the Gospel account of the piercing of Jesus' side. Only the believer can unlock its meaning, for only a believer can glimpse the supreme sign of love in the death of the Son, and thus only a believer can grasp the solemnity of the witness given by the Beloved Disciple. The brutal Roman soldiers, who not only crucify but also smash the bones in the victims' legs and thrust lances into hearts, are instruments who fulfill ancient prophecies while being quite unaware of what they are doing. It is the heart of God himself that is laid open here (for Jesus' heart cannot be separated from the Father's heart and the Spirit's heart). The very last that God can offer up flows out, and the wound remains eternally open, for at the end of the world "they shall look upon him whom they have pierced." One cannot say that the crudity of the sinners has enlarged God's love (which surpasses all understanding), but the behavior of the creature toward the Creator has indeed brought to light the magnitude of the depths encompassed by that love.

[B] Eighth Sunday in Ordinary Time

Hosea 2:16–17, 21–22; 2 Corinthians 3:1–6;
Mark 2:18–22

1. Why no fasting now? John the Baptist appeared under the sign of fasting; Jesus appeared under the sign of eating and drinking (Mt 11:18–19). The "disciples of John" wonder why the disciples of Jesus do not fast. Jesus makes a distinction. As his instructions on fasting in the Sermon on the Mount (Mt 6:16–18) indicate, he does not reject fasting. However, as both God and man, he symbolizes the marriage between heaven and earth, and his existence is the supreme wedding gift of the Father to Israel and to the whole world.

In contrast to the long period of expectancy, lasting all the way to the Baptist, he is the New Cloth that cannot be sewn onto old rags; he is the New Wine that cannot be poured into old wineskins. Things will be completely different after Israel, having rejected its Messiah, has missed out on the period of wedding feasting. Then "the Bridegroom will be taken away" from his disciples, and an entirely different, Christian, fasting will begin. It will be oriented toward the Lord's Passion rather than toward the Old Covenant. And then it will be the Church who, out of Christ's Passion and Resurrection, must give expression to both profound austerity and supreme joy. To that end she will have both a season of Lent and a season of Easter. Inwardly and in outward symbols she will share her Bridegroom's movements.

2. The first reading returns to God's *first marriage* with Israel, making allusion to two scenes. The first is God's espousal of Israel in the wilderness during the exodus from Egypt. This was a time of love in which God and his bride were entirely alone together. The wilderness meant both spiritual wealth (manna, quail, water from the rock) and need (Israel groused quite adequately about the latter). And now that the people has become an unfaithful Bride, a second wilderness period is predicted, a time in which God will woo her all over again, "espouse her in fidelity", and promise her "knowledge of the Lord" (which the Jews understood as a reference to the most intimate union between man and woman). Here too the wilderness, meaning the Exile, unites both fasting and wedding feast. One realizes how final God's covenant with Israel is, yet one also realizes that the marriage of the two natures will only be completely achieved in Jesus Christ.

3. The Church as fulfillment. The covenant made by Jesus' life, death, and Resurrection is indissoluble because God's Holy Spirit is now placed in the hearts of the believers. The Mosaic "tables of stone" have been replaced, in the second reading, with "hearts of flesh", just as the stone temple is replaced by the temple of the Holy Spirit "built of living stones", a temple "which you are". Whatever is true of Christ's Church as a pure, unblemished Bride should be reflected in each congregation, hence the Apostle's imploring tone: just as he is "a minister of the New Covenant", "of the Spirit", so too the believers ought to be a community of the New Covenant, of the Spirit. "Through Christ" he has "such great trust in God" that the community which is causing him such great concern might nonetheless be a credible part of the whole (the *catholica*), uniting abstinence ("seeks not its own" [1 Cor 13:5]) with an abundance of gifts (1 Cor 12).

[B] Ninth Sunday in Ordinary Time

Deuteronomy 5:12–15; 2 Corinthians 4:6–11;
Mark 2:23–3:6

1. "Observe the Sabbath day." The Sabbath which, according to the first reading, God has instituted and commanded to be kept, is "holy" because it is the "day consecrated to the Lord, your God". This means not merely that a man must not work on that day (since he actually works for himself), but also that, during this day, he ought to think about God as the Lord of all work and of all man's being and activity. Otherwise the Sabbath would be merely a dead, negative, meaningless day. God is not dead on this day, rather, precisely on the Sabbath he is more alive for men than ever. Jesus alludes to this when he explains his relationship to the Sabbath: "My Father is at work until now, so I am at work as well" (Jn 5:17). If men misunderstand worldly rest for the sake of God's activity as mere formal inactivity it only illustrates their inability to grasp religious matters. Jesus himself demonstrates this.

2. *"The Son of Man is Lord over the Sabbath."* Although the disciples are criticized for stripping off grains of wheat on the Sabbath in order to feed themselves, in the Gospel Jesus corrects the critics: if the Sabbath is God's day, then there are God-approved actions that a person may do on the Sabbath. Then he offers the example of David who, with his men, ate the sacred bread that was reserved for the priests. Elsewhere Jesus mentions watering livestock (Lk 13:15) or rescuing a child or an animal from a well-shaft (Lk 14:5). These are deeds in which man is not working for himself but is fulfilling God's commandment of love. And since Jesus came to proclaim love as the supreme commandment, he is "also Lord of the Sabbath". Thus he heals the man with the withered hand on the Sabbath, because, by acting in the Spirit of God's free, healing grace, he thereby honors God on his day. For those obsessed with formalities this is a slap in the face, and thus they decide, right at the beginning of the Gospel, to destroy Jesus.

3. *"Delivered to death for Jesus' sake."* In the second reading the Apostle Paul is not talking about the Sabbath. Instead, he says that he, who lives out of God's radiant grace, nonetheless continually dwells at the edge of collapse, indeed, that Jesus' life and Jesus' death are constantly taking shape in Paul's life. For him the Sabbath becomes Good Saturday not only when he narrowly manages to escape death for his apostolic activity (2 Cor 1:9), but also while he languishes in prison, unable to do anything, and when, scarcely able to endure the blows of

"Satan's angel" (2 Cor 12:7), his pleas for relief go unanswered. Paul has to experience fully the paradox of the Passion of Jesus —that Jesus' activity reaches its climax precisely when, nailed to wood, every movement is denied him. "When I am weak, then I am strong." (2 Cor 12:10)—these words of Paul could have been uttered by Jesus on the Cross. Here we find the meaning of the Sabbath fulfilled beyond all human imagining.

[B] Tenth Sunday in Ordinary Time

Genesis 3:9–15; 2 Corinthians 4:13–5:1;
Mark 3:20–35

1. "He is possessed." Two charges are leveled at Jesus in the Gospel: his relatives consider him insane and want to "fetch him home by force", while the scribes say he is possessed by demons—because he acts, clearly not like an insane person, but as one gifted with superhuman powers that seem uncanny to the scribes. Jesus has a single answer for both accusations: what he is constructing is characterized by unity and by the power of God and his Holy Spirit (a work of the Evil one cannot pass that test) and this sort of a new spiritual fellowship cannot be mingled with old, earthly society. Therefore his relatives cannot be granted entry, and those who accuse him of having an evil spirit are equating the Spirit of God with Satan, which is the most unforgivable of blasphemies. For the latter is open contradiction of God, whose effective Spirit is visible for all to see in Jesus' constructive activity for them. Wherever men work—even in the Church—their deeds may be criticized as contrary to God's mission, but where God himself is at work, the man who contradicts that work condemns himself.

2. "The serpent seduced me." He whose sins contradict God always tries to extricate himself from self-condemnation by blaming someone else, as the first reading teaches. Adam and Eve are guilty in God's sight. Their awareness of their nakedness and their fear in God's presence, both of which grow out of their sin, betray them. A sinner is aware of his inner contradictions in the sight of God. He sees no way out except to accuse someone else of being the cause. Adam blames Eve; Eve blames the serpent, who is the deceptive power of seduction to disobedience. Yet God will punish all three (omitted in the reading), ignoring all their maneuvering to blame each other. Men receive a double penalty: first, a laborious existence through which they can repent of some of their guilt; second, a continued struggle against the power of seduction, a struggle that should keep them vigilant about the possibility of resisting this power. Both of these point toward paths by which man can escape the inner contradiction caused by sin. The final escape will take place only when Jesus, who constructs in the Spirit a reality beyond all contradictions, gathers men into his equally uncontradictory unity.

3. "Limitless abundance." In the second reading Paul portrays man between Adam and Christ. Here Christ's constructive activity has integrated Adam's work of repentance into itself. That the "outer man is being worn away day-by-day" is not merely part of the process of adamic repentance, rather, it must also be ascribed to the work of atonement that Jesus has begun. The "limitless abundance" of the "eternal glory" promised to the followers of Jesus does not lighten the burden of the cross at all. The heavier the cross, the more disproportionately weighty is the subsequent glory and resurrection.

[B] Eleventh Sunday in Ordinary Time

Ezekiel 17:22–24; 2 Corinthians 5:6–10;
Mark 4:26–34

1. "He knows not how." In the Gospel Jesus tells two parables about the growth of the Kingdom of God. Each has a different purpose. The first emphasizes the seed's own growth. The farmer can neither give the seed-grain the power to grow nor influence its gradual growth: "The soil produces its fruit by itself." It is not as if the man has nothing to do—he must prepare the field and sow the seed. Yet the main work is done by God, while the man "goes to bed and gets up again day-after-day". The Kingdom of God has its own rules that are not forced on it by men; it is not a product of technology. The seed, the blade, the ear, the full grain, the ripeness—all belong to the Kingdom's own structure and are not human achievements. The second parable indicates this as well: the fully grown fruit, from a seed that initially seemed contemptuous to men, proves in the end to be larger than anything man could have accomplished by himself. And the harvest? It will be God's harvest, but will be on behalf of the man who has prepared the soil and sowed the seed. God harvests, as the lazy servant in the parable of the talents put it, "where he has not sown". Yet fundamentally the harvest is for both God and man: for God appoints the industrious servant to rule over a large realm.

2. "Always confident." The man of the soil has an attitude of steady confidence that the law God established in nature will prove trustworthy. So too, in the second reading, Paul's confidence is constant, regardless of the current spiritual weather patterns in his life or in that of his congregation. "We walk by faith." Man wants to be able to control the weather, to be lord of the imponderable; Paul would rather live where he can gaze on the Lord than to "live away from home" in faith, but, as with the farmer, submission to God's direction is more important to him than his preferences: "whether we are home [with him] or away from home". The Apostle himself is merely a farmer: "I planted, Apollos watered, but God gives the increase" (1 Cor 3:6).

3. "The largest of all shrubs." The second parable of the King-dom of God told in the Gospel is another example of the nu-merous statements Jesus made about the "least" in the King-dom becoming the "greatest", precisely because of having made himself small and having occupied "last place". In his earthly life Jesus himself gave an example of this, an example he contin-ues to give in his Eucharist. The imagery he employs reaches back to the passage in Ezekiel that forms the first reading, describing how, through the power of God, the delicate twig of his people grows into the mightiest of trees, so that the "birds of heaven" can make their nests in it. For the prophet this is completely attributable to God's power—all other trees (nations) should recognize that "I am the Lord" who has the power to lay low the lofty and raise up the lowly, to parch what is green and make parched land lush with green growth. In the Old as well as the New Covenant, this parable has nothing to do with human morality. It refers to the sublime power of God, who deals with man according to his rules, if man will submit himself to him.

[B] Twelfth Sunday in Ordinary Time

Job 38:1, 8–11; 2 Corinthians 5:14–17;
Mark 4:35–41

1. "Who shut the sea within doors?" It seems like the sea, created by God, has the upper-hand over the land in this world. To many ancient peoples the sea's wild, formless power seemed like ungodly chaos. Yet, in the first reading, God shows Job that he has channeled this seemingly overpowering force, that he has enveloped the waters spewing forth from the fountains of the deep as one would wrap a nursing infant in diapers, that God has locked up the raging waters "behind bars". Job learns this lesson: if God can rule over natural forces that infinitely surpass human powers, then he can certainly tame and direct human destinies even more completely.

2. "The waves were breaking over the boat." Then the Gospel shows us that this power to tame the forces of nature has also been given to the Son of Man—he possesses it to such a degree that he can sleep in the boat during a "bad squall"; he can rest in the care of his Father, who keeps watch over his mission and his life and who will not permit any natural power to overpower his Son. Even when, at the insistence of his disciples, Jesus does command the storm to "quiet down!" and "be still!", he does so not to show off his power, nor because he himself is afraid, but solely on account of his disciples' fearful lack of faith. "Why are you so terrified? Have you no faith?" The faith they lacked ought not be limited to this sort of miracle, but should extend to a much greater miracle rooted in Jesus' mission: he came to quiet a very different raging storm —the chaos of our sin. And he tamed it in his death on the Cross, which indeed removes him from all "human standards" and leaves us really asking, "What kind of a man is this?"

3. The second reading takes account of this complete faith, which recognizes that Jesus slips through *all* human standards because he has brought about the ultimate marvel: as an individual he "died for all so that those who live might live no longer for themselves, but for him who for their sakes died and was raised up". This marvel does not merely return men to the safety of their old, mortal lives, as happened in the miracle of the storm on the lake. Rather, "if they are in Christ", they are transported to a completely "new creation", in which "the old order has passed away, and all is new". For the sake of their lack of faith Jesus calmed the storm on the lake—so that they might begin to place their trust in him. His death on the Cross, which calms a much worse storm, requires that all who believe, even haltingly, no longer "live for themselves".

[B] Thirteenth Sunday in Ordinary Time

Wisdom 1:13–15, 2:23–24; 2 Corinthians 8:7, 9, 13–15; Mark 5:21–43

1. Against sickness and death. Today's readings bring to the fore terrifying questions about the plan. Christ heals a sick person, awakens someone from death. This is his mission. Why then must so many people after Christ become sick again? Why must all die? Does God want death? If nothing has changed in the world, to what end did Christ come?

We shall draw only two phrases from the Gospel reading's long story with its two interwoven miracles. Jesus says of the synagogue official's daughter, who according to our perceptions certainly was dead, "the child is merely sleeping", and he is laughed at. When, in the middle of a crowd, a woman with a discharge of blood touches his robe, he asks, "Who touched my clothing?", and his disciples can only look on in puzzlement. In the face of bodily death he speaks of sleep (something he does again in the case of his friend Lazarus [Jn 11:11]), whereas he is anything but casual about real death, what Revelation calls the "second" (final) death. On the other hand, sickness (which the Jews considered a foreshadowing of death) was no trivial detail for him. To heal sickness "power" has "to go out from him" (in Luke this happens with each healing [6:19]). He calls himself "the Life" (Jn 11:25; 14:6) and this life must flow into his powers if the lifeless or feeble are to be revived.

2. Only from this perspective can the statements of the first reading be understood: "*God did not make death.*" This is repeated: "The netherworld has no domain on earth, for justice is undying." The presence of death in the world is ascribed to the devil's envy. How can the sage say this when he knows that everyone, righteous as well as unrighteous, must die? Like Jesus, he distinguishes two deaths: natural death is a corollary of the finitude of existence; unnatural death is the result of man's resistance to God. Consider Jesus' mysterious but in this context very enlightening words: "Whoever believes in me will live, even though he die", followed by words that by no means contradict: "Whoever lives and believes in me will never die" (Jn 11:25–26). Though God created man as a finite creature, man has created the second death, real death, through his sins.

3. "*For your sake he made himself poor.*" To overcome man's efforts at self-destruction is no small matter for God. The second reading states it plainly: Jesus Christ, "who was rich, for your sake made himself poor, so that you might become rich by his poverty". He did not overcome our death through omnipotence but by descending into death's powerlessness. This second death could only be conquered from within—only if

divine power leaves Jesus in order to flow into us on the Cross and in the Eucharist. Paul hopes that we will imitate this, at least in a broad sense, by giving out of our material power to those who are needy to the extent that we at least achieve the sort of "balance" that suits a fraternal attitude. To this end, Jesus' example of descent from complete wealth to utter poverty ought to serve as an, admittedly unattainable, ideal.

[B] Fourteenth Sunday in Ordinary Time

Ezekiel 2:2–5; 2 Corinthians 12:7–10;
Mark 6:1–6

1. The scandal. Scandal occurs when, on penultimate grounds, one rejects what he ought to have accepted on ultimate (and well known) grounds. Quite obviously this is what the people in Jesus' home town do in the Gospel. In the first place, they cannot help but be amazed at his teaching. They cannot figure out "where he got all of this". They readily admit that his wisdom, effectiveness, and miracles are far beyond them. Yet they cannot admit that this is all true, and they justify their refusal by their knowledge of his family and his earlier life among them. After all he was an ordinary carpenter. Where did he suddenly get all of this? Jesus generalizes from this contradiction, extending it to the fate of every prophet in his home town, among his relatives and family. As long as man maintains this contradiction within himself, he can have no part in healing (which presupposes submissive faith). However, the One sent from God must pass the test of this situation. The first reading indicates this incontrovertibly.

2. Sent to the obstinate. It is precisely to "deserters", "apostates", the "obstinate", "rebels",[1] and the "hard of heart" that God sends the prophet Ezekiel (like Isaiah, Jeremiah, and others before him): "It is to them that I am sending you." Ezekiel dare not enter into any compromises with them. He can only speak the word of the Lord. The success or failure of his message cannot be a concern to the prophet—it has no effect on his mission. Many prophets preceding Jesus had to experience the rejection he encountered in his home town. According to Jesus' words, most of them were murdered in the belief that this would finally silence their voices (Mt 13:37; Lk 13:34). Only later, perhaps, will people realize that "a prophet has been among them."

3. "When I am weak, then I am strong." The riddle of God's deployments is unraveled in Jesus' overall destiny, which then also governs the destiny of his followers. No one was ever so radically and generally rejected as Jesus: he was betrayed by a Christian, cast off by the Jews, condemned to death by a Gentile. "His own people did not accept him", even though they were "his own" (Jn 1:11). Jesus himself located his destiny among that of the prophets (Lk 13:33), yet he is distinguished from them because of his divine-human mission, which is to accept rejection by his own people yet produce in their hearts the ability to say Yes. Paul understood this well, as indicated by the second reading. The law of the Cross, which also holds true in his own case, is that "grace proves its power in weakness." The Cross was the "power of Christ". From the Cross onward the

---

[1] The words in quotation marks are equivalents for von Balthasar's German, which seems to have been based on the Latin Vulgate. Not all of these words are found in German or English translations made from the Hebrew, since the Vulgate employs two synonyms to translate what German and English versions render with a single term—Trans.

rule for Christians is: "when I am weak"—powerless, badly treated, in need—"then I am strong." That is how Christ's triumphant destiny also takes effect in me.

[B] Fifteenth Sunday in Ordinary Time

Amos 7:12–15; Ephesians 1:3–14;
Mark 6:7–13

1. Called and equipped. In the Gospel, Jesus calls the Twelve without further explanation. Why does he choose precisely these twelve? The text is silent. Neither moral virtue nor quickness of mind nor eloquence sets them apart. If they lack anything they need to carry out their assignment, it will be given them. And they most certainly lack what they will be given when they are commissioned: the right to proclaim the Kingdom of God, and to do so with authority to drive out unclean spirits. This can only be done by someone who has the Holy Spirit, for, as the Holy Spirit expands, he pushes back the sphere of activity of the unholy spirit. Since the disciples receive these gifts from Jesus, they are asked not to confuse them with their own means of aiding and propagandizing. Thus they are forbidden travel bags, bread, money, fresh clothes . . . and are told not to seek out comfortable lodging. They are assigned the task of proclamation. Their call is a call to conversion, not to success. Should no one respond to the call it ought not affect them—they should simply move on and try again elsewhere. All we are told after this point is that the Twelve took to the road and achieved certain successes. The naked Gospel (*sine glossa*) is the most convincing.

2. Called and rejected. The first reading, from Amos, proclaims something characteristic of each of God's messengers. "If any place will not receive you", says Jesus. Not only was Amos not accepted—he was officially chased out of the country. In the process he protested that he was not a prophet—neither by occupation nor by apprenticeship to a prophet. His call is fully comparable to those of the Galilean fishermen. Neither they nor he wished for or chose such an assignment. They are simply placed on the path: "Go and speak to my people." This is a call in the original sense of the word. A man cannot and ought not spend long hours considering whether he can or ought to respond (for example, whether to become a priest or enter a religious order). God gives him a shove, and unless he deliberately ignores it, he will notice it. Whether Amos leaves to go from Samaria to Judea or not, whether the Apostles tell the High Council (Sanhedrin), "One must obey God more than men" or not, is irrelevant. Jesus' simple "Be on your way" can often also simply mean "Keep at it."

3. "Predestined." The great opening of the letter to the Ephesians (second reading) places the person chosen by God into God's all-encompassing, timeless plan of salvation: what I am and what I shall be has been set out from eternity, before the creation of the world. Neither as an individual nor merely within time am I called, rather I exist as someone already fitted into a predestined comprehensive design consisting in Christ's Incarnation, the glorification of the Father's loving grace, and the Holy Spirit's seal. No man is an island, rather, each is comprehensible only as he is embedded in an unsurveyable landscape in which everything is radiant with the "praise of the glory of the grace" of God.

[B] Sixteenth Sunday in Ordinary Time

Jeremiah 23:1–6; Ephesians 2:13–18;
Mark 6:30–34

1. "Woe to the shepherds." In the first reading the kings of Israel are referred to as shepherds, but it was customary throughout the ancient world to give kings the honorific title of "shepherd". God granted his people a king only reluctantly, for rulers normally "make their authority over their people felt" (Mk 10:42). They think they make their people their own by power when in reality this very power "destroys and drives away my sheep". Pure power cares nothing for the well-being of subject people, who can only "fear and tremble" before it; rather, it merely represents the oneness of those who rule, those who insist that they be called "Benefactors" on the basis of their pervasive power (Lk 22:25). God promises to judge those exercising power and to replace them with the true Shepherd from the house of David who will rightly bear the title "The Lord is our Righteousness."

2. "Like sheep without a shepherd." The crowd of people flocking to Jesus seemed like this to him. The people instinctively sensed that he was the Good Shepherd sent from God, who is not intent on exercising his power over them but who gathers and guides them for their own sake. The powerful have had plenty of opportunity to rule them—not only Assyrian, Babylonian, Persian, Greek, and Roman rulers, but also their own merciless lords, to whom they were merely an ignorant mass "entirely born in sin" (Jn 9:34). Jesus wishes for a moment's rest, but the crowd pursues him and makes such claims on him that he does "not even have time to eat". Ultimately he will have to offer himself as food for these hungry people. He is here not for rest but to permit himself to be worn to the bone. "I give my life for my sheep" (Jn 10:15). "And he began to teach them at great length." His disciples are with him but nothing more is said of their attitude. Yet the consequence of the example Jesus gives to them is that essentially they will experience the same pressures and fatigue their Master is experiencing, even if on a different level—the level of disciples.

3. "Breaking down the barrier of hostility." The second reading reveals the concluding work of the Good Shepherd. He succeeds—if only by giving his life, if only through death—in uniting the flock that has been separated into two parts. This is indeed the explicit task and plan of his life: "I have other sheep; . . . these too I must lead, and they will hear my voice" and thereby become "a single flock" through the "single Shepherd" (Jn 10:16). Yet Paul places all his emphasis on the way in which this "peace" comes about: The Shepherd, by making his own body on the Cross into the locus of ultimate slaughter, gives his torn body itself as the source of unity offered for all. And yet another tyrant is dethroned in the process: "the law, with its commands and precepts", whose multiplicity shreds life into pieces. Henceforth peace reigns through the sole love of the One who has made himself, in Cross and Eucharist, into the powerless yet all-powerful reconciler of all human conflict.

[B] Seventeenth Sunday in Ordinary Time

2 Kings 4:42–44; Ephesians 4:1–6;
John 6:1–15

1. "They ate and there was still some left over." The first reading depicts a food miracle by Elisha that apparently is a preview of

Jesus' multiplication of loaves as told in the Gospel. The two accounts are comparable in a number of details: the insufficiency of the available food, the command to "give the people something to eat" (cf. Mk 6:37), the eating and leftovers (in the case of Elisha this corresponds to the Word of the Lord). In the first reading the extent of the miracle is smaller: the food available is more plentiful, the crowd of people (one hundred men) is smaller, and the miracle takes place through a word from God, not by Jesus' authority. Still, the parallels are striking. One can see clearly that Jesus does not act according to his own fantasy but obediently fulfills the Scriptures, surpassing them by a wide margin in the process. Up to his final words on the Cross he focuses steadily on the fact that he "must fulfill the Scriptures completely" so that "everything might be finished" (Jn 19:28). The works that God began in the Old Covenant through the service of his prophets are thus completed by his Son in the New Covenant out of the Son's authority, which is in fact his obedience to the Father.

2. *"What good is that for so many?"* By surpassing the prophet's miracle, the miracle that Jesus works when he feeds the five thousand reveals his divine grace to humanity: as in Cana, from the far-too-little that men have to offer, Jesus makes an incomprehensible much-too-much. Already incomprehensibly lavish in the natural order, God reveals himself to be even more lavishly carefree in the order of redemption. In the second instance, however, the manna no longer falls from heaven, rather, he makes use of the meager resources of men and then has the remnants of his immense generosity gathered up rather than letting them go to waste. This gives the disciples, the Church, an eternal store from which they can distribute to anyone in need. Just as the master of the feast at Cana viewed the ten jars of superb wine as folly, so here the divine folly that gives far

more than can be consumed is also divine wisdom—this folly permits the "much-too-much" to continue throughout history, for "anyone who thirsts will receive water without cost" (Rev 21:6; 22:17).

3. "One body and one Spirit." The second reading points to Jesus' real multiplication of bread—the distribution of his body in the Eucharist, which, in John's account, is promised in immediate conjunction with the miracle of the multiplication of the loaves. The apparent inadequacy of a bit of bread turns into the more-than-enough of the self-giving of Jesus' body, which satisfies the recipient's hunger, not only for itself, but as it does so, it also unites each individual into one Spirit of Jesus. This Spirit is evident when all share in the humility, peaceableness, and patience of Jesus, and these qualities make the true Christian a participant in the miraculous power of Jesus, which can bring a hungry and desperate world together into "a common hope" in the "one God and Father of all".

[B] Eighteenth Sunday in Ordinary Time

*Exodus 16:2–4, 12–15; Ephesians 4:17, 20–24;
John 6:24–35*

1. "Bread from heaven." From a human perspective one can understand the mood of the people (in the first reading), who have been led into the wilderness by God and find no food there. An entire nation in such a desperate situation could hardly be expected to wait docilely for a miracle from heaven. Instead of scolding the Israelites, God promises a double miracle: meat in the evening (he sends the flock of quail into the camp) and bread in the morning (the "fine flakes" on the ground of the desert that they were to gather up as something unknown [Mân-hu? "What is that?" = Manna]). Once more the Old Testament miracle (meat and bread: bread that is meat and meat that is bread) is merely the foreshadowing of that which God will give the world in Jesus. Many have died of hunger in the wilderness and continue to die there today. God's ultimate concern is not to keep mortals alive a bit longer but to give them heavenly bread for eternal life, to use Jesus' own expression.

2. *"I am the Bread of Life."* The miraculous multiplication of loaves is over. Now men pursue the Wonderworker so that they can continue to be fed by him. It is just like the Samaritan woman at the well: "Give me this water so that that I may not be thirsty or have to keep coming here to draw water" (Jn 4:15). This too is understandable from a human perspective. Jesus instructs them to "work" for something else: food that endures for eternal life, which obviously is God's doing. Hence the follow-up question: "What can we do to accomplish the works of God?" They do not realize that they are giving voice to a contradiction: man cannot "do" the works of God. Jesus points out the contradiction and shows how to overcome it. God's work is that man believes rather than achieves, that he offers himself, and that he offers himself to the One sent from God. Here the people insist on a sign as a basis for belief— they still imagine faith as a work. Now Jesus links himself, the true Bread from heaven, to the manna—something one can gather up. Intellectual hunger cannot be better quieted than by believing acceptance of Jesus, whom God has sent to the world as the "true Bread from heaven". The believer must also work, but he does so solely out of faith rather than in order to believe. For, instead of being a human accomplishment, faith is a complete giving of oneself to God who accomplishes things.

3. The new man. Therefore the "old man", who "is headed for ruin through illusory desire", who decays precisely in his lasting longing to possess and is robbed of everything, has to be put aside. This must be done so that "the new man, created in God's image" can be put on. This primal image of God is Christ, who knows not desire but is pure self-giving. Man was created according to this primal image, to be conformed to it by giving up his human desires so that only the work of the Father will take place in him. And that work of the Father is the impressing of the Son's primal image in us through the Holy Spirit.

[B] Nineteenth Sunday in Ordinary Time

1 Kings 19:4–8; Ephesians 4:30–5:2;
John 6:41–51

1. "Get up and eat." Once more the Gospel reading gives us part of the discourse in which Jesus promises the Eucharist and the first reading presents us with a marvelous Old Testament prefiguration of the Eucharist. The prophet Elijah is at the end of his physical and intellectual strength. Everything he has done seems to him to have been done in vain, and he wants to die. Then, in the middle of the wilderness, he is given miraculous food: a hearth cake and a jar of water. These gifts are forced upon him—he has to feed himself because the path to the mountain of God would otherwise be too much for him. "Strengthened by that food" he is thus able to walk "forty days and forty nights". He thought it was all over for himself; the food God gives him empowers him to turn the end into a new beginning—and not at his own whim but under obedience. Yet what Jesus gives in the Gospel and what he thereupon demands, is far more. The prophet's experience should keep Jesus' gift and demand from seeming impossible to us.

2. "The bread I will give is my flesh." In place of the manna, Jesus calls himself the true bread brought from heaven. Who could believe this, when, after all, people know his father and mother, which proves that he by no means came from heaven? In light of that, Jesus points not to himself, not to his words and wonders, but to his Father. He points to the God in whom one must believe, who then directs those who have in truth been taught by him to the Son. The Father points to the Son, who, as the only one who truly knows the Father, can reveal the Father's being and direct people to his eternal life. The manna, to which the Jewish listeners pointed, could in no way reveal the Father as eternal life, for the manna's recipients had died. But now, since the Father leads to the Son and the Son leads back to the Father; now, since the Father offers himself in the Son (since all recipients of the Son will be instructed by God) and the Son reveals the Father's love in offering up himself, now earthly death has lost all power and meaning. "Eternal life", the reciprocal revelation of Father and Son, is infinitely more sublime than bodily death. In order that all Jesus says here not be taken as a spiritually exaggerated mental fantasy, a final statement follows: "The Bread I will give you is my flesh; I give it for the life of the world." As truly as the hearth cake and jar of water were suddenly tangible for Elijah in the middle of the wilderness, so this Body, which will become Bread for the life of the world, is tangible when it is offered up.

3. "Imitate God." In the second reading, Paul once more draws out the implications for Christians of the wonder of the Eucharist. Just as Christ, out of love, "offered himself up as a sacrifice", so his eucharistic attitude must become the motif of Christian life, a life lived in imitation of God's love, an imitation that can only consist in mutual love, compassion, and forgiveness. Through these the "beloved children of God" become for each other a sort of eucharistic nourishment for the journey—something like food that unexpectedly materializes for our neighbors in the middle of the desert of our lives, like Elijah's piece of bread and jar of water.

[B] Twentieth Sunday in Ordinary Time

Proverbs 9:1–6; Ephesians 5:15–20;
John 6:51–58

A CONTINUATION OF JESUS' DISCOURSE in which he promises the Eucharist. This time it is not the prophet, as last Sunday, but Wisdom who prefigures the invitation of Jesus.

1. "Come, eat of my meal." In the first reading God's Wisdom has prepared God's meal for men, has everything ready, has sent out her maidens to invite everyone to the celebration. Since it is divine Wisdom who is doing the inviting, it is not those who are already wise who are approached, rather, to the contrary, the "inexperienced", "simpletons", those "lacking understanding", the "ignorant". The foods that she sets out are those that cure "foolishness" or "credulity" and lead one "along the path of insight". The problem with this invitation is that it is directed at those who are not wise, yet who are supposed to let themselves be brought to Wisdom. Such people are unwise either because they consider themselves wise (like the Pharisees and scribes) or because they cannot even understand Wisdom's invitation, thinking it to be absurd.

2. In the Gospel the incarnate Wisdom of God issues an invitation to a banquet that likewise is comprehensible only within the framework of divine wisdom. Hence the unwise, who think they are wise, quarrel among themselves: "How can he give us his flesh to eat?" Within the world of foolishness it is a perfectly understandable objection. Here one man stands among other men and offers himself as food. What could be more nonsensical? Yet God's Wisdom incarnate in Jesus chooses not to reply to the objection, rather, stresses all the more the utterly indispensable character of his offer: "If you do not eat the flesh of the Son of Man and drink his blood, you have no life in you." Those who are foolish in relation to God are outdone by God's foolishness: they must do what to them is completely absurd. Nor is it merely some earthly advantage that is at stake, rather, they are being offered eternal life: whoever refuses to come to this banquet will not be raised to eternal life at the Last Day. By way of explanation Jesus pushes forward into the ultimate, impenetrable mystery of God: just as the Son lives solely through the Father, "so the man who feeds on me will have life through me". Those who think themselves wise are confronted with the incomprehensible mystery of the Trinity so that they might comprehend that they can attain ultimate life only through the power of this mystery. God's love has never spoken with more harshness to short-sighted people. Rather than working with them by gradations, God's love confronts them at the outset with the Absolute.

3. "Don't be ignorant." In the second reading Paul admonishes us to "pay close attention" to be sure that we lead lives characterized "not by foolishness but by prudence". Instead of a sterile, calculating soberness, the discernment he has in mind includes within it the heartfelt exultation that rings out to God, whether silently or aloud, from Spirit-given songs. This is merely the response to the exultation in Jesus' heart as he praises the Father for the fact that he, the Son, dared offer himself up for men. It is the exultation of a supernatural joy that is entirely contrary to natural noise. Christian exultation can ring out in every situation of life, even in the darkness of the cross.

[B] Twenty-first Sunday in Ordinary Time

Joshua 24:1–2, 15–17, 18; Ephesians 5:21–32;
John 6:60–69

1. "Decide today." The first reading tells how, at the assembly held at Shechem, Joshua confronted the entire nation of Israel with the necessity of deciding whether or not they were willing to serve Yahweh firmly and finally. He introduces other gods they might worship, but announces that he and his household will be faithful to Yahweh. The people pay little heed to Joshua's warning against deciding lightheartedly, to his warning that God will punish those who stray (omitted from the pericope). They make their final decision for God, and it will have tragic consequences throughout the history of Israel, because, remaining faithful to his people, God will indeed punish each of Israel's departures. "God repents of none of his promises" (Rom 11:29). The Yes that Israel proclaims on this solemn occasion decides its destiny, all the way to the most tragic moments when it is "blinded", "hardened of heart", and "cut off".

2. "Do you want to leave me too?" Jesus confronts his listeners, including his disciples, with an even more merciless decision, in the light of his promise of the Eucharist. Because he refuses

to back away in the slightest from his statements about the
Eucharist, these words seem so "intolerable" to his listeners
that they are faced with the toughest test of all. Indeed, for
his disciples Jesus hones his assertions even more finely when
he predicts his ascent to the Father and claims that all his
words are "Spirit and life". This draws a line among his disciples, a line that Jesus knew existed from the outset—it was
already clear who would follow him in faith and who would
betray him. There could be no neutrality. The account refers
to "many disciples" who excused themselves. Judas is not the
only one who does not believe. Jesus is not concerned about
numbers, hence he even confronts the Twelve with the same
choice: "Do you want to leave me too?" As spokesman for the
small group of faithful ones, Peter gives voice to the word of
faith, to the belief that Jesus is "the Holy One of God". Faith
had brought him to a realization, and that realization made
possible the virtually blind faith needed for such a decision.

3. "As Christ loved the Church." In the context of these other
readings the great passage in Ephesians regarding the union of
husband and wife as an image of the union of Christ and his
Church takes its meaning from the irrevocable nature of the
eucharistic self-offering of Jesus to his Church, which makes
her into an "immaculate bride" (prefigured by a man's self-
offering in marriage). This eucharistic self-offering makes the
Church far more "spotless" than the fickle Synagogue, but it
also means that "reverence for Christ" and "subordination" is
required of the Church as wife. For the Church truly becomes
the "body" of Christ and believers become "members of his
body" through the Eucharist. That is the ultimate fulfillment
of the promise made by the God who chose Israel, a promise
solemnly sealed at Shechem and brought to completion by the
Eucharist of the Son.

[B] Twenty-second Sunday in Ordinary Time

Deuteronomy 4:1–2, 6–8; James 1:17–18, 21–22, 27;
Mark 7:1–8, 14–15, 21–23

1. God's command. The first reading depicts the incomparable superiority of the divine command over all human wisdom. The great nations have their laws and have thought their way to a degree of human wisdom. These laws are modified to conform to changing times and circumstances. In contrast, the law God has issued for Israel is immutable—nothing dare be "added to or taken away from it", for it originates in the eternally valid vitality of the lawgiving God himself. Even though Israel is a small and politically insignificant nation, the "great nations" cannot avoid recognizing the law given by God as more than other human legislation and the nation that lives according to God's law as "wiser and more intelligent" (in divine things) than other nations, who perhaps have recognized much of his wisdom. For the cultural formation (*Bildung*) founded on God's law is not merely human culture, rather, it is a wisdom of the heart growing out of obedience to him. Israel's cultural formation (*Bildung*) consists in its being a form (*Gebilde*) of God.

2. "Born to truth through the Word." In sending his Son to men the Father has far surpassed the goodness of his lawgiving. As the second reading says, his "perfect gift" is to have "brought us to birth through the Word of truth", to have made us into "the first fruits of his creation". His Word is no longer merely spoken as instruction for us, rather, it is now "rooted in the heart". Having become so much internalized, more than ever it must not only be "heard" but acted out, in order that the living Word of the Father might truly bear divine fruit worthy of God. Jesus in our hearts is certainly a fulfillment rather than an abolishing of the law's guidance (Mt 5:17), and this fulfillment certainly extends far beyond Old Testament faithfulness to the law (Mt 5:20). For the word spoken to us from outside has now become an inwardly rooted Word.

3. "Wicked designs come from within." This is the sore point of the Lord's invective in the Gospel reading. Man has made the word spoken by God even more exteriorized by adding to it, something that was forbidden in the first reading. It has reached the point where the law has become a "meaningless" form of reverence for God (Jesus' words are as relevant today to Christians who merely go through the motions, as they were to the Pharisees back then). Jesus explains in drastic terms what he has in mind: foods that enter a man from the outside do not defile him, but the evil that comes from his inner heart, whether that evil remains a thought or becomes an act, does defile. And evil is all the more evil when it comes out of a heart in which God's living, incarnate Word has taken root as law. On the other hand, whatever originates from or is inspired by the Word of God living in our hearts is part of what Paul calls a "reasonable" or "meaningful service [worship] of God" (Rom 12:1), whether it is spoken or done with direct reference to God or as part of everyday human existence.

[B] Twenty-third Sunday in Ordinary Time

Isaiah 35:4–7; James 2:1–5;
Mark 7:31–37

1. "Ephphatha, 'Be opened'!" The Gospel relates the healing of a deaf-mute by Jesus. For him this clearly has to do with more than a physical disability. It is a parable for the people of Israel who, in turn, represent all of mankind. As the prophets have said so often, Israel is hard of hearing when it comes to the Word of God, which, in turn, renders it incapable of giving a valid response. Jesus does not make a spectacle out of his miracles. Hence he takes the sick man aside, seeking the middle line between entirely avoiding publicity and helping the people. Physically touching both ears and tongue precedes his upward look toward the Father (in this miracle the Father acts through him) and his sigh, which probably points to his having been filled with the Holy Spirit. This trinitarian fullness indicates that the prayer "Be opened!" speaks not only of physical healing but of effective grace for Israel and for all mankind.

2. *"Streams will burst forth in the desert."* When, at the end of the Gospel, people say with astonishment: "He makes the deaf hear and the mute speak", this is almost an exact quotation from the first reading, taken from Isaiah. "The ears of the deaf are opened again, the tongue of the dumb breaks forth in song." This is something that has to do with the majority, for the Lord's promises are directed toward the entire people. When the text subsequently refers to streams opening up in the wilderness and to rivers in the steppe, this shows that here the physical healings signify more than merely a physician's action—they indicate a transformation of all of nature by the approach of the judging and redeeming God. The approach of salvation is depicted as an eschatological event: as Revelation will say, "The old order has passed away, behold, I make all things new" (Rev 21:1–5).

3. *"The poor are rich."* The second reading adds a new theme. For Isaiah, the "blind, deaf, lame, and mute" were the ones gifted with the Lord's grace. James refers generally to the

"poor", whom "God has chosen in the world to be rich in faith and even heirs of the Kingdom". They are poor in a double sense: because they are despised by the wealthy world and ushered to a humiliating seat. Yet Christians have to view them with completely different eyes. What the world does and, sadly, what James says Christians not infrequently do (taking notice of the rich and disdaining the poor) contradicts not only the explicit words of Christ but even contradicts the entire divinely established world order described in the Old Testament. For the streams open up and gardens flourish precisely in the midst of impoverished nature, namely, in the wilderness. Hence Jesus calls the poor "blessed" [happy] at the beginning of his first sermon. By "blessedness" he means something much more profound than earthly happiness. He means being uniquely loved by God.

[B] Twenty-fourth Sunday in Ordinary Time

Isaiah 50:5–9; James 2:14–18;
Mark 8:27–35

1. "Faith without works is dead." Christian faith, if it is genuine, motivates the entire person. Simply to believe that a few of the Church's teachings are true is no Christian accomplishment. One's entire life must answer God's call. That is what James teaches in the second reading, and he goes on to demonstrate it through the obedient faith of Abraham, who placed his own son, the God-given son of promise, on an altar of sacrifice. No one can meet James' challenge to give an example of "faith without works", to demonstrate faith that lacks effectiveness in life. According to Paul, faith must "be active in love" (Gal 5:6), for otherwise it is loveless and faith without love is dead. James illustrates this with the hypothetical case of a Christian who turns away a naked and hungry fellow man.

2. *"Let him take up his cross and follow me."* Next, the Gospel! To be sure, Peter responded with a halfway correct answer to Jesus' inquiry about what the disciples thought of him: "You are the Messiah." But by that Peter meant a Messiah of the sort that he and most of the other disciples expected: a wonderworker who would liberate the oppressed Israelites from the Romans. There existed in Israel at the time a powerful and widespread theology of liberation that was not limited to the active resistance fighters known as Zealots. Just as the title "Messiah" passes Peter's lips for the first time, Jesus breaks things off. He forbids the disciples to disseminate this title in any fashion. Instead he announces to them, again for the first time, the destiny that awaits the Son of Man: great suffering, rejection, death, and Resurrection. Peter refuses to listen to any of this, and he sends him away as "Satan", as a seducer and gainsayer. Jesus is revealing here the decisive work he has been sent to accomplish, a task not for him alone but for each person who believes and follows him. James' teaching about faith and works really acquires its full stringency at this point: faith without the work of the Passion is not Christian faith at all. A person whose faith involves the hope that he will be safe and avoid loss will lose everything. To want to salvage oneself is egoism, which is irreconcilable with a faith that cannot be separated from love. The core of the work without which faith is dead is the act of total self-offering, whether to God or to one's neighbor. That this act can involve suffering, even to the point of death, is beyond question—even as hypothesized, this act carries within it a death, a renunciation of the "I". Whether this renunciation leads to physical death in martyrdom or not is entirely secondary.

3. The first reading reveals an *Old Testament foreshadowing* of this renouncing of self. The "Servant of God" stands up to the enemies who beat him, rip out his beard, and defile his face with blows and spit. God gives him the strength to make his face as hard as flint. He knows that in this suffering he is obeying and that God is not abandoning him, despite all his feelings of abandonment. Indeed, a "court case" that affects the entire world is taking place, a judicial debate led by the Holy Spirit as legal counsel ("advocate"; Jn 16:8–11), a proceeding that will end with the triumph of the Servant of God, of the resurrected Son "on his way to the Father".

[B] Twenty-fifth Sunday in Ordinary Time

Wisdom 2:1, 12, 17–20; James 3:16–4:3;
Mark 9:30–37

1. "Let us find out what will happen to him." One cannot escape applying the text of the first reading directly to the "Son of God", to Christ. Each verse fits his and his enemies' behavior. He did in fact accuse them of betraying the law and the tradition; they did conclude that he must die a "crude and shameful" death. The mocking words uttered beneath the Cross correspond to those ascribed to the wicked here: if he is truly the Son of God, then God will certainly defend him; we want to test whether God grants him the aid he ostensibly is counting on. From this point of view, the Cross of Christ would be the proof that the enemies who murdered him were right, for, as they wished, it "tested his gentleness and patience": he did not know enough to defend himself.

2. "Must be the slave of all." The Gospel appears to confirm once again the perspective of the "wicked": Christianity is a doctrine suited to defenseless children and those who wish to become defenseless children—a religion for weaklings. Yet the Gospel also inverts everything: instead of opponents lying in ambush, in this instance Jesus' teaching is directed toward his disciples: *he* will be delivered up, put to death, and rise on the third day. He, not his opponents, determines his fate, and he does so in supreme freedom, as a deed of his utterly fearless courage, out of obedience to God. Replacing the wicked we find the disciples. Having heard but not comprehending Jesus' words, they quarrel over which of them will be the greatest. In the process they unmask and caricature the wicked. To be great and mighty stands in opposition to Christ's proven patience and gentleness. As the sound of his misunderstood prophecy fades away, Jesus takes the child, whose nature everyone understands, in his arms to demonstrate the truth proclaimed by his entire existence: the Greatest, God, proves his greatness by stooping down to place himself in the lowest place as a slave. A child, the weakest form of human existence, who by his very nature calls out for care and acceptance, is the real symbol of this God, who is accepted when one picks up a child: when one accepts, first of all, the humbled Son, but accepting in him accepts the Father as well, for the Father agreed to his humiliation. By his freely chosen slave's service, God demonstrates to all the wicked and those obsessed with lust for power that he is supreme over all. Who among us has the courage to imitate him?

3. "You can obtain nothing." The biting words of the second reading, which inexorably unveil man's sinful interior in the sight of God, merely draw conclusions from the above. Man's striving for power and greatness, which unavoidably involves wars and prestige battles, ultimately leads nowhere, for the "envious" and "ambitious" man is torn by inner contradictions. He strives for things that run contrary to his nature, he is in "disorder" and bristles at the "wisdom from above". When he prays for the order granted by this wisdom, he accomplishes nothing; to the degree he wishes to be great, he "obtains nothing", for, in order to receive, he must be like a child: "peaceful, lenient, docile". Only Jesus' teaching resolves the inner conflict within man, a conflict in which he is entangled and from which he cannot free himself.

[B] Twenty-sixth Sunday in Ordinary Time

Numbers 11:25–29; James 5:1–6;
Mark 9:38–43, 45, 47–48

1. "Anyone who is not against us is with us." The Gospel has two parts (Mk 9:38–42 and 43–48). The first part speaks of the permissible and tolerable, the second of the unbearable.

It is tolerable that someone who does not belong to the community of Christ does something wholesome in Jesus' name. If he calls upon that name, he can scarcely be opposed to him. The community needs to know that Christian thoughts and deeds are not limited to the community. God is powerful enough to let a particular Christian stance—offering a cup of water (Mt 10:42)—occur outside the Church and to reward the benefactor.

In contrast, it is unbearable when someone outside or inside the Church misleads those who are spiritually or morally unfortified ("one of these little ones"). The spiritual "superiority" with which he seeks to lead the simple believer astray is satanic and merits merciless annihilation. But man can seduce himself: his evil desires lie in his hands, feet, and eyes, and he ought to move as mercilessly against these as against the seducer of others. Whatever leads astray should be destroyed; in graphic terms, the member that stimulates one to evil should be hacked off. A spiritually divided man does not reach God; anything in him that is contrary to God belongs in hell.

2. *"Two men inside the camp."* The other two readings can be viewed as explications of the two parts of the Gospel. In the first reading two of the seventy men singled out by God to receive the Spirit stayed behind in the camp instead of leaving it with Moses. The Spirit descended upon them too, and they began to speak prophetically. Joshua wanted to stop them, but Moses let the Spirit alone—he would have been happiest if the Spirit had fallen upon the entire nation. The limits one would like to burden the Spirit with do not matter to him, who "blows where he will" (Jn 3:8). His order does not always coincide with the Church's order, even though he himself prescribes the ecclesial order that the Church has to follow. Nor dare the Church turn the Spirit's freedoms into rules for her own privileges and tolerances. God's thoughts are high above man's thoughts, which must follow God's instructions.

3. *"Your wealth has rotted."* The second reading reveals what is unbearable for Christians: a wealth that feeds on the wages withheld from workers; a surfeit that does not abate even though God's judgment day is dawning (here it is referred to as the day of slaughter); a wealth that is already "rotten", and piles of "gold and silver that are corroded". In the Old Testament the righteous one at whose expense the powerful have enriched themselves, is the "poor of Yahweh". In the New Testament it is Jesus and those who follow him: he "offers no resistance" but, like a lamb led to slaughter, does not open his mouth.

[B] Twenty-seventh Sunday in Ordinary Time

Genesis 2:18–24; Hebrews 2:9–11;
Mark 10:2–16

1. "What God has joined. . . ." The Gospel settles the question
of marriage, as Jesus bypasses Moses to appeal to God's original order of creation. Unlike positive law, which, having been
passed, can be changed, the creation-order is written into the
nature of man. This nature is both physical and spiritual, inseparably so. Physically wife and husband become "one flesh",
and, because the man "leaves father and mother in order to
cling to his wife", and because their union produces children
who must be brought up, they also become "one spirit". This
union traceable to God's doing is thus final and cannot be broken by men. That the Gospel reading includes the story of the
blessing of the children can be related to what we have just
considered. Here children are explicitly a model for anyone
who accepts the Kingdom of God, including married people.
If they maintain a childlike attitude toward God, they cannot
approach their spouse out of an attitude of superior adulthood.
When both of them remain childlike before God, the mutual
understanding and goodwill that can overcome the unavoidable tensions of married life becomes possible.

2. "God built up the rib into a woman." The corresponding
story of the creation of woman from Adam's rib is added in
the first reading. Jesus' redemptive order confirms the Father's
creation-order without reservation. The underlying meaning
of the naïvely graphic tale is obvious: unlike other sub-human
beings, man and woman are one flesh from their very origin.
Discovering each other and "becoming one flesh" thus corresponds to their deepest and most unique nature. Man rules

over the animals, but in the woman he recognizes himself: "At last, flesh of my flesh." "Therefore", it is said explicitly, a man clings to his wife and they become what they already are: one flesh. The fruitfulness of this union is mentioned in the first creation account (Gen 1:27–28) and, as Jesus underscores, is part of the reason why this union cannot be broken.

3. "He is not ashamed to call them brothers." As the second reading indicates, Jesus himself will not marry, so that "according to God's gracious will he might taste death for the sake of all" and offer himself up for all, not for a single woman. At a higher level, his offering of flesh and blood on the Cross and remaining in the Eucharist is a parable, better yet, the archetype of all married self-giving. All mankind plays the role of the wife, to whom Jesus "clings". Although this entire humanity is also represented by the Church as the Bride or Spouse of Christ, the Church is not expressly mentioned here. Instead the passage states comprehensively that Jesus, who consecrates us, and all members of humanity who will become consecrated through him, "originate all from One", the Creator, who is his Father. Thus "he is not ashamed to call them brothers"—in a natural sense based on their origin and in a more profound sense because of his self-offering on the Cross and in the Eucharist, in which they exuberantly become "one flesh". The One who has established this order of salvation is "God", the Father, "for whom and through whom all things exist and who wanted to bring many sons to his glory".

[B] Twenty-eighth Sunday in Ordinary Time

Wisdom 7:7–11; Hebrews 4:12–13;
Mark 10:17–30

1. "Sell what you have." The story of the man who could not
give up his possessions and the disciples who left everything
for Christ's sake make up an integral Gospel reading. Between
the two episodes we find Jesus' comment about how difficult
it is for the rich to enter the Kingdom of God.[2] Who falls
under the label "rich" as far as Jesus is concerned? He who
clings to his possessions, regardless how large or small those
possessions might be. People may be wealthy without clinging
to their goods. (Jesus surely knew people like this, for presumably the women who employed their assets in his service were
well-to-do [Lk 8:3].) Likewise people may be poor yet unwilling to give up what little they have. Initially Jesus employs
words to speak of the difficulty, then he uses the image of the
eye of a needle to point out the virtual impossibility that the
man who is unwilling to renounce his possessions can enter
the Kingdom of God. Seeing how shocked his disciples are, in
the end he leaves it all to the sovereign power of God. Peter
insists that he and the others had indeed left all to follow Jesus,
who radicalizes this in three ways. First he lists all the people
and goods that must be abandoned. Then he underscores the
phrase, "for me and for the Gospel" (that is, one must act out
of a positive motive rather than out of contempt for earthly
things). Finally he adds, "even under persecution"—the one
who robs himself of his own goods does not thereby sail into

---

[2] In German the word *reich* can be used to mean both a rich person and a kingdom (realm). Von Balthasar plays on this when he refers to Jesus' words about how
hard it is for a *rich* person to enter the *Kingdom* of God: "Jesus Worte über die
Schwierigkeit für den *Reichen*, ins *Reich* Gottes zu gelangen"—TRANS.

a safe harbor, rather, the "hundredfold" return referred to here is ultimately promised only for the life to come. The following of Jesus that Peter spoke of becomes such only in light of the cross in this world and resurrection in the next.

2. *"I pleaded for the spirit of wisdom."* In the first reading Solomon is an ambiguous figure when viewed from the perspective of Jesus' challenge. As a young king he prayed to God for wisdom, and this passage from the Book of Wisdom testifies to the fact that he preferred wisdom to all royal power, all wealth, indeed, he preferred wisdom even to light, health, and beauty. In this way he seems to be close to the attitude required of a New Testament disciple. Yet the Old Covenant, which lacked the example of Jesus, has no real sense for the true value of "poverty in the spirit" and "renouncing everything". Thus, as proof that Solomon's request was the right one, God grants him "countless riches" (cf. 1 Kings 3:13). And precisely this wealth granted by God seduces Solomon into the stupidities of his old age. Only the example of Jesus can make clear to men that the God of all riches has no wealth other than his love, a love that can even become poor for our sake.

3. *"Sharper than any two-edged sword."* The second reading describes how God's Word penetrates and judges our innermost attitudes, the attitudes that are most hidden from the world. This Word cannot be bought off or persuaded to turn a blind eye. It discerns "soul and body"—a soul that perhaps still clings to earthly things and is unwilling to give them up, while the spirit ultimately is "willing" (Mt 26:41). Man cannot of his own accord ultimately penetrate his attitudes; but God's Word sees everything lying "bare and exposed" before it. We are accountable only to that Word, for only through the Word can we gain insight into ourselves.

[B] Twenty-ninth Sunday in Ordinary Time

Isaiah 53:10–11; Hebrews 4:14–16;
Mark 10:35–45

1. "Can you drink the cup?" The Lord does not flatly reject the request by the sons of Zebedee as if it were inappropriate (it would have been inappropriate had they understood its true scope, but Jesus tells them they do not realize what they are asking for). He informs them what they have really asked for—by referring to his cup and his baptism, that is, to his Passion. Unsuspectingly they assure him that they can handle this. Thereupon Jesus makes this promise to them: he promises them participation in the atoning suffering of the Cross. After he has taught the disciples once more that worldly power has no meaning for them, that they must strive for the service of a slave instead, he talks about his own service: to give his "life as a ransom for many". With this he includes genuine Christian suffering—whether it be spiritual suffering, sickness, torture, or martyrdom endured for Christ's sake—in the redemptive fruitfulness of his atoning Passion. Since Jesus' existence is an existence-for and his Passion is a suffering-for, everything suffered in following him and focusing on him is marked by this purpose, by a redemptive fruitfulness.

2. "Who gave his life as an offering for sin." The first reading permits us to hear part of Isaiah's great prophecy of the Servant of God who suffers for others. In what was an almost incomprehensible statement at the time it was made, Christians later recognized perhaps the most important prophecy of Christ's vicarious suffering. Of course there were hints of this idea earlier: Abraham's intercession for Sodom, and, more distinctly, Moses' forty days of fasting before the face of God as intercession for the sinful people. The Servant of God surpasses Moses, however, because the entire meaning of his existence seems to be bound up in his suffering on behalf of the people, a suffering no one can grasp. The Ethiopian eunuch reads this passage and cannot understand it; the deacon Philip explains it with reference to Christ (Acts 8). The Jews later found their own experience mirrored in what happened to this figure scorned and shunned by all. Such a reading is not mistaken, if their suffering has indeed been drawn into Jesus' all-encompassing atoning Passion.

3. "Tempted in every way that we are." The second reading presupposes the Gospel. Because our "great High Priest" has made satisfaction for us, through him we can "approach the throne of grace confidently". We dare never place our suffering, even if it occurs as a consequence of following him, on the same level as his. Only he is the atoning High Priest. He alone has "passed through the heavens" and has appeared before the Father "in the sanctuary with his own blood" (Heb 9:12). It is nothing but a grace that we are permitted to suffer with him. And, above all, this grace grants us "confidence" that we shall "find mercy and favor" through him. Our primary place is among the people reconciled to God solely by the Servant of God. That we then are permitted to "endure various trials" (1 Pet 1:6) and "momentary light affliction" (2 Cor 4:17) with him ought to be "nothing but joy" (James 1:2) for us.

[B] Thirtieth Sunday in Ordinary Time

Jeremiah 31:7–9; Hebrews 5:1–6;
Mark 10:46–52

1. "My Lord, I want to see." The story of the encounter with
the blind beggar as he left Jericho, told in such a lively way
by Mark, is dominated by a single theme: to be able to see.
The man hears that Jesus and a large throng of people are
passing by and recognizes his unique opportunity. Hence his
shout: "Son of David, have pity on me!" By employing the term
"Son of David", which is found in all three Synoptic Gospels,
he meant "prophet" or "wonderworker" (cf. Mt 9:27; 15:22).
Annoyed, people try to make him be quiet, but he cries out all
the louder. At this point Jesus stops, summons him, and asks
him what he wants. Now comes the single and unique wish:
To be able to see! His longing for light is part of what causes
Jesus to grant the healing, which in turn makes it possible for
the man to follow him. This following after Jesus shows that
the longing for light was a longing for something more basic:
a longing for the right path, the path a blind person cannot
find; a longing for the path that leads to God, a path whose
direction and stages one must see if he is to embark upon it.
He who was cut off from light now finds his way home.

2. "I bring them home." The first reading describes this homecoming. It begins "with tears", in a blindness that cries out for
light but does so in vain. "Consoling them, I guide them", so
that, now able to see, they can find the path along which God
leads them. It is "a level road, so that none shall stumble".
Blind people constantly stumble, those who see can glimpse
the already-established road. Yet here we recall that Jesus called
himself the light of the world: "Whoever follows me will not

walk in darkness, but will have the light of life" (Jn 8:12). Then comes the qualification: "While I am in the world, I am the light of the world. Night is coming when no one can work" (Jn 9:5, 4). "If one walks at night, he stumbles, because the light is not in him" (Jn 11:10). This means that the light is no more within our power than the sun, which recurrently disappears from sight, is within our power. The Lord does not abandon us, but we dare not stop whenever we want to and hold onto him, as if he were our possession. As long as we keep following, the Light never leaves us behind.

3. "Christ did not grant himself this honor." Christ calls himself the light of the world, but he is, as the Creed says, *"lumen de lumine"* [light from light]. He did not take upon himself the dignity of the High Priest of mankind, rather he received it from the Father, who forever has "begotten" him "today". Because he is sent from the Father "to offer gifts and sacrifices for sins" and "is able to deal patiently with ignorant and erring sinners because he is himself beset by weakness", he warns his own people that his day on earth will come to an end, that he must enter a night of suffering for the sinner. Yet precisely in this night he is "priest forever", precisely in the darkness of our sins, unknown to himself, he radiates his loftiest light. That is his mission, which in its entirety—even in hell and darkness —is the Light of the world. Whoever follows him can indeed enter into darkness, the very darkness that Christ experienced, but in this darkness his follower cannot stumble.

[B] Thirty-first Sunday in Ordinary Time

Deuteronomy 6:2–6; Hebrews 7:23–28;
Mark 12:28–34

1. "Which is the first commandment?" In today's Gospel it becomes clear that strife between Judaism and Christianity need not have arisen. They agree about the prime commandment and they agree that the commandment to love one's neighbor should take its place alongside the all-surpassing command to love God. We are even told that Jesus viewed the scribe (Pharisee) who interrogated him as being "not far from the Kingdom of God". The unanimity goes even a bit farther: at the end of his approving response to Jesus, the scribe asserts that this two-part great commandment "is worth more than any burnt offering or sacrifice". In this he is saying that a believer carrying out the love-commandment in life does better than someone who venerates God merely by means of ritual observance. This was already prefigured in Hosea: "It is compassion that I desire, not sacrifice" (Hos 6:6, cf. Mt 12:7). Yet the unexpressed divide between Jewish and Christian perceptions may become apparent in this last-mentioned aspect (as also affirmed by the second reading): if the sacrifices of the Old Covenant become superfluous with the arrival of Christ, this is so because his fulfillment, in his death on the Cross and in the Eucharist, of the commandment to love God and neighbor permits lived love and formal worship to coincide completely. Through this ultimate offering of love, Jesus' love for the Father and for us takes on an intensity that was inconceivable in the Old Covenant. This by no means denigrates the astonishing "first commandment" that Israel had come to formulate, for the New Covenant cannot find a better way to state it. The difference lies in the fact that, before Jesus, no one was able to travel "all the way to the end of love" like he did (Jn 13:1).

2. "Hear, O Israel!" In the first reading the great commandment is stated for the first time and in its complete perfection. It is introduced by the claim: "Yahweh, our God, Yahweh is one." There are no other gods: "our God" is the only one. To have many gods divides the heart of man and its worship; a single God demands the undivided integrity of the human heart and all its powers. Hence there can be no dichotomy between God's demand for love and the human heart—it is not as if the heart were located within while the command comes from outside or above. Instead these "obligatory words" to men "are to be written on your hearts". In other words, love for God requires man's entire heart and all its powers from the inside out.

3. "Jesus has an everlasting priesthood." The second reading underscores yet again and in the clearest possible terms that Jesus' priesthood is an existential one that no longer ritually offers animals in the temple, as the former priests had to do for their sins and the sins of the people. Instead Jesus offers himself as the Spotless One whose entire sacrificial self-offering was "necessary" to make genuine expiation for us. And, because "Jesus remains forever", his priestly act of sacrifice on the Cross is not a thing of the temporal past. His is an "everlasting priesthood" and his self-offering takes place now and always, "for he lives forever to make intercession for us." Thus, by virtue of his "everlasting priesthood" and out of his eternal standpoint, his Eucharist is able to make make his one-time offering now and always present in our own time.

[B] Thirty-second Sunday in Ordinary Time

1 Kings 17:10–16; Hebrews 9:24–28;
Mark 12:38–44

1. "First make me a little cake." The story of Elijah and the
widow of Zarephath in the first reading reveals all the greatness of the Old Covenant. It has to do with obedience in a
life-and-death situation. The prophet asks the woman to give
him the bit of food she had planned to prepare as a final meal
for herself and her son before they would die of hunger in
the famine that Elijah had invoked upon the region. Elijah's
request for her last resource is not an abrupt one. He begins
with "Do not be afraid"—the words that God so often employs to introduce a command for men. It calms the despairing
woman, she becomes willing. Only then comes Elijah's request
to make a small cake for him, the same cake she had planned
to make for herself and her son. His request is followed by
God's promise that the woman's supply of flour and oil will
not fail until the drought ends. The decisive point of the story
is that obedience, even an obedience that risks her life, is prior
to the promise that assures life for her and her son.

2. "Everything she owned." In Mark and Luke, the story of
the poor widow found in today's Gospel, is the concluding climax of Jesus' words and deeds before the "little apocalypse"
and the story of his Passion. An ultimate decision takes place
here. The wealthy throw something of their surplus into the
alms-box, an act that means no loss for them and gives them
prestige in the eyes of men. (At the beginning of the pericope
Jesus insists on this theme of ambition, concluding with these
words: "They will receive the severest sentence.") When the
widow tosses her two tiny coins in the box she is throwing in

all she had to live on. She does it of her own free will and without attracting the attention of anyone except God. In this her deed surpasses that of the woman in the Old Testament. No words were exchanged, not even between Jesus and her. But, at the conclusion of his public teaching activity, Jesus lifts her up as an example: perhaps without recognizing him, she has understood better than anyone else the meaning of all his words. Significantly he says nothing about a reward, in contrast to Elijah. The woman's act is so radiant that it carries within it its own reward.

3. "Offered up once for all." If one reads the second reading in the light of the Gospel, Christ's unique sacrifice, unlike the multiple animal sacrifices of the Old Covenant, becomes significant as the self-offering of the final One, the One after whom no one else comes. His sacrifice is compared explicitly with human death: just as each man's death is a unique event (the Bible says nothing about reincarnation), so this sacrifice is sufficient to atone for the sins of the world once for all. And behind Jesus' self-giving we glimpse the Father's sacrifice, which is fully comparable to that of the widow in the Gospel. For the Father also tosses everything he has—not merely what is dearest to him but what he needs most—into the offering box: "For God so loved the world that he gave his only Son" (Jn 3:16).

[B] Thirty-third Sunday in Ordinary Time

Daniel 12:1–3; Hebrews 10:11–14, 18;
Mark 13:24–32

1. "No one knows that hour." The Gospel regarding the end of the world is unusually multifaceted. Instead of merely reporting the coming events, it unites various aspects whose unity is not apparent to us. First, imagery of cosmic catastrophe is employed to announce the sufferings of the end times, then comes the proclamation of the arrival of the Son of Man to judge those assembled by the angels, an assembly which, oddly enough, includes only the elect. Next Jesus refers to the signs by which one can recognize the approaching end, followed by the signs of its imminent arrival, only to emphasize the fact that the exact day is not recognizable, since only the Father—not even the Son—knows it. Yet Jesus insists that his words will outlast the destruction of heaven and earth. Without seeking to unite all of this into a comprehensible system we should permit each statement to have its significance, above all the statements about the lasting imminence of the end, which is valid in each generation. For even these words about the end are more imperishable than are we or any people or nation. Hence the signs of the end are recognizable, but not by virtue of threats or catastrophes of world-historical significance. Instead, the very state of the world itself points to its own end. Calculations will do us no good if "not even the Son knows the hour." Only lasting readiness is unconditionally required of us.

2. *"Many shall awake."* Daniel (in the first reading) is the first great apocalyptic spokesman, in many respects the model for later ones. In him too the lines are crossed: supreme suffering yet simultaneously the protection of God's people—which, however, also involves a separation of the elect from the non-elect, a separating of those who awake to eternal life from those who awake to eternal disgrace. Once more we are not offered a simple report, rather, the purpose of the passage is to make people conscious of the ultimate decision of man for God and God for man.

3. "A single sacrifice." Above the uncertainty that man must endure if he is to be truly vigilant hovers (in the second reading) a single certainty that is beyond our manipulation: Jesus has offered the one, single sacrifice for the sins of the world for all time. His act is so unique and unrepeatable that the passage can speak of his "waiting until his enemies are made into his footstool". Yet we are immediately deprived of any grasping or sleepy certainty, since it says that this all-sufficient sacrifice is made for "those who are being sanctified"—in other words, for those who let this sanctification process take place in them by God's act of love, for those who do not refuse it. Thus we are indeed granted genuine Christian hope if we recognize God's work of sacrifice, but are not given the sort of certainty that is unsuited to the pilgrimage of men on earth.

[B] Christ the King

Daniel 7:2, 13–14; Revelation 1:5–8;
John 18:33–37

1. Christ first makes himself known *as King in his Passion.* Up to this point he always slipped away when people tried to make him king—such attempts were merely misunderstandings (Jn 6:15). But now, as he approaches his crucifixion, he can and must reveal himself for who he is: the origin and goal of the world, as the Book of Revelation names him. The unavoidable misunderstandings no longer matter: Pilate will fail to comprehend the essence of his claim to kingship, the Jews will reject him. But he persists: "You say that I am a king" because I "came into the world to testify to the truth". The truth is the Father's love for the world, which the Son represents in his life, death, and Resurrection. The Cross is the proof of the truth that the Father loves his creation so much that he permits even this to happen. And the inscription Pilate has placed on the Cross in the three world languages of that time unwittingly proclaims this truth to everyone. One can certainly say that Jesus, who was humbled to the point of crucifixion, has been installed as ruler of the whole world through his Resurrection from the dead. But this is only possible because he was chosen for this kingship from all eternity, indeed, he always possessed this kingship insofar as the creation of the world would never have taken place without foreknowledge of his Cross (1 Pet 1:20–21). He is given an honor which he always possessed.

2. *"His Kingdom shall not be destroyed."* Daniel's vision in the first reading offers images for the words of the Gospel reading: the Father will bestow the dignity of an eternal Kingdom on the Son in a timeless moment—for we cannot distinguish between a plan of creation and a plan of redemption here. "All peoples, nations, and languages must serve him": in the Old Covenant this is said with reference to the Cross; in Revelation the same thing is said of the "Lamb who was slain".

3. *"I am the Alpha and the Omega."* In the second reading it is the resurrected Lord who, even as judge of the world, remains the "pierced One", who calls himself the "ruler of all creation", the King per se, the "ruler over the kings of the earth". Yet because he, the One who revealed himself a king before Pilate, has "freed us from our sins by his own blood", he has made us redeemed ones into "kings before God, his Father", into kings who, like him, are also "priests"—because we rule only by spiritual authority. This refers not to the earthly office in the Church but to the priesthood of all genuine believers. As king, Christ says of himself: "He is, he was, he is to come." His

transtemporality ("he is") is at the same time the historically unique fact of his suffering and death ("he was"), which, as such, is always coming at us head-on.

[C] First Sunday of Advent

Jeremiah 33:14–16; 1 Thessalonians 3:12–4:2;
Luke 21:25–28, 34–36

1. "Watch and pray constantly." In the Gospel the Church year begins by looking forward—toward Christ's return. In the process the Gospel teaches us something unusual—to view Christmas (Christ's first coming) and the world's judgment (his second coming) together. This should not surprise us, for the Scriptures say again and again that the end times begin with Christ's Incarnation: God says his final Word (Heb 1:2), all that remains is to wait to see if men listen to it or refuse to listen to it. The final Word, which appears upon the earth at Christmas, "is destined for the fall and rise of many" (Lk 2:34). It is "sharper than any two-edged sword, a judge over the thoughts and reflections of men, . . . everything lies naked and exposed to the eyes of him to whom we must render an account" (Heb 4:12–13). The incarnate Word of God is *krisis*, that is, "separation". This Word comes to save the world, but whoever "rejects and refuses to accept my words has his judge; the word that I spoke will condemn him on the Last Day" (Jn 12:48–50). What we view as a huge space between Christmas and the Last Judgment is nothing but the time granted us to make up our minds. Many will say Yes, but it looks like the No's are on the increase during the allotted period. Significantly, "all of Jerusalem was troubled" (Mt 2:3) at the first inquiries about the presence of the Redeemer for whom the entire Old Covenant yearned; and, already by the third day after Christmas we have to celebrate the Slaughter of the Innocents. Right at the outset of his public activity people conclude that he must be killed (Mk 3:6). He came into world history not to bring peace but a sword (Mt 10:34). Christmas is no festival of niceness, rather it celebrates the powerlessness of God's love, which can over-power only by means of death. During the time of our testing the word for us is, "Watch and pray."

2. *"Yahweh our justice."* The Old Covenant certainly looked ahead to the day when God would fulfill his word of salvation for Israel (first reading). The promised shoot sprouting from David will, in terms of God's covenantal justice, be a "just shoot". And God's covenantal justice cannot simply be mea-sured along the lines of human justice, rather, it is identical to the rightness (*rectitudo*) of all the divine deeds of salvation, which in turn is identical to his faithfulness to the covenant into which he has entered. This includes rather than excludes the fact that God will have to punish the unfaithfulness of men in order to bring them to their senses and out of their apparent forsakenness. For that is what covenant and justice in truth mean (cf. Lev 26:34–35, 40–41).

3. *"Blameless, when Jesus comes."* Christian living, in accord with the Church's "admonitions" (second reading), is thus a life lived expecting the coming Lord. It is a life that takes its norm from the future. Priority is given to the commandment of love, love not merely for fellow Christians, but "for all", so that the Church might shine out over her own boundaries with a message that can reach and persuade the hearts of men. Second, a "strengthened heart" is necessary to achieve that purpose, and this is something one must ask God for. Only strength from God will help us to keep our love of neighbor Christian rather than letting it drift off into a vague human-itarianism. When we eventually appear before Christ's judg-

ment our holiness has to be so "blameless" that he can add us to the cluster of his "holy ones" who are coming with him, for together with them he will judge us (Rev 20:4–6; 1 Cor 6:2).

[C] Second Sunday of Advent

Baruch 5:1–9; Philippians 1:4–6, 8–11;
Luke 3:1–6

1. "Make ready the way of the Lord." The detailed historical and contemporary references to the time at which the decisive salvation events were inaugurated by the appearance of John the Baptist indicate the depth of the Gospel's concern to place these events into the framework of world history. Instead of imagery, symbols, and archetypes, we are given exact, datable facts. The first fact is that God's Word comes to John. He is called and sent as the last prophet and thus, both in his existence and his task, he brings to a close the series of anticipatory prophetic missions within history. This corresponds to and, as the Gospel says, "fulfills", the great promise given through Isaiah. John's specific mission, which does more than merely repeat ancient words, is symbolized by his baptizing: at the end of the time of promise the simple calls to repentance enunciated by earlier prophets are now surpassed by an action that spreads over the entire nation. In being immersed and then emerging from the water the "convert" testifies that he lives on as a different, cleansed person who wants to make his crooked path into a straight one. The entire Old Covenant recognizes in John a trial run for the decisive event that is on its way.

2. "Arise, Jerusalem." The first reading shows that the old promises of a new time of salvation (at the return from ex-

ile) promise a glory that has not yet arrived. The return from
Babylon was anything but a triumphal march. The promised
glory was a promise that will be fulfilled later and in a completely different way than the prophetic imagery suggests. The
true glory that is promised to Israel here is the arrival of Christ
as proclaimed by the Baptist, but this glory will be no earthly
luster. Instead, it will be precisely what the Gospel of John
describes as the visible glory of believers: the life, death, and
Resurrection of Jesus. This, after all, is the straight path—"I
am the way"—by which God comes to us. And the God who
comes is the One who, out of his "compassion" (which will
be perfected on the Cross), brings his covenant-"justice" with
him, as the conclusion of the reading says. In order that all
this might happen to her, Jerusalem is challenged to "Wake
up" and "look to the east."

3. "That he will also complete the good work." The second reading transfers us to the New Covenant. With the advent of Jesus
we have not simply arrived at the destination, for he "is the new
and living Way" (Heb 10:20). Even for the pilgrim Church he
remains a "forerunner", the "One who precedes" (Heb 6:20),
and no Christian can retire prematurely: "Therefore, let us be
on our guard while the promise of entering into his [God's]
rest remains, so that none of you might be found to have been
negligent" (Heb 4:1). Paul's words to the Philippians constantly
refer to this "being underway", but it is a pilgrimage undertaken with greater "confidence" than under the Old Covenant,
since Christ "has already begun the good work" and, if we remain on his path with "insight and understanding" for that
good work, he "will also complete it" at the day of his final
coming. The "way of the Lord" promised by Isaiah as a path
requiring preparation, the path which the Baptist declared was
now really ready for travel, has become the "Way" which is

"the Lord" himself, the Lord who is ready to take us with him along this path.

[C] Third Sunday of Advent

Zephaniah 3:14–18; Philippians 4:4–7;
Luke 3:10–18

1. "Then what should we do?" The Gospel describes how the Baptist instructed those who wanted to begin a new life. (In the preceding passage he dismissed as a "brood of vipers" the self-righteous who had come to hear him solely out of curiosity.) The answer he gives to those ready to repent, which includes people despised by the Jews (tax collectors, soldiers), reveals that Jesus' radical love-commandment was thoroughly anticipated in the Old Covenant. Indeed it was something that could dawn on any unspoiled conscience. The teaching of John the Baptist has to do with sharing when my neighbor lacks sufficient clothing or food. It has to do with justice in the course of collecting taxes and other dues. It has to do with observing limits in matters of power, something that can be difficult for military people (no theft, extortion, or pressure for more pay). What John insists on can be defended out of the prophets; there is no need to confuse him with the coming Messiah. The Messiah, before whom the Baptist humbles himself, will bring a completely different means of purification: the Holy Spirit, who will reveal our sins to us from God's perspective and who can burn them away with his fire. He will also confront us with the ultimate decision between Yes and No, wheat and chaff. Giving this sort of direction places the Baptist, who is the "greatest born of woman" (Lk 7:28), at the extreme end of the time of preparation, already fully able to catch sight of the new beginning, and perhaps, because of his profound humility, to cross the boundary: as "friend of the Bridegroom" (Jn 3:29), whose baptism is adopted by the Bridegroom so that it can be filled with new meaning.

2. *"Fear not, O Zion!"* The first reading, which calls on Israel to exult, speaks to its own time but also points to the future: "On that day it shall be said to Jerusalem. . . ." This means that today man can already rejoice over what is yet to come. And he can do this not with a mixture of joy and fear, but in a joy that is based on God's own joy: "The Lord rejoices and exults over you as one sings joyfully at a feast." For the believer, Advent is not a time of vacillating between fear and hope, for the arrival of the Redeemer that has been announced is a certainty. The feast is sure to get underway. All that is asked of us is that we not let our heads droop in unbelief or mistrust about whether God will keep his promise. This applies to his first advent as much as to his second.

3. *"The Lord is near."* In the second, New Testament, reading, this joyful hope grows stronger, to the point that we are commanded not to be anxious about anything. We are told not merely to be free of anxiety, but to have a "joy in the Lord", which alone can bring "peace", which "surpasses all understanding", and which eliminates any thought that our hope might be in vain. But this joyful glimpse of the Lord's approach must prove itself in mutual love within the community, a "kindness" recognizable even to non-Christians. The joy with which we approach the Lord must be an apostolic joy. A trust that lets God take care of all earthly concerns (as the Sermon on the Mount insists) is a Christian trust only if it is bound up with prayer that asks for daily bread and is thankful for what has been received.

[C] Fourth Sunday of Advent

Micah 5:1–5; Hebrews 10:5–10;
Luke 1:39–45

1. "Blessed is the fruit of your womb." As the final preparation
for Christmas, today's Gospel tells how Mary, bearing her child
within her, traveled to her relative, Elizabeth. Mary is not the
one who tells Elizabeth she is pregnant (she also said nothing
about it to Joseph). Instead the Holy Spirit causes the child in
Elizabeth's womb to "leap for joy". This is a marvelous inter-
twining of the Old and New Covenants, carried out by God
himself. Later the Baptist will at first not know who the Greater
One to come after him is (Jn 1:33: "I knew him not."), yet here,
already in his mother's womb, he is blessed by this Greater One
and thereby chosen to be his forerunner. By extension we can
say that Christ's fulfillment of the Old Covenant turns all of it
into a forerunner, so that it acquires its full meaning only when
explicated in the light of Christ. A sign makes sense only if the
destination to which it points exists. This is also true because
men in the Old Covenant had only a pale impression of the
Savior whose future coming they awaited. Not so Elizabeth—
like her child filled with the Holy Spirit, she knows precisely
and can thus greet the chosen woman who stands before her
as the one who possesses the perfect faith that permits God to
bring his ancient promise to fulfillment. Many a man in the
New Covenant only recognizes long after the fact that he has
been "chosen" and "called from his mother's womb" (Jer 1:5;
Is 49:1; Gal 1:15).

2. "You, Bethlehem-Ephrathah." Seen from the perspective of
salvation history, Micah's astonishing prophecy in the first reading glimpses more of the future than the prophet could have

possibly realized. In the time of tribulation following the destruction of Samaria, he returns to the origins of David, who had come from Bethlehem and the tribe of Ephraim in the distant past. According to the prophecy, after the tribulation of the exile has passed, the Shepherd of Israel will come from that place to establish a worldwide peaceable kingdom. Isaiah had spoken of the young woman who would bear the "God-with-us"; here the mother of the Messiah is simply called the "birth-giver". The prophet reaches back to David, but the "distant past of Jesus" is eternity, and his eschatological peaceable kingdom will far surpass Israel's expectations. Perhaps the fulfillment in Mary and her Son reaches back to the Old Covenant only in order to tower high above it.

3. "I come to do your will, O God." Now the very spirit and mission of the Messiah who comes into the world are revealed (in the second reading). His task is pure obedience, for even to enter upon this mission is a matter of obedience. This obedience does not engage in external liturgical activities, rather, his own body, created by God for this purpose, will be the object of his sacrificial obedience. The ancient external sacrifices in the covenant of man with God disappear into the man-become-offering. True "once and for all", this completes the covenant and sanctifies all of us. Here the reference of the New Covenant back to the Old Covenant is merely formal: the concept of sacrifice is taken up, but its meaning is totally changed—from ineffective to infinitely effective.

[C] The Christmas Masses

(See Year A, pp. 21–28.)

[C] Holy Family

1 Samuel 1:20–22, 24–28; 1 John 3:1–2, 21–24;
Luke 2:41–52

1. "Unknown to his parents." As portrayed by the Gospel, the Holy Family is a family that is painfully opened up, undergoing suffering that surpasses that known by earthly families, yet in a manner exemplary for all. The father claims as his own the son implanted by the Holy Spirit, something he has to do if he is to obey God and let God's son be the Son of David. The mother has been told that her heart will be pierced by a sword (Lk 2:35); she has already given the Son back to the divine Father. And the Son recognizes this divine Father as his own in such a matter-of-fact way that he says nothing about it to his parents, who would not understand. God and obedience to him stand at the center of this family and constitute the glue that holds it together, creating a bond tighter than the physical bond between the Mother and the Son. The Son has been obedient to his parents and will continue to be obedient, but obedience to the eternal Father rules obedience to earthly parents—even though they cannot understand it and are filled with the anxiety of an unsuccessful search and an even deeper anxiety caused by the words, "Didn't you know?" *"Dieu premier servi* [serve God first]" (Joan of Arc).

2. "I will return the boy to the Lord." The first reading offers a moving drama, a preliminary stage on the way to the Holy Family, in which Hannah returns to God the son she asked for and received from the Lord. A woman who wishes to become a mother in order to give her son to God is unique in the Old

[For this feast, von Balthasar offers reflections on additional readings which are options given in the German Lectionary—ED.]

Covenant and points ahead to Mary's sacrifice. Indeed, it becomes a model for all Christian families, who are prepared to return one child, perhaps more, to God—if he so wills. More than many mothers Hannah is aware that she owes her fertility to God, and she expresses this thankfulness by giving back to him. She does not simply let go of the child; instead, she herself brings him to the temple. She does this not to get rid of the child but because she sees something valuable, something she certainly loves, and something she can offer as a gift that will please God.

3. "We are called children of God, and so we are." In the second reading the spirit of the Christian family is traced back to the fact that all its members are children of God. All of them owe their existence to God, and they owe all human fertility to the eternal fruitfulness of the triune God. In this Godhead there is an order of processions (the Father's place is before the Son's and that of both is before the Holy Spirit's) yet all three Persons in God are of the same being and worth. So too, there is a derivative order in the earthly family by which the parents' place is before the child's, even though the child has the same worth as the parents. Being placed ahead or behind in the order does not impede unity of love, the same unity of love that dominates the triune God and joins all three Persons in the same being. If those who belong to each other in an earthly sense obey the God of love, they receive this unity of love as a continually renewed gift from God. All they have to do is ask for it: "We receive from God whatever we ask, because we keep his commandments and do what pleases him."

[C] January 1:
Mary, Mother of God

(See Year A, p. 30.)

[C] Second Sunday after Christmas

(See Year A, p. 32.)

[C] Epiphany of the Lord

(See Year A, p. 34.)

[C] Baptism of the Lord

Isaiah 40:1–5, 9–11; Titus 2:11–14, 3:4–7;
Luke 3:15, 21–22

1. "Jesus let himself be baptized, with all the people." The fact
that Jesus let himself be baptized with the people who sought
to turn away from their sins contains a profound mystery: it is
as if already in his first public act he wanted to make known
that he stood alongside all sinners. Later he will receive his
own into his Church through Christian baptism, through the
humiliation of a descent into water as an element of both death
and new life. He does not wish to burden his own with anything he has not also gone through. If baptism is really to
become a sharing in his death and burial and a resurfacing
to everlasting life (as Paul portrays it in Romans 6), then for
him this first baptism is already an advance commitment to

[For this feast, von Balthasar offers reflections on additional readings which are
options given in the German Lectionary—ED.]

his own Passion and Resurrection. Everything that happens between his baptism and the Cross is framed by an integrated meaning and action. For Jesus the baptism in the Jordan is a baptism "with the Holy Spirit"; the baptism on the Cross is a baptism "with fire". The first means solidarity with sinners who need cleansing, the second burns away the sin of the whole world. God as triune makes all of this activity known: the Father who sends confirms his "beloved Son" who, out of free love, fulfills the triune willingness to save; the Holy Spirit hovers in the form of a dove between the Father in heaven and the Son who prays on earth. The Holy Spirit brings the Father's will to bear and brings the Son's prayer to the Father. Everything between the baptism and the Cross-Resurrection will correspond to this visible form of God's triune decision to save.

2. *"Behold, there is your God."* In the first reading the comforting words that the time of redemption has dawned are spoken to Jerusalem and, through her, to all mankind. On the one hand, the Redeemer comes "in glory" and "with power", for Jesus' work of redemption will triumph over and subordinate all of world history. On the other hand, he comes with the solicitude of a shepherd who carries the young lambs on his shoulders and personally looks after the ewes. This union of power and loving care proves that he is God become man, for only God joins these two characteristics in perfect unity.

3. *"So that we might become heirs of eternal life."* The second reading locates us at a point at which Jesus' work of salvation is complete ("he has given himself for us") and Christian baptism ("the bath of rebirth") now gives us a share in Jesus' first baptism in water and his final baptism in blood ("there is a baptism with which I must be baptized, and how great is my anguish

until it is accomplished" [Lk 12:50]). Again the heavens open over the Christian baptism and God reveals the completeness of his "goodness toward mankind". The Father's grace has "appeared, saving all mankind", not because of their deeds, "but because of his mercy". Jesus himself is simultaneously (in all likelihood) referred to as "Savior" and "our great God". And baptism accomplishes the renewal "in the Holy Spirit" that has been "richly poured out on us", both for our justification and for our sanctification—which makes us worthy to attain the hoped-for eternal life. The miraculous theophany of Jesus' baptism continues in his Church through all ages.

[C] Second Sunday in Ordinary Time

Isaiah 62:1–5; 1 Corinthians 12:4–11;
John 2:1–12

1. "In Cana he revealed his glory." The Church's liturgy sees a threefold dawning of God's glory in Jesus in the feast of the Epiphany: God's glory dawns on the Magi, in the theophany at the Jordan (celebrated last Sunday), and in Jesus' first miracle, at Cana, where he "revealed his glory". Poor folk invite Jesus, his mother, and his disciples to their wedding, but they run out of wine. Mary, already representing the caring and interceding Church, turns to the Son, which may seem odd, since she has probably not seen any outward miracle by him yet. Yet she knows all that is necessary: she knows of the holy power within him. Aware that the only wonder God has assigned to him is the Cross, Jesus does not want to be forced into the role of a wonderworker, which the insatiable throng will demand of him again and again from this point onward. Then comes what is probably the most beautiful word from Mary, by which she leaves everything up to him and at the same time instructs the servants about obeying him: "Do whatever he tells you!" Although unnoticed by others, this is really the dawning of her glory. Jesus does not resist her, for his mother's word is very close to that which occupies him most inwardly. The account does not tell us whether people even noticed the transformation of what was useless into a very precious commodity, whether Jesus was celebrated as a wonderworker, something he always wanted to avoid. The account merely says that his disciples "believed in him". That is the only outcome that he would consider a success. Although he tried to keep his later miracles quiet, many of them were bandied about as sensations, making his mission more difficult.

2. *"As the bridegroom rejoices in his bride."* The first reading compares God's joy at a converted, purified people with the joy between bridegroom and bride. The comparison is intended to point out simply that, through his miracle at the wedding feast of Cana, Jesus blesses human marriage and elevates it to serve as an image of a completely different kind of wedding joy. "As a young man marries a virgin", so it is between God and the people. Erotic love is not a lower form of love or a distant parable for God's love for the land which he now refers to as "espoused" and "my delight". Natural, human love should be a point of departure by which men can sense how much they are loved by God. Indeed, the sexual union of husband and wife becomes an, admittedly inadequate, image of the intimate union between Christ and us in the holy Eucharist.

3. *"To each person gifts of grace are given for the common good."* The second reading leads us into a different track: the miracle at Cana was a miracle done purely for the joy and benefit of others. Now, in the Church, the Holy Spirit gives each believer a

charism, a gift of grace, "for the common good". Since they are supernatural gifts, one can indeed compare these charisms to the capacity to work spiritual wonders; and one can make this comparison even if these charisms seem inconspicuous from the outside. In the list at hand, Paul includes some conspicuous gifts; in other listings (Rom 12) he mentions more modest ones. When Jesus says in a parable that faith can move mountains, he has in mind his spiritual power, which can remove great burdens in the hearts of men, heaving them out of the way, not by psychological techniques but based on the divine power in which the true believer shares. Many saints have also done material miracles, but the spiritual wonders they accomplished were greater and more important.

[C] Third Sunday in Ordinary Time

Nehemiah 8:2–6, 8–10; 1 Corinthians 12:12–31;
Luke 1:1–4, 4:14–21

1. "Today is holy to the Lord your God." The "today" in the course of Ezra's solemn public reading of the law to the entire, assembled nation (first reading) is an Old Testament upbeat for the "today" of the Gospel. This public reading is described in impressive terms, with parenthetical explanations of the situation. The people are visibly moved, throw themselves reverently to the ground, and weep, because they heard about so many things they had not been taught. Yet they are encouraged to rejoice and are sent off to a festive banquet because the fact that they had received God's word made the occasion a joyful one: "For rejoicing in the Lord must be your strength." This makes it all the more astonishing when a much more important "today" from the mouth of Jesus calls forth completely different reactions from his listeners.

2. "Today this Scripture passage is fulfilled in your hearing." In
the Gospel we hear only the introductory part of the scene, in
which Jesus likewise reads the Scripture in the synagogue of his
home town and says words that seem blasphemous and are incomprehensible to his listeners: Today is fulfilled the prophecy
of Isaiah that "the Spirit of the Lord is upon me . . ." so that I
might "bring glad tidings to the poor, proclaim liberty to cap-
tives, sight to the blind, and freedom to the oppressed." Then
he applies these words to himself. In front of all those who
knew him he steps forward out of the obscurity of his youth
into an immense light, right into the role of the Messiah. His
listeners' reception of this is related in next Sunday's Gospel:
not with tears and rejoicing but with rage. Let us, however,
take it to heart and marvel both at the courageous willingness
of Jesus to stick to his mission and his humility in calling his
work simple obedience to the "Spirit of the Lord" that rests
upon him. Together these characterize his attitude in a most
profound way and indicate its uniqueness: his mission is the
fulfillment of all the most sublime promises of God, but he
carries it out as the true "Servant of God", in whose Spirit the
Isaiah passage was spoken.

3. "All have been given to drink of the one Spirit." But what does
"today" mean for us today? It is something entirely different
from what it meant to the ancient people of Israel. The second
reading describes it: the nation of old was a nation weeping
and rejoicing at the law. We are a body taken up into the today of Christ. The Jews were not members but were individuals within a national community; we are interrelated members
within the body of Christ. Paul describes this in detail. There
are no individuals anymore, only organs, each of which func-
tions for the living whole that constitutes the organism. Only
the Whole, Christ, is indivisible, *in-divid-uum*. Our different-

ness is not for us alone but for all the others, who corporately make up the indivisible Whole. And this is an ethical, not a physiological, matter: in Christ's constant Today we live for him and for one another. Each of us has a personal, irreplaceable task, but not for its own sake, rather for the living whole. Each of us has to carry out our mission in the Spirit of the whole, the Spirit who assigned that which is specific to each of us. Since all of us "have been given to drink of the one Spirit", each of us who has the Spirit must live outside himself, in love to the other, in the other. That is the Today that results from Christ's Today of fulfillment.

[C] Fourth Sunday in Ordinary Time

Jeremiah 1:4–5, 17–19; 1 Corinthians 12:31–13:13;
Luke 4:21–30

1. "Do not cower before them." Our subject today is the courage of someone sent by God to recalcitrant people—in other words, our subject is the problem of provocation. The first reading reveals how difficult is the situation of someone who has to point out and endure tenacious human recalcitrance toward God. For that reason God himself is relentlessly present with him. He dares not fear anyone, neither "kings, officials, priests" nor ordinary "people", lest God himself instill fear of everyone in him. He must portray how God contradicts everyone who contradicts him, and God's gainsaying is so powerful that the person portraying it must become a "wall of brass", who therefore has to set "his face as hard as flint" (Is 50:7). "I am with you", God tells him—therefore they cannot overpower you. How much a mission of this sort costs a weak man is apparent in what happens to Jeremiah inwardly and outwardly.

2. "No prophet gains acceptance in his homeland." In the Gospel Jesus takes up the attitude of a prophet and in so doing, begins to provoke his listeners. He has told them that he is the fulfillment of all prophecy; he responds to all the slap-dash praise for his "charming discourse" with the statement that his prophetic words will not be recognized "in his own country", for people are already saying, "Isn't this the son of Joseph?", that is: How can he say anything new? Jesus' proof follows immediately: the prophet Elijah could do his miracles only in a Gentile country; his successor Elisha could do his miracles only for foreigners. We might well think Jesus was imprudent in the way he provoked his relatives and fellow townspeople. Would it not have been better for him to begin by telling them things they could handle and swallow before gradually moving on to more difficult matters? Is it not his own fault that they are "filled with indignation" and drag him out of the town in order to murder him? Yet later Christian preaching will imitate his method. In his sermon to the Jews in the temple Peter says: "You denied the Holy One and asked that a murderer be released to you; you put to death the author of life" (Acts 3: 14–15). One can tiptoe around diplomatically only for a short time before it leads to the point where he has to jump feet-first into truth-telling. Paul may indeed quote pagan poets to Athenian intellectuals, but all of a sudden he finds it necessary to talk about Jesus, Resurrection from the dead, and judgment. An "inculturation" approach never quite gets around to addressing those topics.

3. "Our knowledge is pieced together." Between these two texts the second reading forms a canticle to love, the "path that surpasses everything else", the only way that leads to the destination. Everything else, even our most profound insight, our heroic ethic ("giving all I have, handing over my body to be burned") is insufficient. When God uses Christ and his Church to provoke men, he is acting solely out of his love. And all those who are entrusted with the task of living and proclaiming his love to the world provocatively must do so in love and out of love. Otherwise instead of being messengers of God, they are speaking solely from themselves, out of contempt for other people, out of contempt for their failings, obsession with comfort, misuse of power, and abuse of nature. That sort of motivation is beneath the standard set for Christian preaching. Love "is not jealous, is not prone to anger, does not rejoice in injustice". Our brothers must sense the love of God effectively at work in us even in the harshest words we have to utter in God's name.

[C] Fifth Sunday in Ordinary Time

Isaiah 6:1–8; 1 Corinthians 15:1–11;
Luke 5:1–11

1. "Here I am, send me." Today all the texts talk about being chosen. Great instances of being chosen are placed before us, but as examples of invisible callings—for each believer is one who has been called to an assignment. In the first reading we have the most solemn call found in the Old Covenant. Isaiah's vision of the Lord seated on a lofty throne, surrounded by seraphic hymns of praise, filling the smoke-filled temple with the train of his garment, cannot but send Isaiah reeling: "Woe is me, I am doomed." In fact, mission always begins with an experience of utter distance, of absolute unworthiness. Then the seraph comes from God with the burning ember, which purifyingly sears the lips of the terrified recipient: "Your sin is purged"; do not persist obstinately in your unworthiness. Next there comes from God more of a question than a command: "Whom shall I send? Who will go for us?" There is no more room for thoughts of worthiness or unworthiness, rather: God needs someone and so, "Here I am, send me."

2. *"From now on you will be catching men."* The calling of Peter in the Gospel proceeds in a very similar manner. The only difference is that an act of obedience on the part of a man who has already heard and been impressed by the preaching of Jesus precedes the vision of Jesus' omnipotence and absolute superiority. Contrary to what his experience as a fisherman would tell him to do, Peter obeys the command to lower his nets. The experience of unbridgeable distance repeats itself. Isaiah: "Woe is me; I am doomed!" Peter: "Leave me, Lord, for I am a sinful man." No genuine mission can dispense with this experience of the gulf between myself and God—and the mission comes, after all, from God. Precisely into the emptiness of this chasm Jesus points Peter toward his mission to be a fisher of men. The "fear not" recurs at each of God's commissionings. This includes Mary's, for, before God "does great things for her" she knows she is a "humble servant" before God. For Peter, being called to be a fisher of men is so far out of proportion to his sense of who he is that it makes no sense to be afraid any more. All that is left is wordless obedience: "They brought their boats to land, left everything, and followed him."

3. *"Last of all by me also, as one born out of normal course."* Now, in the second reading, we have Paul, who, as a persecutor of Christ's Church, had reason enough to emphasize the chasm between his person and his assignment. "I am the least of all the Apostles, in fact, I am not worthy to be called an Apostle." More than others, his mission involved a mighty deed by God: near Damascus he was knocked down and blinded, for,

like Isaiah, he had seen the heavenly Lord in his glory. Thus he had to be led by the hand into the city. His commissioning does not occur personally but, to humble him, is blunt and involves other people: "Go into the city and you will be told what you must do." Ananias' assignment is delivered in even blunter language: "I will show him what he will have to suffer for my name" (Acts 9:1–16). Humiliations of this sort accompany Paul during his entire life of mission. He will be treated as "rubbish, the scum of all" (1 Cor 4:13). And, as if that were not enough, he is given a special rod of discipline from God: the blows of the angel of Satan that "keep him from becoming too elated". All his entreaties to God fail to get rid of it: "My grace is sufficient for you" (2 Cor 12:7–9). If, in today's reading, he notes that he has worked harder than all the others, he immediately has to add, "not I, but the grace of God in me".

[C] Sixth Sunday in Ordinary Time

Jeremiah 17:5–8; 1 Corinthians 15:12, 16–20;
Luke 6:17, 20–26

1. "Blessed are you poor." In the Gospel we find four pronouncements of beatitude and four declarations of woe. What does "blessed" mean? Certainly it does not mean "happy" in the sense that man gives to this word. And it is certainly not a call to continue on his way comforted and contented. Instead of referring to something that belongs to man, something that man feels or experiences, it refers to something in God that affects this man. In the context of blessedness Jesus speaks of "reward", which is also only a metaphor. It has to do with the value that this man has for God and in God, something timeless in God that will be revealed to the man in his own time. It is the same with the declarations of woe. The poor, to whom the Kingdom of God belongs, that is, the poor of God (in the language of the Old Covenant), show that their poverty corresponds to a possession in God: God owns them and therefore they own God. So too with the hungry and weeping and, finally, with those who are hated for Christ's sake: they are loved by the Father in Christ, for he, after all, was hated and persecuted by men for the Father's sake. If the poor are to be understood as poor in God, then the rich are to be understood as rich without God, rich for themselves, full and laughing, praised by men. They have no treasure in heaven and thus all they own makes its appearance merely in passing. The Psalms repeat this constantly, as do Jesus' parables (the rich man and Lazarus, the rich farmer [Lk 16:19–31; 12:16–21]). The poor really are the poor. They own nothing. They are not secretly becoming rich as they pile up capital in heaven. God is not a bank, and giving oneself up to God is not like buying an insurance policy. The blessedness is found right in the sacrifice.

2. *"Cursed is the man—blessed is the man."* The Old Covenant already knows this fully, as the first reading shows. The blessed man is one who trusts the Lord, who extends his roots along God's "stream", or, as Augustine says, has his roots in heaven and grows from heaven downward toward earth. This naked trust in the Lord is enough to make him "blessed" in the sense in which Jesus uses the word. No matter how harsh the earthly privation he has to endure, he need fear no drought. Contrasted with this is the "man who trusts in men", in human and earthly things, thereby "turning away from the Lord". Here we have a commentary on the meaning of Jesus' declaration of woe to the rich and the well-fed. The simple antitheses of this prophet, which we find also in the first Psalm, divides men into two camps with no regard for psychological finesse: either they live

by God for God or they try to live for themselves by themselves. In Jesus' judgment there are also only two classes of men: sheep and goats.

3. The second reading also divides men into two categories: those who believe in the Resurrection of Christ and our own resurrection and those who deny the Resurrection. *Without this "your faith is useless"*, the dead are "lost", and "we are more pitiable than all other men", who at least place their hope in real earthly goods rather than on a non-existent otherworldly God. Their lives were somehow fulfilled: with happy human relationships, with all kinds of pleasure, with self-satisfaction. At least that is something—whereas belief in the Resurrection is a high-stakes game in which the player has bet the bank and, if there is no Resurrection, loses.

ALL THREE TEXTS for today's celebration demand an ultimate decision from us: are we sufficient for ourselves or do we owe ourselves constantly to our Creator and Redeemer? There is no third path between the two.

[C] Seventh Sunday in Ordinary Time

1 Samuel 26:2, 7–9, 12–13, 22–23; 1 Corinthians 15:45–49; Luke 6:27–38

TODAY'S TEXTS SPEAK OF MAGNANIMITY. The Gentile philosophers and ethicists knew of and marveled at it. In the Old Covenant it receives a more profound basis. In Christ, in the form of love of enemies, magnanimity (generosity) becomes a form of imitation of God himself.

1. "David took the spear and water jug." In the first reading David has an opportunity to kill his enemy Saul as he slept. Following the logic of war, his companion, Abishai, advised him to do so. But David did not do it—out of magnanimity, to be sure, but also because: "Who has ever raised his hand against the Lord's anointed and remained unpunished?" Respect and awe for a man consecrated to the Lord motivates his magnanimity, which he does not extend to other enemies— even as he dies he instructs his son Solomon to take revenge on these enemies.

2. "Be compassionate, as your Father is compassionate." Jesus goes a good bit farther. "Love your enemies, pray for those who mistreat you." The issue here is not outer acts of magnanim- ity, but an inner attitude, which is now explicitly compared to God's attitude. "For he is good to the ungrateful and the wicked." And he is good to them not out of an otherworldly goodness existing in and of itself, as the sacrifice of his Son for sinners, for the "enemies" (Rom 5:10), demonstrates. Jesus expressly ascends from limited human generosity (which re- turns love to someone who has given love and gives gifts in order to receive gifts in return) to the absolute generosity of God, which showers love on those who currently hate him and despise him. Jesus dares to make this ascent because he himself is God's gift to all his enemies, a gift of uncalculable love that indeed now causes everyone endowed with it to be "consecrated to God". Each of our fellow men who have been anointed through the atoning death of Jesus thus becomes to us what Saul was to David. Magnanimity has thereby been transformed from a human virtue at which people marvel, as did the Gentile philosophers, to something self-evident and ordinary for Christians, because the Christian knows that he himself is a product of divine generosity. So is everyone else, which is why I do not make the other person aware of my superior generosity but merely remind him through my deeds that we all owe ourselves to God's generosity.

3. "Heavenly men are like the man of heaven." Earthly and heavenly virtues are contrasted once more in the second reading. The man who ascends from nature here below, no matter how much he may see himself as the highest flowering of the cosmos, remains an "earthly living soul" who incorporates the norms that are valid within nature: ordered love begins with my own self. Since the world's goods are limited, the first rule mandates a fair division of them, in which I receive that which is mine (cf. Rev 6:5b–6). But the first Adam, the one who appeared first, is surpassed by the second, heavenly Adam. Because he comes from the limitless God, he does not acknowledge the limits and norms of finitude. He can waste himself and heavenly love without reserve and bequeath the same gift to his "descendant", the Christian, who is formed in his image.

[C] Ash Wednesday

(See Year A, p. 51.)

[C] First Sunday of Lent

Deuteronomy 26:4–10; Romans 10:8–13;
Luke 4:1–13

THE STORY OF THE TEMPTATION OF JESUS, which is always read on the first Sunday of Lent, is accompanied today by confessions of faith from the Old and New Testaments. At the center of the account of his temptation, we find Jesus too acknowledging God and God alone.

1. "The Lord gave us this land." The offering of the first-fruits in the first reading is accompanied by an ancient confession of Israel's faith that recounts in highly abbreviated form the saving act of God: "homeless and wandering Aramean" must refer to Jacob, who served Laban in the land of Aram. He arrives as a foreigner and, in Egypt, becomes an alien in the deepest sense. Only delivery from Egypt by Yahweh's might and the land Yahweh gives to the people brings stability and prosperity to him. Therefore the first-fruits of the soil belong to God. Here, confession is gratitude. The gifts presented in a basket are symbols of an attitude of faith.

2. "The Spirit led him around in the wilderness for forty days." According to this Gospel account, Jesus' ministry also begins with a homeless wandering in the wilderness. In this case it carries overtones of the forty years of Israel's wandering in the wilderness, a time of testing and often of genuine temptation, to which the people more than once succumbed. It was also a time when the people gained practice relating to God, just as Christian confessors, apostles, and saints often begin their mission among men only after years in the wilderness and solitude with God. That their faith is forged into tempered steel during such a time shows that they are following in the footsteps of their Lord, who fasted in the wilderness and passed the test posed by the temptations regarding his messianic mission. We dare not underestimate or doubt the depth of temptation Jesus went through. He who took our sins upon himself also wanted to learn to know our temptations with all their cleverly deceptive power to seduce. "Eve saw that the tree was good for food, pleasing to the eyes, and desirable for gaining insight"

(Gen 3:6). To someone hungry after more than a month's fasting, to have bread within his reach must have been desirable. To possess this world (which he was supposed to bring to his Father) must have seemed a good idea, and the miracle that was proposed to him would have appeared useful to establish his standing with the people. It was all so plausible—why bother with the much more wearisome path of renunciation? The three verses with which Jesus counters the devil are not neatly memorized aphorisms but painfully acquired responses. In a higher sense one can call them an existential confession of faith.

3. "Confession with heart and lips." The confession mentioned in the second reading is not intended to imply that it is subjectively easy: the word (of faith, which the Church proclaims) is "near you, on the lips and in the heart" of the believer— because this word is basically Christ himself, yet it is also a word that the believer himself—and he alone—can voice. It too is more than a mere phrase learned by heart from the liturgy of the community. By this statement one confesses his readiness to accept its consequences for his life: "Jesus is the *Kyrios* [Lord]" and "God has raised him from the dead." Both belong together: as the Resurrected One he is the *Kyrios* over the whole world, but also over me, over my heart and my life. He is, therefore, the *Kyrios* who has "endowed from his riches all those who call on him", whether they are Jews or Greeks or Chinese or Indians. Such confession of this Lord and the self-surrender that it contains grants "justification and salvation"— everything that we might imagine as saving or rewarding.

[C] Second Sunday of Lent

Genesis 15:5–12, 17–18; Philippians 3:17–4:1;
Luke 9:28–36

1. "They talked about his end." The present reading of the story
of the Transfiguration is the only one that reports anything of
the contents of the transfigured Lord's conversation with Moses
and Elijah. They talked about Jesus' death, that is, about the
most important of the events of the world's salvation. The entire scene relates to his death: Jesus reveals himself in changed
form to his disciples because he has already predicted his death
to them. The Father's voice from heaven designating the chosen Son also points toward his redemptive act on the Cross.
And if the disciples in the end see Jesus alone again, they
know now what a fullness of mystery is concealed by his simple form. Enclosed within him are his relationship to the entire Old Covenant and his constant relationship to the Father
and the Spirit, which has also overshadowed the disciples as
representatives of the Church to come. His transfiguration is
no anticipation of his Resurrection (when his body is transformed toward God), rather, it is just the opposite—it is the
presence of the triune God and all of salvation history in his
body, which is destined for the Cross. In his transfigured body
the covenant between God and mankind is sealed with finality.

2. "A deep, uncanny fear came over him." On the mountain of
the Transfiguration, the disciples first fell asleep, then were
overcome by fear. That is how it is when God comes so near
to man. The first reading returns to the first covenant, which
was concluded in an original ceremony between God and Abraham, the father of the nation of Israel. It was preceded by the
Lord's words of promise, just as in the Gospel reading Jesus'

prediction of the Cross preceded the Transfiguration. The sealing of God's promise to Abraham takes place in an archaic ceremony that is known to have been performed by other nations. What is important here is the deep sleep and the fear, which are signs of the numinous character of the event and which, like the Transfiguration of the Lord, essentially point ahead to the fulfillment of God's promise: the gift of the Promised land and the expanse of the Kingdom. Both events are not closed in upon themselves but point both backward and forward.

3. "Our homeland is in heaven." The second reading establishes the provisionality of all human existence, a provisionality which now, like the Transfiguration, points ahead. Whoever establishes himself in the flesh is "an enemy of the Cross of Christ". But whoever follows Christ, expects his return from heaven, where Christ has his homeland already, in anticipation of ours. Heaven is no worldless place, rather it is that place where "our lowly body" will assume the "form of his glorified body", where the Creator's world will take on its final form as the Redeemer's world. Here we will be integrated with finality into the embodied covenant between God and creation in Jesus Christ, who in himself gives body to this covenant between God and man, heaven and earth.

[C] Third Sunday of Lent

Exodus 3:1–8, 10, 13–15; 1 Corinthians 10:1–6, 10–12; Luke 13:1–9

1. "Then perhaps it will bear fruit." The Gospel consists of nothing but warnings. Jesus is told that Pilate has had several men executed, and that many were killed by a falling tower. To him all the others are in equal danger, as long as they continue sinning. Then he tells the parable of the fig tree that bears no fruit. It ought to be cut down—it is a parasite. The tree receives one more chance, at the request of the gardener: "Then perhaps it will bear fruit; if not, it shall be cut down." The events mentioned above should be interpreted in this sense: Pilate's sword hangs over everyone, the tower can fall on any of us at any time. In this story the fruitless fig tree is not cursed, but it has stretched the owner's patience to the limit. That one fertilizes it and works the soil around it is grace—a final grace that it has not earned. It is a grace offered to the tree, a grace that does not automatically produce fruit. Instead he, the man symbolized by the tree, must produce fruit together with grace.

2. *"They have been written as a warning to us."* The second reading surveys the graces granted to the people of Israel in the wilderness: transit through the sea, food from heaven, water from the rock (which, according to the saga, follows them, a rock whose water-of-life points ahead to Christ). Again, the entire overview is intended as a warning to us: the people were ungrateful, craved the delicacies of Egypt so much that they wanted to go back, let themselves be led astray into sexual sins, grumbled against God. Because God punished them for this, most of them never reached the destination God had promised them. The Church, to whom this warning is directed, dare not wrap herself in a greater sense of security in comparison with the Synagogue, telling herself that everything will turn out right for her in the end. Indeed, precisely because she has been gifted with greater graces she may be in greater danger of failing. The worst way to go astray is when a person destined by God for a certain path is unfaithful to his call. Those destined for the greatest sanctity can become the most treacherous apostates, tearing out entire sections of the Church with

them in their departure: "and a third of the water turned to wormwood" (Rev 8:11).

3. "I-Am-Who-Am." Yet, in the first reading, the miracle of the burning bush is recounted and Moses is chosen to proclaim this name of God, "I-Am-Who-Am" as the name of the Savior of the people. In today's situation can this mean anything other than that the warnings directed at a person, which can come to pass, never for a moment place the faithfulness of God in question? It would be perverse to conclude that God's patience with a fruitless person ever comes to an end, that divine love simply gives way to divine justice. God's qualities are not limited qualities. It is man who is limited to his own time, who has only this limited span within which to bear fruit. The warning is not that God's patience is exhausted, rather that our own limited opportunity will soon come to an end. God cannot pay out wages for an unproductive life, as the fate of the worthless servant in the parable of the talents obviously reveals.

[C] Fourth Sunday of Lent

Joshua 5:9–12; 2 Corinthians 5:17–21;
Luke 15:1–3, 11–32

1. "The Father threw his arms around his neck and kissed him." The parable of the prodigal son is perhaps the most moving of the parables Jesus tells in the gospels. The experiences and life of the two sons serve solely to reveal the heart of the father. Nowhere else does Jesus portray the Father in heaven more vitally, more plainly. The impressiveness of the story begins already with the fact that the father grants the son's request and hands over to him his portion of the inheritance. For us a portion of God's inheritance is our existence, our freedom, our intellect, our accountability—all of these are the most sublime goods imaginable, goods that only God could give us. That we waste it all and end up in distress, and that the distress brings us to our senses, is not really as significant as the father's vigil, compassion, extravagant greeting, refurbishing of the prodigal, and the feast announced in his honor. Not even for the refractory and envious brother does the father have a harsh word —he is not scolding him when he speaks to him, he merely speaks the full truth: whoever sticks by God possesses everything in common with God. The remarkable thing about Jesus' glorification of the Father is that Jesus himself does not figure in this portrayal of God's reconciliation with sinful men. He is nothing other than the Word that reports the reconciliation— really an always-already-reconciledness. He says nothing about the fact that he is the Word through which God establishes his eternal reconciliation with the world.

2. *"He made him who did not know sin to be sin for us."* Jesus, the Father's Word, glorified the Father all the way to the Cross. In his preaching he wants to reveal nothing except the love of the Father, who "loved the world so much that he gave his only-begotten Son for the world". That, in all his words and especially in his Passion, Jesus was revealing his own love together with the Father's love, is something the believing Church first realized. To be sure, it lay hidden in his claim to be greater than the prophets, in the beatitudes that only he could express, in the example of love that he gave in all that he lavished on men. But only the primitive Church formulated it openly and with emphasis in the words of the second reading: God has "made the one who knew no sin into sin for us, that we might become the very righteousness of God in

him". Not by bypassing the Son, but "through Christ" and "in Christ" does the Father reconcile us to himself. The Church founded by Christ has received from God the task of proclaiming this "Word of reconciliation". The uncomfortable proximity of these phrases will not let us blithely postpone the event into timelessness or the distant past. The reading warns us that we are "a new creation" and have to live accordingly here and now.

3. "The manna ceased." The first reading is not well known. It reports that the Israelites left the wilderness and entered the Promised Land, where after long delay they could once more celebrate the Passover meal and where they could now eat the produce of the land. From that point onward their heavenly nourishment ended. God has put the people back into their ordinary way of life; supernatural graces are no longer necessary, and they are supposed to recognize God's providence in earthly goods every bit as much as they formerly recognized it in heavenly gifts. The Israelites are not supposed to become so used to the Promised Land that they think it belongs to them, for it has been entrusted to them by God and he remains its owner. Daily life is no less filled with God's grace than are extraordinary times.

[C] Fifth Sunday of Lent

Isaiah 43:16–21; Philippians 3:8–14;
John 8:1–11

1. "Nor do I condemn you." Curiously all the texts of today's Mass point toward the future, toward God's salvation, which creates new things and toward which we are hastening. Moreover, this orientation toward the future serves to introduce Passion week (Holy Week). It is precisely here that the new, the final salvation, is accomplished. Our life, in its entirety, will consist in approaching this act of God.

The Gospel shows us sinners who accuse another sinner in Jesus' presence. Bending over to write on the ground, Jesus seems to be absent. He breaks his silence only twice: the first time to gather accusers and accused together into their shared culpability; the second time to give voice to his forgiveness, since no one is left to condemn another. In the light of Jesus' silent suffering for all of us, every accusation has to fall silent, for "God has locked everyone up in the same disobedience", not to punish them (as the accusers wanted), but "that he might have mercy on all" (Rom 11:32). That no one can condemn the woman follows from Jesus' second rather than first statement. He has suffered for all in order to gain heaven's forgiveness for all and for that reason no one can accuse anyone else in God's presence.

2. *"I give no thought to what lies behind me."* In the second reading Paul is completely overwhelmed by God's forgiveness through the course of the suffering and Resurrection of Jesus. Alongside this truth nothing else has any worth—he abandons everything else as "rubbish" in order to attain the fact of Christ's Passion and Resurrection. He knows that this which has taken place remains our true future, the future for which we live—straightforwardly, without glancing to the right or to the left, with our "eyes fixed on the goal". Because the goal is in the present (mankind has already been "grasped" by Christ) he races toward it without fooling himself into thinking he has already grasped it—something Paul emphasizes twice. A Christian always looks ahead, not behind: his entire existence takes its meaning from the running. If we are heading toward

Christ, then any backward glance to fret over past sin can only damage us—for past sin is forgiven.

3. "Now then, I am doing something new." Even the Old Testament commanded people to look ahead. "Consider not the things of long ago" (first reading). In Israel it was a deeply embedded custom for the people to think back to the origin of their salvation, to the exodus from Egypt—certainly under the assumption that the memory of those beginnings would strengthen faith in the God who walks with them in the present. But God does not want them to be stuck on a rearward view, especially not now, since reflecting on the past would now be reflecting on a time of exile. He promises something new, indeed, something that is now "springing forth", whose arrival can be "perceived". In similar fashion, the Holy Spirit bestowed on believers in the New Covenant will be a "down payment" toward eternal life. Thus God opens for Israel a way toward redemption that passes through the wilderness of history; for us who are redeemed, he opens a path to eternal blessedness.

[C] Palm Sunday

(First and second readings as in Year A, p. 62);
Passion from Luke 22:14–23:56

WE FOCUS HERE on three main emphases that characterize the Passion according to Saint Luke.

1. The legacy. In the other Synoptic Gospels the institution of the Eucharist also foreshadows the Passion. In Luke it is accompanied by a detailed explanation from Jesus that has the effect of a last will and testament. Thus the disciples are entrusted with a task—to look out for the coming of the Kingdom of God. "I assign to you the kingdom." Yet this concern can be taken up only according to the mind of Jesus, which sets itself off from any sort of exercise of power in the world: the greatest among them "will become like a servant", and Jesus himself is "in your midst as the one who serves you" (although he won't call himself what he is: this Greatest One). In terms of office, Peter will be the greatest, but he can only be the servant who "strengthens his brothers" if Jesus has prayed for him, the one who denies him. Jesus expresses the true content of his service with words from Isaiah: he must be "counted among the criminals" and his enemies would now have "the power of darkness" over him. Surrounded by strength and confidence his Passion would not have been perfect suffering; hence Luke's graphic description of Jesus' anguish on the Mount of Olives.

2. *Participation.* Jesus suffers alone. The disciples, represented by Peter, do not accompany him. The Jews, Pilate, and Herod too, play the same roles as in the other accounts. But only in Luke does an angel appear at the Mount of Olives to strengthen Jesus. This can only be a strengthening to permit him to persevere in a situation of extreme weakness, to bear the unbearable—to have to drink the cup of God's wrath against sin. On his way to the Cross women mourners accompany him, but he dismisses them with a reference to the inescapably approaching destiny of Jerusalem, who was "unwilling" (Lk 13:34) and therefore has been abandoned to her fate. The man from Cyrene constitutes an exception: here we have at least an external sharing of the burden of the Cross, but by means of normal human strength, in sharp contrast to the victim, who has been flogged nearly to death. Then there is one more person who turns toward Jesus—one of the criminals crucified with him

addresses a genuine request to him. This man knows something about participation, for he "shares the same condemnation" yet clearly distinguishes between his well-earned suffering and the completely different suffering of the One "who has done nothing wrong". In this situation some of the grace of the pain of crucifixion can overflow into a broad vessel. And it continues to flow after Jesus' death: the centurion is affected by that grace, and the account even says that "All who were assembled for that spectacle returned, beating their breasts."

3. Words of salvation. Whereas Matthew and Mark report only Jesus' cry of abandonment, Luke's account of Jesus' words from the Cross carry a different tone. It is as if we hear, translated into spoken words, what the Word of God essentially accomplishes and intends by his suffering. First he requests of his Father: "Forgive them, for they know not what they do." The Jews are blinded, they fail to recognize their Messiah. The Gentiles do professionally what they have done a thousand times over: crucify a supposed criminal in accord with military orders. In fact no one knows who Jesus is. His request aims at excusing those who are culpable, and it finds a reason to excuse. His words to the thief are part of the grace of forgiveness earned on the Cross. His dying words, "into your hands, Father, I commend my spirit" replace the cry of abandonment found in the other gospels. Even if the Son no longer senses the Father, even if the Father's hands have become imperceptible, he has no other place to place himself. In Jesus' words Luke allows something of the grace so painfully won for us to radiate from the Cross.

[C] Holy Thursday

(See Year A, p. 64.)

[C] Good Friday

(See Year A, p. 66.)

[C] Easter Vigil

(First and second readings as in Year A, p. 69);
Gospel: Luke 24:1–12

1. "Then they remembered." Bringing their spices, the women make their way to the tomb early in the morning, find the stone rolled away, and enter the tomb, but fail to find the corpse they are looking for. They are "at a loss", for what they have encountered makes no human nor supernatural sense. It is much the same with Peter who, having heard the women's story, decides he has to visit the tomb. This shows how inconceivable Jesus' talk of rising again on the third day remained even for the most willing among his listeners. Nowhere in human experience, not in any religion, can one find a preunderstanding of such an Event that inserts itself into the middle of normal history (in which the dead remain dead). Thus it is that the women need a supernatural reminder of Jesus' prediction (made "while he was still in Galilee") that he "would be handed over to sinners and would rise again on the third day". For the women it is as if they hear these words for the first time. What was once incomprehensible now dawns on them in the light of the empty grave and the explicit reminder. What was formerly beyond their knowledge has been transformed by the angels into a pre-understanding that can help them understand the present events.

2. "Nothing but foolish chatter." We do not know exactly what the women said to the disciples, nor do we know whether the disciples had remembered the words of Jesus about his Resurrection. Even if they did, the memory of it did not go far enough to kindle belief within the disciples. Human experience simply offers no instance in which such an event can be considered even remotely possible. Hallucinations do occur, but they prove the opposite. Spiritualistic experiments with various sorts of material apparitions may take place, but nothing that compares to the later appearances of Jesus. Some may believe in reincarnation, but reincarnation does not assume that the same person, bearing the same wounds and possessing precise memory of his former and present self, appears. Therefore the Resurrection can be nothing but "foolish chatter". To many people it has remained precisely that to this day!

3. "Full of amazement." The closing report, describing Peter's trip to the tomb, differs from the preceding accounts. No angels appear. In Luke's Gospel we also find no mention of the carefully rolled up headcloth that appears in John's report. All Peter sees are the linen wrappings. Why has someone taken them off the corpse? What could anyone want with the corpse alone? Somehow this incomprehensible event has to make sense. Having concluded this, thought stands still like a clock—in "amazement", perhaps even "pensiveness". This stage is attainable by many, if they read the Resurrection accounts in their entirety. The path to faith takes off from this point, if the Lord grants the grace to see and worship him with the eyes of the Spirit.

[C] Easter Sunday

(See Year A, p. 70.)

[C] Second Sunday of Easter

Acts 5:12–16; Revelation 1:9–13, 17–19;
John 20:19–31

1. "So that through this faith you might have life." Already during his earthly life the Lord had called himself "the Resurrection and the Life". He proves the truth of his words in his Gospel. By appearing among his disciples he demonstrates beyond any doubt that he is alive (a ghost would not offer them the greeting of peace with such naturalness or show them his wounds), especially because in the Gospel reading he grants his youthful Church the Easter gift of the power to forgive sins. For it is through this gift that the disciples and their successors can best make Jesus' vitality comprehensible to the world. Countless people whose sins have been forgiven have realized that they have received a share in the vitality of the Resurrection from the dead. Physical touching, of the sort required by the doubter, Thomas, is not necessary, for the spiritual experience of sacramental forgiveness of sins, if received in genuine contrition with deliberate intention, can be more profound than anything the senses can offer. Jesus' "life is the light of men" (Jn 1:4). Not only Baptism, but all the sacraments can be included under the label *photismos* (illumination) that was applied to them by the early Church. In the Church, to give life and to bring light into a darkened existence is one and the same deed.

2. "Once I was dead, but now I live for all eternity." The great opening vision of the apocalypse to John in the second reading confirms this without reservation, for here the eternal Lord appears to the Beloved Disciple as the One who has put death behind him in order to live forever. He has not merely survived death as one would survive an accident, rather, he holds death in his living power: "I am the Living One and I hold the keys to death and the netherworld." Life-threatening death is no longer a threat or limit to Jesus' vitality, rather, it has been incorporated into the range of power of his life: "death is swallowed up" in the victory of life (1 Cor 15:54). The overwhelming vitality with which he appears to the seer is such that John "falls at his feet as though dead", yet is immediately put back on his feet by the life that touches him and is strengthened and equipped for his mission. The powers of death may prove themselves ever so mighty within world history, as the whole Book of Revelation reveals, but they cannot face up to the vitality of the "Lamb that was slain". In the end "death and death's kingdom" will be "thrown into the pool of fire", rendered powerless with finality, and given up to eternal self-destruction.

3. "And all were healed." The first reading, as it reports the life-giving miracles of the primitive Church, especially those of Peter, reveals that Jesus gives the Church a share in the power of his Resurrection and Life. Spiritual as well as bodily reviving takes place: "crowds of men and women" come to faith, the sick that people brought out onto the street were "all healed" when so much as Peter's shadow fell across them. The Apostles do not make a fuss about the miracles they do, and Paul only mentions in passing the ones he performed (2 Cor 12:12). Far more important to him is the spiritual vitality of the Word of God proclaimed by the Church. It is not the Apostle's vitality that is effective, rather, just the opposite: "If I am weak, then I am strong", for then the Lord demonstrates the "power of God" through the Apostle. "For power is made perfect in weakness" (2 Cor 12:9–10, 13:4).

[C] Third Sunday of Easter

Acts 5:27–32, 40–41; Revelation 5:11–14;
John 21:1–19

1. "Lead you where you do not wish to go." The Gospel of the
appearance of the Lord at the Sea of Tiberias ends with the
installation of Peter in his pastoral office. Everything that precedes this is preparatory: unsuccessful fishing, then the miraculous catch, after which Peter swims to the Lord and stands
beside him on the bedrock of eternity, while the rest of the
Church brings her harvest to the two of them, at which point
Peter himself hauls the entire netful ashore. Finally the crucial
question to Peter: "Do you love me more than these?" You, the
Denier, do you love me more than the Beloved Disciple there,
who stood under the Cross? Made conscious of his guilt by
means of the threefold question, Peter answers with a repen-
tant first Yes (since he can by no means say No), undoubtedly
gaining the strength to do so from John (in the communion of
the saints). Without this confession of greater love, the Good
Shepherd, who gives his life for his sheep, could not entrust
his flock to Peter's pasturing. For the office Jesus has received
from the Father is identical with his own loving sacrifice of
his life for his sheep. Ever since Jesus bestowed this office on
Peter, this unity of love and office has been unconditionally
required. This unity is then sealed by the prediction of Peter's
crucifixion, the gift of completed discipleship. The cross will be
bound up with the papacy from this point onward, even when
it is given to unworthy popes. The more seriously a pope takes
his office, the heavier the weight of the cross on his shoulders
becomes.

2. "To suffer mistreatment for Jesus' name." In the first reading
the Church on earth gives an example of what we have just

stated. All of Peter's timidity stemming from his denial has vanished. With the other Apostles he boldly fires back at the High Council (Sanhedrin) the following words: "Better for us to obey God than men!" The Apostles are unimpressed by the command forbidding them to preach in the name of Jesus—it neither frightens them nor depresses them, and they seek no diplomatic compromise. Instead "they rejoiced that they had been judged worthy to suffer mistreatment for Jesus' name." In places where the Church is persecuted, if her members stand firm, a very special kind of spiritual joy is found, a joy unknown in other parts of the Church that live in peace. Experience proves this.

3. "Worthy is the Lamb that was slain." In her worship of the divine Lamb the Church in heaven also participates in the unity of office and love, of mission and mistreatment, of vitality and slaughteredness that he models and the Church on earth imitates. For John (second reading), this is simply glory as a unity of Cross and Resurrection. "All creatures in heaven, on earth, under the earth, and in the sea" bow down before this inseparable unity, portrayed by the living Lamb that was slain. For in this unity the entire mystery of divine love is ultimately manifested.

[C] Fourth Sunday of Easter

Acts 13:14, 43–52; Revelation 7:9, 14–17;
John 10:27–30

1. "I give them eternal life." The Gospel for Good Shepherd Sunday contains an extravagant promise, indeed, one might say, a promise that throws caution to the wind. The sheep belonging to Jesus, who are known by him and who follow him, are promised three times that they belong to him and to the Father with finality. And they are promised this on the basis of the "eternal life" they have received in advance. What Jesus grants us here below, through his life, his suffering, his Resurrection, his Church, and his sacraments, is already eternal life. Whoever accepts it, whoever refuses to reject it, can never again "perish". "No one can snatch" such a one "out of my hand"; more than that, no one can snatch him out of the hand of God the Father, who, Jesus says, is greater than he is (since the Father is his origin), yet he, the Son, is one with this greater Father. The sheep, who are sheltered within this unity between Father and Son, possess eternal life. No earthly power, not even death, can find any fault with them. However heaven is not promised here to everyone willy-nilly, rather, it is promised to those who "hear my voice" and "follow" the Shepherd—an infinitesimally small precondition for an infinitely and incomprehensibly immense consequence. One cannot help but recall the words of Saint Paul here: "For this momentary light affliction is producing" for us an overwhelming measure of abundant results, "an eternal weight of glory beyond all comparison" (2 Cor 4:17).

2. *"Who were destined for everlasting life."* It becomes apparent in the first reading that one is not automatically saved. One has to accept the word of Christ and the Church. The Jews, to whom Paul and Barnabas were preaching, become jealous because the preaching is so successful. They contradict and slander, which is why the Apostles say to them: "Because you show yourselves to be unworthy of eternal life, we now turn to the Gentiles." And they explain to the Jews that a light will always emanate from Israel "to the ends of the earth", that is, the Apostles' turning toward the Gentiles takes place in the

spirit of the true Israel. Yet this "true Israel" of the Gentiles will not be permitted to clutch salvation for itself alone—salvation is always planned for all mankind. By egotistically clinging to salvation one excludes himself from heaven. Of the Gentiles the reading says: "All who were destined for life everlasting believed in it"—not in the sense of a limited predestination (which does not exist), but in the sense that the Gentiles too are required personally to accept this faith and to live according to it.

3. "The Lamb will shepherd them." Finally, in the second read-ing, we have a glimpse into heaven, where the Lord's promise in the Gospel is fulfilled, and all who followed him as his sheep on earth make up an innumerable flock drawn from all peoples as they stand before the Lamb their Shepherd. Redeemed by the blood of his Cross, they can now be "pastured" by him and "led to springs of life-giving water". The life promised by him is not static, but is continually springing forth, which is why those who belong to the Lord "shall never again know hunger or thirst".

[C] Fifth Sunday of Easter

Acts 14:21–27; Revelation 21:1–5;
John 13:31–33, 34–35

1. "I will be with you only a little while longer." The Gospel already points ahead to the Ascension of the Lord, the time when he will no longer be visibly present to his Church. Yet he gives them instruction about how to live so that, invisible, yet alive and effective, he might remain present among them. His rule is utterly short and unambiguous: "Love one another, as I have loved you." He calls this "a new commandment", because, even though there were so many commandments in the Old Testament, this one could not yet be formulated, because Jesus had not yet established the model for love of neighbor. Now one need only look at him to know and carry out the single, all-sufficient commandment he gives. Of course, it makes an all-encompassing demand on us: since Jesus gives his life for us, his friends, we must place our entire lives at the service of our neighbor, who ought to be our friend. Yet, as the epitome of Christianity, this new and all-sufficient commandment is precisely what assures Christianity's continued existence: "By this all will know that you are my disciples." By this and only by this. No other characteristic of the Church can convince the world of the rightness and necessity of Christ's person and teaching. Radiant love lived by Christians is the proof of all teaching, dogmas, and moral precepts of the Church of Christ.

2. *"Through many trials."* The first reading shows that, oddly enough, it is the new commandment of Jesus that produces so "many trials" for the witnessing Church. Because they largely seek their own intellectual or material advantage, men are not prepared to face this commandment. They are acquainted with something like love, but what they know is generally marked with their selfishness and thus remains limited by barriers and reservations. During the apostolic journey from which Paul is returning he encountered this especially among the Jews, who had closed the door to him in an effort to maintain these boundaries. In contrast he then declares upon his return that "God has opened the door of faith to the Gentiles." Opening the door, renouncing all barriers to love, is described here as an act of divine grace, without which men have no opportunity to go beyond their limitedness. But they really have to step out of themselves through the door opened for them.

3. "He will dwell with them." The second reading shows how the new commandment issued by the Lord takes effect at the point where it actually defines our existence. In the Gospel mutual love is the legacy of the Lord, who is about to leave yet invisibly remain in the Church in love. In the second reading this "remaining" becomes visible. The holy city, which descends from heaven to earth, is nothing other than the dwelling of God and man together, something that is eternal but is now becoming visible. "Behold, God's dwelling among men." Men can never establish this mutual dwelling by themselves. They can never erect paradise on earth. Just as selfless love itself is God's gift to us, so its ultimate visibility will show that God and man live together in this love, just as divinity and humanity are already one in Christ, something he has proven by *his* love: "as I have loved you".

[C] Sixth Sunday of Easter

Acts 15:1–2, 6, 22–29; Revelation 21:10–14, 22–23;
John 14:23–29

1. "My peace is my gift to you." In the Gospel, which once more points ahead to his departure, Jesus brings home to his young Church a single word: "peace". And this peace is specifically the peace that comes from him, the only genuine and lasting peace. In contrast, the peace the world can give is largely a precarious ceasefire or even a Cold War. In God the disciples have the archetype of true peace: Anyone who keeps Jesus' commandment out of love loves the divine Father. Together with the Son the Father comes to the believer and, within his heart the Holy Spirit explains all the truth Jesus has brought. In his triunity God is the true, indissoluble peace. Joyfully the disciples are supposed to release their beloved Lord into this peace, for there can be no other joy than the triune love, and one ought to grant it to anyone, even if it means letting go of him.

2. *"Therefore we have unanimously decided."* The Church must be a place of peace in a world without peace. Yet she has to overcome internal problems that initially create tensions, problems that can only be solved under the guidance of the Holy Spirit, in prayer to the Spirit, and in obedience to the Spirit. Perhaps the most serious problem is the one described in the first reading, one that posed itself to the Church already in the apostolic period: how will the chosen people, who have a thousand years of revelation from God, live peaceably with the Gentiles who are now joining them and who bring nothing with them from their tradition? To achieve a truly peaceful life together requires that both sides give up something, and the extended conferring among the Apostles unavoidably leads to the requirement that each side give up something. The Gentiles need not follow some important Jewish customs, for example, circumcision. But they have to make several concessions to the Jews in the area of dietary practices and marriage between relatives. The content of these compromises may seem rather strange to us today, but at the time they were acutely relevant, and we need to draw from them a model for how the genuine peace of Christ rather than a mere ceasefire can rule the Church. Neither party is ever completely right or completely wrong. Within Christ's peace people have to listen to each other, consider the reasons for the other side's views, and avoid making one's own views absolute. This may require genuine concessions from us—today as much as ever—for only if both sides manage to give up something can we receive the gift of the peace of Christ.

3. "The names of the twelve tribes . . . the names of the twelve Apostles." In the second reading the form of the ultimate "city of peace", the heavenly Jerusalem, confirms the peace God has provided between the Old Testament of the Jews and the New Testament of the Christians, the closing of the terrible chasm that has split the chosen people since the time of Jesus. While the twelve gates bear the names of the twelve tribes of Israel, the twelve courses of stones bear the "twelve names of the Apostles of the Lamb", and the number of those who surround the throne is twenty-four (Rev 4). This chasm that first opened up because of the coming of Jesus may only ultimately close at the end of time, but it is our responsibility to bridge it as well as we can here within history. Even if a unity of faith is not possible, a unity of love is.

[C] Ascension

Acts 1:1–11; Hebrews 9:24–28, 10:19–23;
Luke 24:46–53

1. "Blessing them, he left." Today Luke tells us, at the end of the Gospel and the beginning of the Acts of the Apostles, about the Ascension of Jesus. In the Gospel it involves a retrospect that is at the same time a commissioning for the future; in the Book of Acts, it involves the elimination of false expectations in order to make room for the coming mission of the Church. In the Gospel the Lord refers to the core of the Holy Scriptures: the Passion and Resurrection of the Messiah, which is to be proclaimed to all nations from this point onward. The disciples were and remain witnesses to this quintessence

[For this feast, von Balthasar offers reflections on an additional reading which is an option given in the German Lectionary—Ed.]

of all revelation, and the unique grace they received ("Blessed are the eyes that see what you see") thereby makes them into the "chosen witnesses". Yet the main witness is God himself —his Holy Spirit—who will grant their human words "power from on high". They must await the Holy Spirit, and their commissioning will thus require a constant obedience to him. Jesus' departure to the Father follows, accompanied by a con-cluding blessing that reveals the entire future of the Church. That blessing remains effective throughout all ages, and we must place all our efforts under it.

2. "My witnesses to the ends of the earth." The first reading, the opening of the Acts of the Apostles, wipes away the cramped expectations of the disciples, who are still looking for the restoration of the kingdom of Israel. It expands the field of mission, beginning with Jerusalem, to include Judea and the heretical land of Samaria, and then extends it to the ends of the earth. The reconciliation that God has brought about in Christ affects the entire world. All nations have to experience it. The Apostles are not supposed to propagandize for a partic-ular religion, rather, they proclaim a divine event that applies to everyone from the outset and has already affected them even if they do not realize it. Still, they ought to realize it, because they can then place their lives in, and order them according to, this Light that gives meaning. The universality of the truth of Christ requires that its objective truth also be subjectively affirmed by men—affirmed or rejected, for even rejection is a form of knowing.

3. "A new and living path . . . through the veil." The second reading emphasizes the uniqueness and finality of the Christ-event. Were it repeatable, it would have no universal validity. The Old Covenant was characterized by repetition, because the offering of animal blood could accomplish no ultimate atonement before God. Jesus' sacrifice of himself was so once-for-all and sufficient that in him we can collectively pass through the veil that still separates us from God and enter his sanctuary. What seemed to separate us from God, our mortal flesh, has become, in Christ's Ascension, precisely that which penetrated all the way to the Father, washed our "bad conscience" clean, and granted us an "unchanging confession of hope" in God's "faithfulness", which has now proven itself definitively.

[C] Seventh Sunday of Easter

Acts 7:55–60; Revelation 22:12–14, 16–17, 20;
John 17:20–26

1. "They shall see my glory." We await the Pentecost Spirit of God. Today all the readings speak of existing in transition. All of us live in transition all the time, not only at the time of death. "For we who live are constantly being given up to death so that the life of Jesus may be manifested in our mortal bodies" (2 Cor 4:11). In the Gospel Jesus ends his high priestly prayer to the Father with the prospect of entering into the Father's glory, but without leaving behind those who belong to him, rather, with the prospect of taking them with him into this glory. Here we hear him say: "Father, I would. . . ." They are to be permitted to follow him in his transition to God, for Jesus has brought them the declaration of the love of God and they have accepted it. Thus already on earth they have been introduced into the triune love of God, and Jesus' wish that they follow him corresponds to the will of the Father, who, after all, sent the Son into the world for this purpose. Behind this one will of Father and Son is the Holy Spirit, who will bring to completion in the believer the work of introduction that Jesus began. Jesus' mission is already fulfilled in this Holy Spirit; now it remains for the Spirit of God, who binds Father and Son together, to finish the work of binding heaven and earth together. Then the world, if it opens itself to the Spirit, will be able to realize that the eternal love of the Father for the Son already includes love for men: "that you have sent me and that you have loved my own as you loved me".

2. *"Lord Jesus, receive my spirit."* The first reading portrays the first Christian martyr, Stephen, in the same transition. He has made his great confession of faith. At its conclusion, already "filled with the Holy Spirit", he sees "the glory of God (the Father), and Jesus standing at God's right hand". As with Jesus, his passage to the Father is a witness of blood; he imitates Jesus even to the point of appropriating his words from the Cross: "Receive my spirit", "Do not hold this sin against them." In this way his death becomes not only a witness (martyrdom), but a representation. This can happen only as part of following a Jesus who has already breathed his Spirit upon the Church.

3. *"The Spirit and the Bride say: 'Come!'"* Finally, in the second reading, we see the entire Church in transition. She is all the more in transition because the Lord has promised he will soon return and has accentuated her longing for the Tree of Life and the glory of the Eternal City. It is this yearning that permits the Church and the Holy Spirit to call out "Come!", inviting all people to add their voices to the call. We await the approaching feast of Pentecost, but our waiting is already in the Holy Spirit. We beg for him, with his refining light and fire, so that together with him we might all the more longingly call for the Bridegroom to come. The Spirit calls out in us better

than we ourselves can, and heaven understands this call of the Spirit from the earth, "for he intercedes for the saints, according to God's will" (Rom 8:27).

[C] Pentecost

Acts 2:1–11; Romans 8:8–17;
John 14:15–16, 23–26

1. "All were filled with the Holy Spirit." The Holy Spirit is the most mysterious Person in God, which is why he can appear in so many forms: as a stormy wind and fire (in the first reading's portrayal of the Pentecost events), but also very quietly and inwardly, as described in the second reading—where it is a matter of letting oneself be led by his inner voice and stirrings. No matter how the Spirit communicates himself to us, he is always the one who expounds Christ, the one Christ sends us so that we can understand him, his word, his life and sufferings in their true depth.

The arrival of the Spirit as a stormy wind reveals his freedom: "The Spirit blows where he will; you hear the sound he makes, but you do not know whence he comes or whither he goes" (Jn 3:8). If, in addition, he arrives with tongues of fire that rest on everyone, he does so in order to set the tongues of his witnesses on fire spiritually as they immediately begin to speak and in turn ignite the hearts of their listeners. With the Spirit, outer phenomena always have an inner meaning: his windstorm blows the crowd of listeners together and his fire makes it possible for each to hear the message in a language that he knows intimately. This means that the message each

[For this feast, von Balthasar offers reflections on additional readings which are options given in the German Lectionary—ED.]

encounters is not an alien message that he must first study and translate. It is a message that goes directly to the heart.

2. *"All who are led by the Spirit of God."* With that we have arrived at the second reading, which reveals the Spirit active in heart and conscience. Something remains here of the wind-storm, which we are to permit to "drive us" if we want to be sons of God, indeed, "driven" free sons rather than slaves who are motivated by an external, alien command. Paul calls this "spirit of slavery" the "flesh", by which he means think-ing, concentrating on, and longing for earthly, passing, often demeaning goods that charm us powerfully. If, however, we follow the Spirit of God in us, we learn that being charmed by earthly things need not be determinative, that we "don't owe the flesh anything", rather, as spiritual men we can dominate our urges. We do not do this out of arrogant contempt for the body, rather, because like the Son of God who became flesh, we can be sons of God. That is the decisive difference about the divine Spirit—he does not turn us into haughty spiritual men, rather, he makes the Son's call, "Abba, Father!" resound within us.

3. *"He will teach you everything."* The Gospel proclaims this paradox: the Spirit is sent to us in order to lead us into the whole truth of Christ that the Father reveals to us. He is the Spirit of the love between Father and Son, and he introduces us into this love. By communicating himself to us, he com-municates to us the triune love, and the Son, as the One who reveals the Father, is our entry into this love. Thus the Spirit deepens our recollecting insight into everything of God that Jesus shared with us through his life and teaching.

[C] Trinity Sunday

Proverbs 8:22–31; Romans 5:1–5;
John 16:12–15

1. "He will guide you to all truth." In the Gospel Jesus promises
the disciples the Holy Spirit, who will lead them into the entire truth. This entirety is the inner mystery of God, his being, which he alone knows. For just as a man's inner self is
known only to his spirit, so it is even more that God's innermost mystery is hidden from all except where he himself
permits it to be expressed and participated in (1 Cor 2:10–16).
This self-revelation of God is, in turn, the "entire truth", for
behind, or rather above, the truth of God there can never be
any other truth, and all the truth found in the created world
is only a shadow and reflection of his truth. The inner truth
of God is this: as Source and Father, he continually and absolutely communicates his "Word" or "expression" or "image",
which is "begotten" in this very act of total self-giving, an act
of the most original love that can only be answered by equally
absolute reciprocal love. Yet the more unconditional love is,
the more fruitful it is: a mere I–Thou that was eternal would
exhaust itself unless the encounter also brought forth fruit that,
like the child produced by the encounter of his parents, is gen-
erated by the eternal encounter of the Father and Son. Finite
beings, even when they love each other and conceive and give
birth in love, remain beings that are next to one another. The
infinite Being that is God, however, can be only one, and in
him the lovers can only be integrated in one another. If the Son
becomes man, he can reveal nothing else to us than the Father's
love and his love for the Father, and both of these for us. Yet
we can understand and participate inwardly in this mystery if
the Spirit, who is both the mutuality and fruit of this love, is

made to penetrate us. The Spirit can say nothing else, nothing new; yet his guidance is as boundless as divine love itself. If the revelation of the Son has "expounded" (Jn 1:18) divine love to "the end" (Jn 13:1), and if this end is reached at the point of death and Resurrection, then the exposition of the Spirit will be just as limitless as that which the Son expounded.

2. *"The love of God is poured out in our hearts through the Holy Spirit."* The second reading underscores this truth once again. Through his suffering and death Jesus has made effective the love of God toward us and for us. This love can be nothing other than his own triune love. For God does not love us in a manner different from the way he loves in himself. In the midst of tribulation and patient suffering, we are confirmed in the hope that we who have received "access" to this love have received a share in his love. In other words, we have confirmation that suffering in this world does not lead us away from God but toward God, a confirmation that grows into certainty through the Spirit of the love of God that is poured out in our hearts. Suffering makes us more fluid in the flowing Spirit, makes us flow into the eternally circulating stream of divine love.

3. *"I was with him as a beloved child."* The foregoing applies to Christians. But the triune mystery of God was impressed upon his entire creation from the beginning, as the first reading shows. This Wisdom of God, here described as his child, was prior to the primal seas, and is also depicted as helping at the conception of the creation. In the Old Covenant this Wisdom can refer both to the Son and to the Spirit, something divine and yet distinct from the fatherly Creator; hence all creatures carry a trace of this eternal self-giving and fruitfulness. Christ and the Holy Spirit whom he sends are not merely the reve-

lation of a totally new, alien mystery, but are indeed the revelation to the creature of his own ultimate meaning and being.

[C] Corpus Christi

Genesis 14:18–20; 1 Corinthians 11:23–26;
Luke 9:11–17

*1. "Jesus raised his eyes to heaven, blessed the loaves, and broke
them."* The mystery of today's feast has three aspects, as is
the case with all the great feasts after Pentecost and Trinity
Sunday. First, the Gospel portrays it through the image of the
multiplication of the loaves. This is no bit of magic on Jesus'
part—to accomplish it he looks toward heaven, toward his Father, with both petition and thanksgiving (*eucharistia*): "Father,
I thank you for hearing me" (Jn 11:41). His lavish giving away
of himself in the loaves will be a sign of the way the Father's
love utterly lavishes his Son on the world. Then he blesses the
bread, for the Father has left everything to the Son, including
the bestowal of heaven's blessing. He breaks it, which points
both to his own brokenness in the Passion and to the way his
gifts will be limitlessly multiplied by the work of the Holy
Spirit in every Eucharistic Celebration. Thus through this visible image we realize that triune Love itself becomes present
in the eucharistic self-giving of Jesus.

2. "This is my Body for you." The inexhaustible fullness of the
divine sacrifice of love lies hidden in the terse words of institution, which are quoted in the second reading. It is as if, after
a stone has been lifted away, a never-ending stream flows from
a spring. Paul merely reports what he has heard from the first
disciples, without daring to add a single word. Setting them

within the context of Jesus' action in the "night in which he was handed over" is essential, for ultimately it is the Father who hands him over to the Cross for mankind and into the Eucharist, likewise, for us. Jesus expresses his gratitude for this: his gratitude that the Father is doing this, that he himself is permitted to do it with him, that the Spirit will accomplish it unceasingly. He not only distributes the broken bread, that is, himself, but he bestows it on those who receive it as the supreme fulfillment of the gift, and also the command and the power to continue to do it themselves. They do this not in place of his gift of himself, rather they do it "in his remembrance", so that his Gift never becomes something in the past, a mere object of thought. Instead, it is something always newly present for which one looks up to the Father and thanks him, and in the name of the Son, by the power of the Holy Spirit breaks the Bread and enjoys it. The breaking of the eucharistic Bread is inseparable from the crushing of the life of Jesus on the Cross, and thus every Eucharistic Celebration is a "proclamation of the death of the Lord" for us. Paul does not need to mention the Resurrection, for it goes without saying that it is implied in the fact that the death of Jesus in the past can only become present now if this dying was already an act of a life of supreme love.

3. "Melchizedek brought out bread and wine." The demeanor of the king of Salem in the first reading remains a most significant archetype for Jews and Christians. Long before the system of plant and animal sacrifices was established in Israel we find this simple presentation of bread and wine by a king of Salem, the place which had not yet become Jerusalem. Melchizedek is a mysterious priest-king who (according to the Epistle to the Hebrews), points ahead, past the entire levitical priesthood, to the priesthood of Jesus. The earliest (alpha) often points more clearly to the last (omega) than to the stages in between, of which one need not be aware.

[C] Sacred Heart of Jesus

Ezekiel 34:11–16; Romans 5:5–11;
Luke 15:3–7

1. "He follows the lost one until he finds it." Although we find express mention of the heart in none of the readings for this feast of the Sacred Heart of Jesus, they do speak explicitly of the special form of love that we associate with the heart. The Gospel reveals this in all its paradoxical nature. A shepherd, after all, concerns himself with his entire flock in equal measure; how then can one imagine him leaving behind ninety-nine in the wasteland in order to concern himself with only one of them? There is no sign of any sort of calculating or deliberating over the risk of leaving most of the flock unshepherded— the shepherd has eyes only for the danger that threatens one sheep; it alone seems to matter. No weighing of the odds takes place. God will not let himself be indifferent to the straying of one or two people in order to save the majority of mankind. A human heart that has here become a vessel for divine love simply does not think in those terms. The one beloved and ir-replaceable sheep is important to him. Believers who celebrate the feast of the Sacred Heart seldom sense how much God loves each individual. He loves each individual so much that many a saint has expressed the idea that Christ would have died on the Cross even if only in order to save him, this one single person. The thought seems perverse to us, but it takes its justification from the parable Jesus tells here. And the joy at finding this single sheep is no different from the concern that makes him search it out. Yet one can say with certainty that the Good Shepherd loves each and every sheep among the ninety-nine in the same way, for they are, after all, all sinners for whom Jesus dies on the Cross. And he dies for them not as an anonymous mass, but as unique persons.

2. *"While we were still godless men, Christ died for us."* The second reading underscores what we have just said. In the parable, what was lost is truly the one who runs from God, who is a stranger and an enemy to him. The love of the Good Shepherd is not based on any reciprocity, but is love that seeks to generate mutuality out of its own perfect self-giving. Carried back on the Shepherd's shoulders, the sheep who has been saved begins to consider how valuable he is to the Shepherd and how much he owes to him. Yet Jesus does not tell this parable in order to generate reciprocal love. His love "lacks a why". And the second reading really says nothing about a love-response owed to him, rather, it speaks only of the certainty of being held safely and securely, of being cuddled, by God's love, of having been brought to "atonement". That this certainty obligates us to reciprocal love, indeed, that it spontaneously calls forth love from us, will be an obvious conclusion to anyone who realizes what has just been expressed.

3. *"The lost I will seek out."* The first, Old Testament, text relocates the love of the heart of Jesus in the heart of God. God wants "to seek out his sheep himself", to bring them home from the "cloudy and dark" places to which they have scattered. This reveals one final point to us: the archetype is not the human heart of Jesus, to which we ascribe this remarkable personal love—as if only the Incarnation gives God's love this remarkable personal quality. Jesus' human heart is simply the more comprehensible expression of the incomprehensible love that the eternal God has always possessed toward his creatures.

[C] Eighth Sunday in Ordinary Time

Sirach 27:4–8; 1 Corinthians 15:54–58;
Luke 6:39–45

1. "The mouth speaks from the heart's abundance." We shall consider today's Gospel from the perspective of this concluding maxim (the passage contains several other proverbs). Normally one finds a correspondence between inner attitudes and
outer expression, between heart and word. God's expression,
his Word become man, is the precise expression of the Speaker:
the Father. Subhuman creatures reveal their being through external forms: if an animal barks we know it is a dog. With men,
who can tell lies, one has to test and observe—in the long run
it is not an individual word but a man's behavior that reveals his
inner attitude. Just as a tree is known by the fruit it bears, so a
man is known by his entire conduct. Jesus gives us two hints in
this regard. First, a man who is to judge someone else should
have spiritual vision, not be spiritually blind or blindly assume
the worst or best about people. Second, he should first test
the relationship between his own heart and mouth before he
undertakes to correct someone else's problems. He should first
measure himself against Jesus Christ, who is the utter truth of
his Father. If he has really appropriated the measure of Christ,
he will have drawn near to the right way of being truthful.
Jesus' guidelines for judging men move between practical, human discernment and his own divine-human understanding of
truth.

2. "The defects of a man appear when he speaks." The Old Testament text (first reading) establishes the same relationship between a man's attitude and its expression. (The text has to do
not with testing of a man but with the criteria by which testing

proceeds.) Jesus' wish that the heart be judged according to the mouth (the tree by its fruit), is anticipated here by the sage. We are warned here not to praise a man until his words can be known to be the expression of his heart. Since men can lie and distort themselves, each person must be observed to see if his heart and words correspond.

3. "Ever more fully engaged in the work of the Lord." To fit the second reading into this context, we need to note Paul's exhortation that the Christian carry out his work (which can include testing and judging men and earthly situations) "ever more zealously" in the same manner as the Lord judges the things of this world. He judges in the light of eternal truth, where the perishable attains its imperishable final form. If he says to us that men "will have to give account at the day of judgment for every careless word" (Mt 12:36), then not only Jesus but also his disciples can distinguish fruitful and unfruitful speech already on earth. "This toil is not in vain when it is done in the Lord." Of course there is speech that only has to do with temporal situations, but even it should be expressed in light of an ultimate accountability.

[C] Ninth Sunday in Ordinary Time

1 Kings 8:41–43; Galatians 1:1–2, 6–10;
Luke 7:1–10

1. "I am not worthy to have you enter my house." In the Gospel, the manner in which the Gentile centurion transmits his request for healing for his servant to Jesus is touching. He feels unworthy to appear before him and thus sends Jewish acquaintances in advance, so that they can recommend him to Jesus.

As Jesus approaches, the centurion does not leave the house but once more sends friends who are supposed to tell Jesus how much the centurion trusts him: just as his soldiers obey him, so, he is convinced, the power of sickness must obey Jesus. Expressed from a distance twice removed, this trust "astonishes" Jesus, for it is different from the behavior of the Jews (who either ask for signs from him or often abuse the miracles he grants by letting them feed their lust for sensationalist gossip). True belief is not limited to Israel, indeed, it can be found in a purer form outside the chosen people—as was the case with the Canaanite woman. Even ancient Israel was aware of wise and holy Gentiles who became models for it (Ezek 14:14; 28:3).

2. "Do all that the foreigner asks of you." In Solomon's temple prayer this universal tone can already be heard (first reading). He expands his prayer for the people to include the foreigners who, after long journeys, will pray in this temple—may God hear them "so that all people of the earth may know your name and fear you". Even though this theme does not appear commonly in the Old Covenant, in the Church of Christ it is not merely permitted, but expressly prescribed. For the Church is to offer "supplications, prayers, petitions, and thanksgivings" "for all men", including Gentile kings, "and for all in authority" (1 Tim 2:2). God's saving will is universal, openly known since the Incarnation of his Word, which has power "over all flesh" (Jn 17:2).

3. "There is no other Gospel." This explains Paul's anger in the second reading over the fact that the Galatians have "so quickly" abandoned the Gospel of "the grace of Jesus Christ", intended for all men, to return to a particular religion in which one carries out "weak and destitute" practices (Gal 4:9) that can never justify a person before God even if one, quite logically, were to keep "the entire law", with all its prescriptions. For in that case the "scandal of the Cross would have been abolished from the world" (Gal 5:11). This stumbling block has revealed God's love to all men and obligates us to no other command than the command of love. If this love is genuine its byproduct is the fulfillment of "the entire law" (Gal 5:14). The commandment of love is the only universal commandment, because it is nothing but a response to the Cross-event of God. As "love of neighbor" it is thus the universal means of salvation by which the peace of God is brought into a quarrelsome world.

[C] Tenth Sunday in Ordinary Time

1 Kings 17:17–24; Galatians 1:11–19;
Luke 7:11–17

1. "Let life return to this child." The raising of the dead found in the first reading differs from the one carried out by Jesus for the young man in Naim. The widow bitterly accuses the prophet of having come to her to remind her of her sins, which she assumes have caused her son's death. Elijah pleads with God (ultimately to beg him to restore the woman's faith), stretches himself over the child's body three times, and gives the boy who was brought back to life back to his mother. As a result, she confesses her faith.

2. "The Lord had pity on the woman." In the Gospel the raising of the dead man is motivated entirely by Jesus' compassion. No one challenges him to do it, as is the case in similar miracles elsewhere in the Gospels. To complete the miracle he employs no particular pleading with God or method of resuscitation (such as Elijah's threefold stretching out over the child). Instead, we have only the majestic gesture by which he stops the procession of mourners and commands the dead man to rise. Jesus shows here (as with the dead daughter of Jairus and at the grave of Lazarus) that he himself is the ruler over life and death. Thus, raising the dead is no more difficult than healing the sick, and in the same breath he can command his disciples, as he sends them out, "Heal the sick, raise the dead" (Mt 10:8). For him, both of these acts are simply signs of the decisive matter: the awakening and liberating of men from the spiritual death caused by sin. This is clear from the episode found in Mark 2:1–12, where the paralyzed man has his sins forgiven before his paralysis is cured: "Which is easier, to say to the paralytic, 'Your sins are forgiven' or to say, 'Rise, pick up your mat, and walk'?" Because Jesus possesses, through his efforts on the Cross, the authority to forgive sins, he also possesses the "lesser" authority to heal the physically sick and to raise men from physical death.

3. *"But when God revealed his Son to me."* Through the conversion of Paul the second reading confirms the exalted Lord's unsurpassed power to undertake a spiritual raising of the dead, whose effects seem more powerful than any physical awakening to physical life. The sovereignty of the glorified Lord toward Paul is far more sublime than the his physical gesture at the young man's bier. In Paul's conversion we have an entire existence being transformed into its spiritual opposite. His life was devoted with every ounce of zeal to the cause of "the tradition of the Fathers", which is why he persecuted the novel proclamation of the following of Jesus. Suddenly his life is dispossessed of this entire cultural tradition so that he can proclaim the gospel, something he has learned not by means of a tradition but "by the revelation of Jesus Christ". Yet this very dispossession in the course of serving something alien is precisely

what "God has set me apart for before I was born", that is, it is something that impressed Paul's person more deeply than any traditions he learned after his birth. This violent alienation that takes place outside Damascus is really a return to a prior calling. This is also shown by the fact that, for Jesus, physical death can be called a mere episode (twice he calls it "sleep"; Mt 9:24; Jn 11:11). He himself is undivided "life", rather than a synthesis of life and death.

[C] Eleventh Sunday in Ordinary Time

2 Samuel 12:7–10, 13; Galatians 2:16, 19–21;
Luke 7:36–8:3

1. "I have sinned against the Lord." David's sin, reported in the first reading, is great: through lust for a woman he has become a murderer. His sin is all the greater because God had so richly endowed him. He had been anointed king over Israel, his enemy had become subject to him, and he had taken his enemy's wives into his arms. Yet these were not enough for him. He lusted for another, who was married to the Hittite Uriah. A sentence is passed: the sword will not depart from his house and Bathsheba's child must die. Only now does the king break down and confess his sin, and after his confession he is forgiven.

2. The forgiveness described in the *Gospel* is quite different. The sinner, who disturbs the Pharisee's dinner party, is forgiven many sins because she has loved much. What a mysterious statement! Certainly "much love" does not refer to her sexual sins. Yet, even if she was a perverse and sinful lover, she was and is in some sense a lover, rather than a person preoccupied with her own righteousness. God's forgiving grace connects with her impure love, moving her to testify exuberantly of her contrition. "Tax collectors and prostitutes are entering the Kingdom of God ahead of you" (Mt 21:31). It is not that the prostitute's love moved God's mercy to excuse her so that she could then give evidence of a great and pure love for the Lord. Yet the interplay between constantly prevenient grace and the onset of genuine love in the woman is a totality that we dare not try to unravel. Certainly God's love can take hold on the very limited love of a self-righteous person only inadequately and with great difficulty. The parable about the five hundred and the fifty denarii owed [to the moneylender] that Jesus tells to the host is and remains a paradox: for the Pharisee really remains more in God's debt than the sinful woman. The parable is told from the Pharisee's spiritual horizon.

Yet a link to the story of David can perhaps be constructed, for, in his case, his great sin arises not out of an evil and obstinate heart but from love that has gone sinfully astray. That is why he breaks down under the accusation and confesses his guilt. The difference is that, in the Old Covenant, he has to pay the penalty for his sin, whereas in the New Covenant the sin-forgiving Lord takes the penalty for our guilt upon himself.

3. "A man is not justified by works of the law." The teaching of Paul in the second reading can be seen as an explanation of the Gospel reading. He is a Pharisee and sinner who was forgiven. Yet Jesus confronted him with his sin ("Why do you persecute me?") and grace transforms his perverse zeal into genuine zeal. Thus "through the law" he has "died to the law", by persisting in the path of the law (which brings sins to the fore [Rom 7]) he reached the end of that path. This occurs not out of his own insight but by the grace of the one who revealed himself as the Crucified One—crucified *through* the law but *for* me. In love for Christ Paul is crucified with him, as Paul puts it—which is the only reason for his conversion to pure surrender. Now it is no longer my "I" and the law I must keep that face each other, rather, the Christ who loves me and gives himself for me faces my faith (that is, my self-surrender) in him. Or, put in better language: confrontation has been overcome because the Lord who carries me and my sins holds me in himself, so that I live in him rather than in myself. Better yet: "Christ lives in me."

[C] Twelfth Sunday in Ordinary Time

Zechariah 12:10–11, 13:1; Galatians 3:26–29;
Luke 9:18–24

1. "The Son of Man must first endure many sufferings." The scene found in the Gospel reading forms a climax of the Synoptic Gospels. It constitutes the watershed in Jesus' life. To this point, in accord with the mission given him by the Father, he has acted messianically and has aroused a sense of who he is, especially in his disciples. Because the shift that takes place in this scene is so important, Luke places it in the context of a prayer of Jesus in solitude. By asking his disciples about his identity, he takes the opportunity to reveal the core of his mission. Yet the people's perception of who he is is so imperfect that he cannot use it as a point of departure. Peter's statement, "you are the Messiah of God" hits the target, yet Peter's image of the Messiah remains an Old Testament and contemporary one: the Messiah as Israel's liberator. That is why Jesus forbids them to use the title and, more profoundly, that is why he lays out clearly what is the true task of the Messiah: to be rejected, to die, to rise again. So that this will not be received as some sort of incomprehensible, mythological event, he immediately explains its implications for anyone who wishes to be his disciple: "Take up your cross daily" and "follow" the Messiah in this way. The required faith embraces the act it includes: discipleship, but not by scheming to gain something, rather by unconditional loss: "Whoever loses his life for my sake. . . ."

2. *"Mourning as for an only son."* In its proximity to the Cross of Christ the first reading, from Zechariah, will probably always remain mysterious, permitting only partial interpretation. Perhaps the prophet himself does not know the identity of this "only Son" for whom such great mourning arises, mourning like that which the Gentile Syrians brought forth for their dying and reviving God, Haddad-Rimmon, mourning for One whom the mourners themselves have murdered, have "thrust through". Moreover, this mourning is triggered by a "spirit of compassion and prayer" that comes from God, and because of this mourning "a fountain shall flow" in the Holy City "for cleansing from sin and impurity". Could the prophet really have had a notion that all of this would come together: the pierced Son of God, the fountain (that ultimately flows from the Son himself), and the Spirit of prayer who is poured out on the people through the death of the Pierced One? There is no other possibility than to assume that we have here a vague premonition of what the Gospel states clearly: the Messiah has to suffer and die and the Spirit of prayer and purification will make an inner com-passion possible.

3. *"Sons of God in Christ Jesus."* The second reading closes the gap that threatens to open up between the fate of the pierced Messiah and the call to completely ordinary men to follow him. If such men "lose their life for my sake", they enter the very realm of this primal and vicarious Sufferer. They thus become "sons of God" in him—not in the manner of the heathen

mysteries surrounding Haddad-Rimmon, but in the sense revealed by Paul when he shows how the believer "puts on Christ like a garment" in baptism. Paul is not referring to anything external here, like the way a garment remains external to the body. Rather, he means a reality into which man loses himself. Therefore Christians do not each wear their own personal garment, rather, they put on the garment of Christ. The living Christ takes all of them into himself so that they become "one" in him, thereby also inwardly participating in his unique destiny ("daily taking up their cross").

[C] Thirteenth Sunday in Ordinary Time

1 Kings 19:16, 19–21; Galatians 5:1, 13–18;
Luke 9:51–62

1. "Go, but come back." Today's readings have to do with the call to discipleship. We find an already quite radical model from the Old Testament surpassed by Jesus' call. In the first reading the prophet Elijah throws his cloak over Elisha as he is plowing—a sign that he has chosen him as his successor. Elijah grants his request for time to say good-bye to his parents; Elisha demonstrates his determination to follow Elijah by slaughtering two of his twenty-four plow oxen and giving the meat to his servants to eat. "Then he arose, followed Elijah, and entered his service." It is no pure human service, rather, because Elijah himself is a man of God, it is already service to God. This is a marvelous Old Covenant example of obedience to God's call as mediated by the prophet.

2. "Let the dead bury their dead." Nonetheless, Jesus' requirements exceed those of the Old Testament. Three men present him with their wish to follow him. In response to the first Jesus points to his own example and fate: he has no place to call home. Even the house in which he grew up, his mother's house, no longer counts. He does not look back. He is worse off than the animals; he lives in utter insecurity. He owns nothing but his mission. And the destination of his mission is announced at the opening of the Gospel: he is headed for a "lifting up"—whether on the Cross or into heaven Luke does not specify. Typically, in the Samaritan village where he wanted to rest, he was not welcome. But he rejects the idea of calling down fire from heaven upon the village—that "his own people do not accept him" (Jn 1:11) is normal. The second would-be follower first wants to bury his father. Here the Lord of life answers: "Let the dead bury their dead." The dead are the mortals, who bury each other. He is above life and death, he dies and rises again "in order to be Lord of both the dead and the living" (Rom 14:9). The third potential disciple wants to say good-bye to his family. Here Jesus exceeds Elijah. For the person radically called there can be no compromise between family and the decision for the Kingdom. The decision he has to make is an immediate and indivisible one. Relationships with family and other men are governed by the norm provided by that decision.

3. "Called to freedom." The freedom mentioned in the second reading is the freedom "for which Christ freed us", and no other kind of freedom. It is no individualistic freedom, since this freedom consists in service to one's neighbor: "Serve one another in love." It is no libertine freedom, for sensual lusts directly contradict the freedom that the guiding Spirit of Christ grants us. That man has to struggle against himself and his lusts in order to receive true freedom is no denial of his having been given freedom, for Christ himself had to struggle during his "temptations" (Lk 4:1–12). It is impossible to be free to do contradictory things simultaneously, but, in order to be free, one must overcome the contradictions within himself. The freedom of Christ is constantly to do the will of the Father. To follow him in that makes one "truly free" (Jn 8:31–32). The freedom to which Christ calls us is his own. In that freedom we receive a share in God's inner, trinitarian, absolute freedom.

[C] Fourteenth Sunday in Ordinary Time

Isaiah 66:10–14; Galatians 6:14–18;
Luke 10:1–12, 17–20

1. "Like sheep in the midst of wolves." In the Gospel's great commissioning speech Jesus sends his disciples out "like sheep among the wolves". If one permits the image to sink in, it is frightful. Humanly considered such a commission is irresponsible. Jesus dares to do it only because the Father has sent him as the "lamb" among men who act like wolves toward him, so that he can win the victory of the "lamb that was slain", a victory that makes him worthy and able to break all the seals of world history (Rev 5). Fully defenseless, Jesus appears among men. His only weapon is his mission which, as long as it lasted, protected him from his enemies' attacks even if occasionally he could escape them only by taking flight. Jesus completely disarmed those "few workers" sent to announce his message —their primary wish was to be for peace, whether people accepted him or not, and even where he was rejected, his messengers were simply to leave and go elsewhere, rather than try to force him on people. But his messengers were to proclaim the imminence of the Kingdom both to those ready to receive it and to those who resisted, so that the people could take ap-

propriate account of how little time was left. His disciples were
not to rejoice or despair over success or lack of it. Success is
not part of the assignment, for true success remains with the
Lord who hands out assignments, the One who by his Cross
has thrown Satan out of heaven. Only the Lamb of God "has
triumphed", the "lion of the tribe of Judah". The great hymns
of praise in heaven are sung to him (Rev 5:5, 9ff.). Those he
commissions will find in him—not in themselves—the "authority" "to overcome all the power of the enemy". This will
have to suffice to console those he sends out.

2. *"I bear the brand marks of Jesus in my body."* In the second
reading the Apostle Paul speaks in the name of the Church of
Christ. The defenselessness of Jesus and his disciples has now
been transformed into their crucifixion, in which apparent de-
feat has proven to be true victory. The seemingly victorious
world has been crucified, has been rendered dead and harmless, while the Apostle is "crucified to the world", that is, has
made the world in him harmless. Both of these are possible
by the power of the Cross of Christ, the only thing he boasts
of. That he bears the "marks of Christ in his body" is merely
a sign of close discipleship, which alone reveals the true distance between him and the Lord ("was Paul crucified for you?"
[1 Cor 1:13]). Only from the perspective of the Cross of Christ
can he promise everyone "peace and mercy" in the name of
the Church (the "Israel of God"), peace and mercy "based on
this rule of life": that the victory over the world is found only
in Jesus' Cross and its impact on the Church and the world.

3. *"As a mother comforts her son."* In this "rule of life" we find
the entire treasure of the Church, who suckles us as our mother
and from whom, according to the first reading, we should drink
our fill. The Church has no other consolation for her children

than the one she has received from God: that the love of God has finally been made comprehensible to the world in Jesus' Cross, that only from that Cross can "peace like a river" be channeled into the Church and through her into us and into the world.

[C] Fifteenth Sunday in Ordinary Time

Deuteronomy 30:10–14; Colossians 1:15–20;
Luke 10:25–37

1. "Go and do the same." The Gospel parable of the compassionate Samaritan would seem to be a story in which Jesus does not appear. And yet it bears his mark, for no one except Jesus could tell it in such a way, namely, that those who should have been compassionate (the priest and the Levite) pass by, while the foreigner takes pity on the "half-dead" victim, ministers to him, cares for him, and concerns himself with him even after departing. Only Jesus tells it this way, but he does so not out of a humanitarian concern, rather, because he himself has done everything that the foreigner did and he has done it lavishly for everyone. "Samaritan" is a pseudonym for Jesus and thus, when he tells the lawyer to "go and do the same", he is inviting him to become his disciple. A humanitarian would have done something falling somewhere between the do-nothing response of the first two and the extravagant deeds of the third: he might have called the Samaritan police, reported the incident, and gone on his way. The mark of Christ is found in the extravagance of involvement, which points back to the answer that Jesus gave to the question about eternal life: "Love with your whole heart", not only God, but also your neighbor.

2. "Through him all things are reconciled." Jesus is hidden behind the foreigner in the parable. In the second reading he is the "first-born" in whom all creation "has its existence". If that is so, then there would be no creation at all without this first-born, this archetype. Creation exists only because God "in all his fullness desired to dwell in him in order to reconcile all things through him", in order to dissolve all the dissonances of the world, in order to bring all strident contradictions to an end in his peace—the peace "he established on the Cross through his blood". This includes the social injustice described in the parable, injustice that leaves a person lying half-dead on the roadside while the upper classes of society, the intellectually and physically well-off, pass by unconcerned. This too is atoned for by the Samaritan's bloody work for the world. Here we dare not forget the concluding words: "Go and do the same." Yet Jesus' universal work of reconciliation precedes our work of reconciliation, and preceding his reconciling deed is his election to be the foundation and archetype of all creation. The linkage between these three elements is indissoluble.

3. "The word is very near to you." Precisely this is what the first reading, from the Old Covenant, brings home, by eliminating the apparent distance between God (together with his commandment) and men who are supposed to hear and obey the commandment. Excuses come easily: the commandment in heaven is intangible in our ordinary lives or it is far away, across the sea, that is, only practicable for emigrants or rare ascetics! Not at all—because all things have their existence in Christ, the word is near you, your conscience can perceive it, it is within your capacity to understand, consider, implement. If the Logos is the archetype of all being, then you are his image, you bear his mature impression in yourself. Humanism does not deny that it is possible to have this primal rule and follow its imperative, but it simply does not understand that a man is only an impression in the wax, not the seal itself, and that one has to look at the seal itself in order to know how far the duty of love extends.

[C] Sixteenth Sunday in Ordinary Time

Genesis 18:1–10; Colossians 1:24–28;
Luke 10:38–42

1. "Do not pass by your servant." Hospitality is one of the loftiest principles among simple folk, and Abraham offers generous hospitality to the three pilgrims. We hear the story in the first reading. He prepares a festive meal for them, as if he sensed that a supernatural power was seeking him out through these strangers. Although they are three in number, Abraham addresses them in the singular. God appears to him in a multiplicity that is not comprehensible to him (later, when God proceeds against Sodom, we find two angels involved [Gen 19:1]). Abraham's conduct toward God here provides the prelude to the divine promise that Sarah will bear a son within a year.

2. The Gospel is different: *"One thing only is required."* Rather than Martha's busy hospitality, it is the word of God spoken by Jesus that takes precedence. No service to God can earn this word, for it is given to Mary gratis, because she is open and able to listen to it. It would be nonsense to reverse the obvious import of the story and ascribe greater perfection to Martha (despite the scolding she received) because she understood how to be *"in actione contemplativa"*. Man cannot act rightly if he has not first listened to God's word. One can even see this in the story of Abraham at Mamre, since the story began with obedience to the active and efficacious word of God. Even in the Old Covenant everything begins with "Hear, O Israel". Action must follow upon and obey this listening. No ortho-praxis dare imagine that it can replace orthodoxy or produce orthodoxy out of itself. Mary's *praxis* was shown to be the right one at this last banquet in Bethany, since she anointed Jesus in anticipation of his burial, the Lord defended her deed against all attacks, and thereby established her example as a model for all activity throughout Church history.

3. "Christ in you, your hope of glory." In the Church, too, the word of proclamation must precede *praxis*, as the second read-ing shows. "How shall they believe in what they have not heard? How shall they hear of him if no one preaches to them?" (Rom 10:14). God's greatest deed, sacrificing his Son for us, is the epitome of his Word to us. To perceive this Word as God's deed means that we must also enter into this deed. Thus the Apostle Paul can utter the audacious words: "In my earthly life I fill up what is lacking in the sufferings of Christ." Insofar as Christ the head has suffered for the entire body, this suffering lacks nothing. But insofar as Christ is "head and body", the body must participate in Christ's suffering. The "communion in Christ" into which the Apostle wishes to lead everyone, including the Gentiles, through his preaching, requires more than a distance between the speaker and the listener, it requires deeds done in common.

[C] Seventeenth Sunday in Ordinary Time

Genesis 18:20–32; Colossians 2:12–14;
Luke 11:1–13

1. "Will you sweep away the innocent with the guilty?" Abraham's intercession for the righteous in Sodom, as related in the first reading, is the first great example and the lasting model for intercessory prayer. It is simultaneously insistent yet humble. It constantly dares to go a little farther: from fifty righteous as enough to stave off destruction, to forty-five, forty, thirty, twenty, ten. Even if the petition in the end falls short, since not even ten righteous people could be found in Sodom, such an account can only serve as a unique stimulus to a believer to penetrate into God's heart so far that compassion begins to flow there. Later examples, for instance, when God listens to Moses' intercession, confirm this. If God has entered into a covenant with men, he has no wish to behave like a tyrant toward his covenant partners. Instead, he is willing to let himself be shaped (in human terms, one might say, "be persuaded"), as we see often enough from Old Testament pleas that moderate Yahweh's wrath. God has granted the man who is in covenant with him power over his heart.

2. "Forgive us our sins." In the Gospel, Jesus asks of the Father and knows that he "always hears" him (Jn 11:42). Since he is praying, his disciples ask him to teach them to pray. They receive Christ's own prayer, the Our Father, and, in addition, the parable of the man who wakes up his friend at midnight in order to ask him for three loaves of bread. In the parable the man has to be persistent if he is to receive what he has asked for. Not indiscretion but persistence in pleading, seeking, knocking at the door is necessary if God is to open up the door as a Father to his creatures. Far from being asleep, God is ready to "give his Holy Spirit to those who ask him", but he does not toss his most precious gifts at those who have no desire for them or who request them only half-heartedly. For what God gives is his own, zealous love, and this can be received only by those who genuinely hunger for it. To ask God for something that he in his own essence is unable to give (a "scorpion", a "snake") is absurd, but he will infallibly and immediately grant every petition congruent with his will and his attitude, even though we may not notice it within the passing of time in which we live. "All that you ask in prayer, believe that you will receive it and it shall be yours" (Mk 11:24). "If we ask anything according to his will, he hears us. And if we know that he hears us in regard to whatever we ask, we know that what we have asked him for is ours" (1 Jn 5:14–15).

3. "In company with Christ God has given you life again." The second reading gives the presupposition underlying what otherwise would be a presumptuous hope. The presupposition is that we have been buried with Christ in baptism and have been raised with him at Easter through faith in the power of God. In this way an immediacy has been established in Jesus Christ between God, the Lord of the Covenant, and us, his partners, an immediacy that has removed every obstacle (our sins, proofs of liability, and all accusations pending against us). The Cross of Christ is the means to this immediacy, for it constitutes the "razing of the wall of division", it constitutes the "peace" that has been concluded (Eph 2:14–16). Therefore the children can ask the Father for all they need.

[C] Eighteenth Sunday in Ordinary Time

Ecclesiastes 1:2, 2:21–23; Colossians 3:1–5, 9–11;
Luke 12:13–21

1. "To whom will all this piled-up wealth of yours go?" In the
Gospel Jesus distinguishes between having and being. Being is
a man's life and existence; assets are the larger or smaller as-
semblage of possessions [having] that permit him to continue
living. The simple warning is given here so that man does not
confuse means with purpose, nor equate the meaning of his
being with the size of his accumulated assets. The absurdity of
such an equation leaps out at us if we reflect not only on man's
death, but on the fact that he must account to God for his
life. Even if the Old Testament parallel has not yet come into
focus for us, even though Jesus asks the question: "To whom
will all this that you have assembled belong [if you die]?", this
is not the central question for him. His point is "Do not store
up for yourselves treasures on earth, where moth and decay
destroy, . . . but store up treasures in heaven" (Mt 6:19–20).
We know that in the sight of God it is not the quantity of our
assets but the quality of our being that is in question (cf. 1 Cor
3:11–15). This is apparent especially in the tiny word "self". He
who wishes to have things, collects treasures "for himself"; he
who has a rich being renounces this "self" and thinks about
his being in God. God is the treasure. "Where your treasure is,
there your heart will also be" (Mt 6:21). If God is our treasure,
then we must be dominated by the thought that God's endless
wealth is found in his self-giving and self-emptying, that is, in
the very opposite of the wish to have everything.

2. "All things blow away in the wind." In the first reading Qo-
heleth brings home to us the absurdity of the fact that the

goods one has assembled artfully and industriously can be inherited after one's death by a lazy ne'er-do-well. Thus a contradiction lies at the heart of lasting striving for passing things, a contradiction that is renewed with each new generation. It thereby clearly reveals the vanity of all earthly desire to possess things.

3. The second reading draws the comprehensive conclusion: "*Set your heart on what pertains to higher realms . . . rather than on things of earth.*" But "heavenly things" are not the treasures, merits, and rewards we have piled up in heaven, rather, they are simply "Christ". He is "our life", the truth of our existence, for we owe to him everything that we are, in God and for God —we are this precisely in him "in whom all treasures are hidden" (Col 2:3). "Build yourselves on him", the Apostle counsels us (Col 2:7), even if that means that the essential meaning of our life is thereby hidden from earthly view. All forms of the desire to have, which Paul proceeds to list (vv. 5ff.) and which are merely various degenerative forms of yearning, must now be "put to death" for the sake of being in Christ. This putting to death is in truth a birth: the "becoming of a new person". In the course of this putting to death, all divisions that delimit the being of man ("slave" or "free") fall away, while everything valuable about our specific being (Paul calls this the "charisma" [the giftedness]) contributes to the ultimate fullness of Christ (Eph 4:11–16).

[C] Nineteenth Sunday in Ordinary Time

Wisdom 18:6–9; Hebrews 11:1–2, 8–19;
Luke 12:32–48

ALL OF THE TEXTS for today's celebration require us to live in a
state of departure: departure on the basis of faith, on the basis
of what God has said, on the basis of the accounting soon to
be required of us.

1. "Confident assurance concerning what we hope for." In the second reading a pilgrim existence is simply called "faith". Faith
is based on the Word of God that has been received but which
promises what is unseen and belongs to the future. This is illustrated by Israel's existence, which begins with Abraham's departure and continues through the centuries. This faith might
be tested severely, as when God dares ask Abraham to sacrifice
his son, but also as is evident in the fact that all representatives of the Old Covenant "died without having obtained what
they were promised". In a more drastic way than Christians,
they learned what it means to live here below as "strangers
and guests", seeking a homeland that lies entirely beyond their
present, passing existence. For in Jesus' experience and by receiving the Holy Spirit, Christians have not only glimpsed
their heavenly homeland "from afar" but, as John says, they
have "seen, heard, and touched the Word of eternal life", and,
as Paul says, they have received the Holy Spirit as a down-
payment. Thus they can and must journey toward the fulfillment of the promises with greater certainty and responsibility.

2. "The night of liberation announced beforehand." The first
reading shows that even in the Old Covenant faith did not
entirely lack certainty. There were proclamations of events that

came to pass, as in the night of the Passover or in God's promise to King David or the prophets' statements about the exile and its duration. Every attentive person receives signs of this sort. Through these signs God is showing him that he is on the right path. If he is going to require faith of him, he does not leave him in uncertainty even though he may occasionally put him to a severe test, as was the case with Abraham or many of the prophets. Ultimately, faith dare not depend on signs and wonders, but on the faithfulness of God, who keeps his word inviolably.

3. "To whom much is given, of him much is required." In various ways the Gospel modifies the challenge to Christians to live in a constant state of departing. The more richly God has endowed Christians with gifts, and thereby with assignments, the more God varies the requirement to live "underway". God's assignments are carried out best if his servant never loses sight of the fact that he might be called to account at any moment— in other words, if every temporal moment is lived and shaped directly in and toward the light of eternity. If he forgets this immediacy, he has forgotten the content of his earthly mission and the justice and righteousness (*Gerechtigkeit*) it incorporates (he "begins to beat the housemen and servant girls"). It now becomes clear that this justice-righteousness can only be retained if the believer looks beyond the world to the requirements of eternal justice-righteousness, which is not merely an "idea" but is the living Lord, for whose appearance all of world history waits.

[C] Twentieth Sunday in Ordinary Time

Jeremiah 38:4–6, 8–10; Hebrews 12:1–4;
Luke 12:49–53

1. "Not peace but division." The fire that Jesus has come to cast upon the earth (in the Gospel reading) is the fire of divine love that will ignite men. It will begin to burn from the Cross, which is the baptism he fears. But by no means will all men permit themselves to be set ablaze by the unconditionality of this fire. Because some will resist the very love that could and would lead men to unity, humanity will be divided. More clearly and inexorably than before Christ, humanity will divide itself into two kingdoms or states. Augustine called them the "city of God", where love rules, and the "city of this world", where cupidity rules. Jesus reveals that the division severs even the closest family ties, while Saint Paul depicts this division as splitting apart even the individual human heart, where the flesh fights against the spirit (Gal 5:17) and the "wretched man" "does not do what he wants but does what he (fundamentally) loathes" (Rom 7:15). Yet neither for Jesus nor for Paul is this a fatalistic tragedy. Instead, it is a fight that will be fought all the way to victory. Love and hate are not two co-eternal principles, as the Manichaeans thought, rather, we can "conquer evil through good" (Rom 12:21). It is to that end that God has granted us the power of his grace.

2. "Jeremiah sank into the mud." The struggle is harsh because the "kingdom of this world" is filled with cruelty. From time immemorial war, torture, and all manner of injustice have ruled this world, and, after the appearance of Christ, the "Prince of Peace", it seemed as if they only increased. Christ divides and thereby sharpens the contrasts. What happens to Jeremiah in the first reading is a single parable for the countless abominations that take place in the world, at times in the name of religion. The prophet is exposed to this torture, which was intended to kill him, for the sake of the word of God, which was spoken against Israel's blind insistence on making war. In the Psalms the devout pray repeatedly that God would rescue them from the mud in which they are sinking (Ps 40:3; 69:15). Job compares himself with this mud (10:9; 13:12 etc.). Paul says he has been relegated to the last and lowest place and has been treated as "the scum of all" (1 Cor 4:9, 13).

3. "Heedless of its shame." In the "contest" referred to in the second reading, a contest in which the Christian might be inclined to give up, there is only one thing to do: look steadily at the "One who inspires and perfects faith", the One who "has endured the opposition of sinners", to himself. Long before us, countless others (a "great cloud of witnesses") have done this and have been tested even more severely than we—even to the "point of death". Jesus took upon himself plenty of shame in the sight of the world—his entire path to the Cross was accompanied by nothing but scorn and mockery. He has made his way through this mud to "the right of God's throne". Anyone who looks at this example would be ashamed to lag so far behind him in absorbing shame.

[C] Twenty-first Sunday in Ordinary Time

Isaiah 66:18–21; Hebrews 12:5–7, 11–13;
Luke 13:22–30

1. "Some of these as priests and Levites." The first reading's prophecy, taken from the end of the Book of Isaiah, tells the people of Israel with complete clarity that God will call men to himself from the most distant lands that "have never heard anything of me", and that he will make some of them into his priests and special servants. It is a hard task for Israel to know itself as the chosen people yet to permit itself to be relativized by the knowledge that God will extend the same chosenness to others—at a time known only to him. God will now refer to nations that Israel, for the most part, considered the enemies of God as "your brethren". The sacrifices that they offer in the house of the Lord are not blemished and worthless like the heathen offerings, for they will be offered in "pure vessels". How will Israel behave toward this promise?

2. *"I do not know where you come from."* The Gospel provides an answer, for it addresses primarily those in Israel who will not accept the truth of the promised expansion of the chosen people. Strangers come "from east and west, north and south" to "take their place at the feast in the Kingdom of God" with the patriarchs of Israel. This is so intolerable to those Jesus is addressing that they will "grind their teeth" and will be transformed from "first" to "last", indeed, will no longer be permitted entry. They will learn that they "did evil" when they insisted on their prerogatives, even though they ate and drank with Jesus and he "taught in their streets". The harsh words they hear from Jesus are words of warning and admonition which can have no other source than love. And if, in the end, they are the "last", this lowest place (as confirmed by many prophecies: Ezek 16:63) may be a place of shame but it is not a hopeless place. There is hope for all of Israel (Rom 11:26).

3. *"Whom the Lord loves, he disciplines."* When the second reading speaks of God's discipline, which follows from love, it surely addresses itself primarily to Christians. They should consider

themselves addressed also by the warnings of the Gospel reading. For they too, like the Jews, are capable of insisting on their election and supposed prerogatives, and thereby might find themselves left standing at the door or shown to the last seats. They ought to remember that discipline in life must be understood not simply as punishment but as a necessary instrument of formation, a means to put new tension into their slackened faith and Christian life. Yet Israel after the arrival of Christ also ought to recall the words that were spoken to it already in the Scriptures of the Old Covenant (Prov 3:11–12). If it is true that God's gifts and callings are irrevocable (Rom 11:29), then Israel can only see its long suffering as an event within its calling to be God's chosen people.

[C] Twenty-second Sunday in Ordinary Time

Sirach 3:17–18, 20, 28–29; Hebrews 12:18–19, 22–24;
Luke 14:1, 7–14

1. "In the lowest place." One might say that the Gospel deals with humility. The only problem is that it is hard to define humility as a virtue. One cannot really strive for humility, for then he is trying to be something. One cannot really practice humility, for then he is trying to attain something. No one who has humility can know or establish that fact. One can only express it negatively: a man ought not to seek anything for himself. For if he does not, then he will not place himself in the most prestigious place, where he can be seen, held in respect, and valued highly. Neither will he calculatingly invite to his banquet those who will invite him back. If he takes the lowest place, he does not do this calculatingly, in order to be considered humble. If he is asked to move to a higher seat, his joy is not for himself but because he experiences the host's goodwill. He simply does not assess himself, because he has no interest in the rank he occupies among men. If the Lord tells him that his attitude will "be rewarded in the resurrection of the just", presumably to him this means simply that he will be present with God. For only this concerns him: that God is so infinitely higher in goodness, power, and majesty than he is.

2. *"To the city of the living God."* The second reading assures the humble man that he already belongs "to the city of the living God", which is inhabited by thousands of angels, first-born, righteous ones, above whom tower God, the "judge of all", and "Jesus, the mediator of the new covenant". He rejoices to belong to this city and understands that it is a gift of God to be a member of a society drawn together by God. He does not ask himself whether he is worthy or unworthy to belong, just as a child does not ask himself whether he is worthy to take part in a banquet for adults—he simply takes pleasure in the good things and the gracious guests who treat him kindly. This could serve as a model for us as children of God, for we have also been permitted to participate in something equally beautiful. Of course we do not deserve it—how could we have "earned" it? Yet we participate in such a way that we feel at home in this company and need not be strangers.

3. *"God is glorified by the humble."* The ancient sage in the first reading knew this already. God is honored only by those who make nothing of themselves, for God too makes nothing of himself, since he simply is He who is, the Lord, the Mighty One. He is the One who hands out good gifts, hence a man ought not put on airs of "magnanimity" and patronizing gift-giving. He may have received many goods, other people may consider him important, but he himself knows that he owes

all he has been given to the only Magnanimous One. He is all ears for the wisdom of God, for that is his joy, a joy that makes him forget himself.

[C] Twenty-third Sunday in Ordinary Time

Wisdom 9:13–19; Philemon 9–10, 12–17;
Luke 14:25–33

1. "Whoever does not renounce all his possessions." In today's Gospel, that is what Jesus requires of anyone wishing to be his disciple. In this context, "possessions" includes relationships to other people—Jesus mentions close relatives and one's own family among the things to be renounced. And he uses the harsh word "hate", which applies wherever fellow men disturb or question the disciple's relationship to the Master. Because he is the representative of God the Father on earth, Jesus demands the same undivided love that the old law demanded toward God: "your whole heart, all your strength". Nothing can compete with God, and Jesus is the visibility of the Father. Whoever has renounced everything for God's sake has moved beyond all calculating. A man has to deliberate and calculate as long as he aims for a compromise. If he has that prospect in mind, he will never finish his tower or win his war. Jesus issues this provocative challenge to a great crowd of people who outwardly are his followers, yet is there anyone in this crowd who is willing to take up his Cross? (The Romans crucified thousands of rebellious Jews, everyone knew what Jesus meant by the word *cross*: willingness to suffer a despicable death in utter nakedness.) Jesus gave up everything: his relatives, his mother. He had no place to lay his head. He "considers his life as nothing", he will "carry his own cross" (Jn 19:17). Only he who has abandoned everything can receive it back—in his mission from God—"and persecution besides" (Mk 10:30).

2. *"Your good deed should be freely bestowed."* In the second reading, Paul tries to shape Philemon into this selflessness, which is not only compatible with but coincides with pure love. Paul sends the runaway slave [Onesimus] back to Philemon, but tells him that, although the slave would be useful to him [Paul]; the decision to let him serve him must be Philemon's own (the slave belongs to Philemon). By doing this, Paul both relieves Philemon of his possession and releases him from any calculating (Philemon gains nothing by sending him back to Paul). Indeed, Paul dispossesses Philemon in a yet more profound way: he returns the man to Philemon not as a slave, but as a beloved brother, for that is what the man has become to Paul, and "how much more a brother to you". Even that is not enough, for Paul raises the stakes—he returns him "both as a man" (for the man has become a fellow man to Philemon by means of Paul's love) and "in the Lord" who is selflessness himself, surpassing any sort of longing to possess.

3. *"They were rescued by Wisdom."* One cannot struggle by human means to accomplish Jesus' command of complete dispossession for the sake of pure willingness toward God, for this is Wisdom that must be granted from on high (according to the first reading). He who thinks solely in this-worldly terms, has to be "anxious" about many things simply because earthly things are so precarious. This anxiety distorts his perspective on heavenly carefreeness. The necessity to calculate keeps him from gaining any concept of "God's counsels", which are based on generous surrender rather than calculation. Only "through Wisdom" can he be "rescued" from this distorting fixation on cares.

[C] Twenty-fourth Sunday in Ordinary Time

Exodus 32:7–11, 13–14; 1 Timothy 1:12–17;
Luke 15:1–32

1. "But I have found mercy." All of the texts today speak of
God's mercy. Already in the Old Covenant mercy is the quality that grants access to his innermost heart. In the second
reading Paul reveals himself as a pure product of divine mercy.
Twice he says "I have found mercy", and this that he might
serve "as an example for all those who will believe in Christ
in the future". "Although I was once a blasphemer, a persecutor, and filled with arrogance, he has made me his servant and
judged me faithful." Even Paul's blasphemy, persecution, and
arrogance occurred out of blindness, which God was able to
transform into a healing blindness through his immense light,
permitting his blindness to "fall like scales from his eyes". So
that the entire paradox of God's mercy might be apparent, Paul
reduces himself to the lowest place, referring to himself as "the
first among sinners", an occasion for all of "God's patience" to
be displayed. Thus he becomes an object through which God's
mercy is demonstrated for the benefit of all subsequent ages
of the Church.

2. "And searches tirelessly." The Gospel tells the three parables
of God's mercy. He is not merely the Kind One who forgives a
sinner when he returns, rather, God "pursues the lost one until
he finds it". This is true of the parable of the lost sheep and
that of the lost silver piece. In the third parable the father does
not wait at home for the lost son, rather, he hurries to meet
him and throws his arms around his neck. God's search for
the lost does not mean that he does not know where the lost
one is. Instead, it tells us that he searches to find which paths

will be effective, which paths will permit the sinner to find his way back. This is God's "exertion", which expresses itself in the culminating risk of giving his Son for the lost world. If the Son descends into the most profound abandonment of sin, to the point of losing the Father, then this is God exerting himself to the uttermost in his search for the lost. "When we were still sinners, God had mercy on us through the sacrifice of his Son" (Rom 5:8).

3. Appeal to God's heart. Initially, the first reading, in which Moses talks God out of his wrath in order to change God's mind, seems to contradict what we have just said. Yet when considered more deeply, this is not the case. Moses appeals from God's fully justified wrath to his deeper attitude, to his faithfulness to the patriarchs, and thereby to the nation. This points beyond his anger to his innermost attitude. Moses appeals to what is the most godly in God. This heart of God does not stop beating even when the nation virtually renounces the covenant, for which he has to send it into exile. No exile of Israel can be final. "If we are faithless, he remains faithful, for he cannot deny himself" (2 Tim 2:13).

[C] Twenty-fifth Sunday in Ordinary Time

Amos 8:4–7; 1 Timothy 2:1–8;
Luke 16:1–13

1. "We will buy the helpless man for silver." In the first reading the theme of "wicked mammon", which is continued in the Gospel, is broached in such a way that all the wickedness rests not in the money but in the way it is employed by the oppressor. The issue is not unprincipled manipulation of the market economy ("reduce the measure and raise the price"), but open fraud ("fix our scales for cheating"), combined with offering poverty-stricken men as wares ("we will buy the poor man for a pair of sandals"). All of this collides directly with Israel's covenant with God, which not only condemns lying and theft, but requires that a man love his neighbor as he loves himself. In the world's way of thinking, outside the covenant, these sorts of things can be considered "normal" (although even there, statesmen have repeatedly striven to achieve justice for all). In the Gospel Jesus can make use of such "normal" and "clever" behavior as a point of departure for his teaching.

2. *"The children of this world are more clever than the children of light."* The steward who was called to account for having wasted his rich lord's property chooses fraud as the "clever" way out. He finds a way to extricate himself at the last minute from the mess—his clever calculation consists in ensuring that, when he loses his position, he will find refuge with those whose debts he had written off. Christ ("the Lord" in verse 5) praises, not the deception, but the cleverness that often exceeds the cleverness of Christians in worldly affairs, in the practices of the world economy. For Christians it is a matter of being or nothingness. They ought to take steps to ensure in advance that they "will find lodging in eternal mansions". At the very least this means giving their money away as alms rather than idly awaiting the judgment and eventual dismissal.

The last four statements Jesus makes about mammon (vv. 10–13) insist on trustworthiness in money matters even in the Church, for money entrusted to the Church for good purposes must be administered conscientiously. Ultimately, his words here demand a clear decision: God and money cannot share dominion.

3. "God wants all men to be saved." The second reading expands the horizon. The Church ought to pray even for the non-Christian realm, for God has included it in his plan of redemption. The Church cannot leave political, economic, and social problems to themselves, but must instead do all she can to ensure that the equal dignity of all men (which has been highlighted by Christ) finds implementation in all of the above-mentioned areas. Since God's plan of salvation encompasses all men, the Church has to extend herself beyond her own sphere and be concerned about this entirety. Paul refers to himself here as a "teacher of the Gentiles". This means not merely that he converts some of them to faith, but that he wants the norms of genuine humanity that come to light in the New Covenant to have force beyond the boundaries of the Church.

[C] Twenty-sixth Sunday in Ordinary Time

Amos 6:1, 4–7; 1 Timothy 6:11–16;
Luke 16:19–31

1. "Lounging comfortably upon their couches." Once more the first reading, from Amos, is important for understanding the Gospel. The prophet thunders not simply against property and wealth, but against what property and wealth often produce in men: carousing, indolence, being comfortable without caring about the nation's situation (Israel was already seriously threatened at that time, but "you are not made ill by the collapse of Joseph"). The prophet reads the riot act to men with this sort of selfish "carefree" and "self-assured" attitude: "Their wanton revelry shall be done away with" and "they shall be the first to go into exile."

2. "The rich man likewise died and was buried." The Gospel underscores the unbridgeable gap between the carousing life of the rich man and the misery of the poor man. "Lying at [the rich man's] door" the poor man sees what goes on inside, but only the stray dogs care about his sores. This is all Jesus emphasizes. We need not expand the portrait theologically in any direction (for example, by considering the details of the view of the afterlife given here). Outwardly it seems that this portrait does not go beyond that of the prophet, but Jesus, who has drawn the lines of the commandment of love of neighbor much more concretely, expands the implications of the screaming chasm between rich and poor far beyond those of the Old Covenant. In the next life this gap will become a "final" and "unbridgeable" abyss between repose in Abraham's bosom and torment in the fiery netherworld. Even Abraham cannot bridge the chasm. The request to send the poor man —precisely the one who was formerly despised and ignored —to the five brothers makes no sense, since Moses and the prophets speak to them far more penetratingly than this poor man could. Jesus' simple parable is no more and no less than a concretization of words we might otherwise scarcely grasp: "Blessed are you who are poor . . . but woe to you who are rich" (Lk 6:20, 24).

3. "Take firm hold on everlasting life." Once more the second reading expands on the others. Two attitudes are contrasted with each other, but now one of them, the right and salvific one, is clearly understandable. Paul's disciple Timothy has already made the decision, publicly, "before many witnesses", just as Jesus made his decision and gave his witness before Pilate and the entire nation. From this point on what counts is to hang on to what has been chosen and thereby to "take firm hold on everlasting life" by anticipation. Persistence in this choice will require constant struggle, and "the good fight of faith" must be carried on "without blame or reproach" as an assignment from Christ and the Church. Yet to "take hold of everlasting life" does not mean grabbing at God. The doxological conclusion here is important. The God "who dwells in unapproachable light, whom no man has ever seen or can see", can only be worshiped, never grasped by men. To decide for God, to bear witness to him, means just the opposite: to be grasped by him and placed under assignment.

[C] Twenty-seventh Sunday in Ordinary Time

Habakkuk 1:2–3, 2:2–4; 2 Timothy 1:6–8, 13–14; Luke 17:5–10

1. "I cry out to you, 'Violence!' but you do not intervene." The prophet in the first reading can no longer endure the situation the world finds itself in. Violence, abuse, and oppression are everywhere! He cannot comprehend how God can simply stand by and watch. Men cannot improve the world's situation by themselves. If anything is to change, God will have to become involved, and at least help men to change things. Initially God's reply has an Old Testament tone: Be patient, Messianic salvation will soon arrive. "It presses on to fulfillment and will not disappoint." Essentially, this will also be the New Testament answer, for example, in Revelation, when man can no longer offer resistance to the devilish powers of the netherworld and cries out to God: "Come!", the Lord answers "I come quickly" (Rev 22:17, 20). Yet a difference is to be found: in the New Covenant the Christian not only waits ("wait for it, for it will surely come" [Hab 2:3]), but also fights alongside the Lamb, rides with him into the battle (Rev 19:14). In that fight, to appear to be defeated with the Lamb is already a form of victory.

2. *"God has not given us a cowardly spirit."* The second reading hints at the same. The chosen one should remember the Spirit that was given him in the laying on of hands. He ought to let the fire inside him, which perhaps is only smoldering, be "kindled anew", for it is "a Spirit of strength, love, and wisdom". All three words may be viewed together: strength is located precisely in love (and this is love that is prudent and deliberate rather than ecstatic), which is needed to fight against powers inimical to God. This strength, which is love, is the weapon of the Christian. Paul brings this home yet again: One ought to persist in the strength granted by the Holy Spirit, "abide" in the "love" that has been given, and do so according to the example of the saints, who retained strength to suffer for the Gospel even in prison. This can indeed be the "good fight" (2 Tim 4:7), the most fruitful struggle, since it is fought alongside the Lamb.

3. *"Prepare my supper."* The Gospel clarifies things even more. To believe is not simply to sit back and wait until the Lord comes and serves us with his grace. Faith receives its incomprehensible efficacy (tossing a tree into the ocean) in the course of serving the Lord, who, after all, has become the servant of us all and cannot stand to see anyone lazily let himself be served by him (*sola fides*). Instead, he takes it as self-evident that his followers serve alongside him, which really means they serve him, for "where I am, there will my servant also be" (Jn 12:26). Moreover, this serving does not take place in haughty pride over how useful to the Lord my co-service may be (as if he could not do anything without me). Just the opposite— in modesty the servant knows the words of Jesus: "Without

me you can do nothing" (Jn 15:5). Since he has already done everything for us, the correct estimation of ourselves is the one commanded by the Lord himself and expressed in the confession, "We are useless servants; we have only done our duty."

[C] Twenty-eighth Sunday in Ordinary Time

2 Kings 5:14–17; 2 Timothy 2:8–13;
Luke 17:11–19

1. "Where are the other nine?" In the Gospel the Lord heals ten lepers—by sending them to the priests. The priests were responsible for declaring lepers unclean (Lev 13:10–11), but also to establish the fact of recovery from the disease and to rescind the verdict of uncleanness (Lev 13:17). Clearly Jesus alone accomplished the miracle that took place while the lepers made their way to the priests, but the liturgical prescriptions of the law were so decisive for the lepers who were Jews that they located the meaning of their healing entirely within the prescribed ceremonies. This is not unlike many Christians who consider "practice" to be the center of religion and thereby forget the grace bestowed by God who is the origin and goal of "going to church". The end disappears under the means, which often have little to do with genuine Christian life, and which have often become little more than pure custom, unexamined tradition. In such circumstances we need a "foreigner", someone unaccustomed to the traditional ways, who, on the way to the "health authorities", realizes that grace underlies his path, and then expresses gratitude to the proper source.

2. "Please accept a gift of gratitude from your servant." Preceding the first reading's pericope, the Old Testament parallel to the healing of the ten lepers in Luke began by sketching the Syrian's outrage at having to obey Elisha's requirement that he bathe in the Jordan River in order to cure his leprosy. Do we not have rivers aplenty at home? His servants are the ones who have to persuade him to obey Elisha. He is healed, not really by faith but on the basis of his obedience. Now come his immense astonishment and exuberant gratitude. He would like to show his gratitude through gifts, but the prophet will accept nothing. He is simply "at your service". This leads to the second, inward healing of the Syrian, followed by renewed amazement, no longer at the miracle-working powers of the prophet but at the power of God himself. Now all he wants to do is worship God on the soil of the land that belongs to God, some of which he takes back to Syria with him. A distance from religious custom is necessary in order to experience what a miracle is and how much gratitude one owes to it. Jesus said this very clearly in his programmatic sermon at Nazareth (Lk 4:25–27).

3. *"My gospel, for which I must suffer."* The second reading shows that beneath a spiritually deadening deformation into mere traditionalism true Christianity takes the unnerving form of martyrdom, which is nothing other than a (not necessarily bloody) suffering for one's confession of Christ. Here Paul endures suffering for the "sake of those whom God has chosen", so that despite their sleepiness they "may obtain the salvation to be found in Christ Jesus and with it eternal glory". One ought not focus merely on the concluding phrase of this little hymn that ends the pericope: "If we are unfaithful he will still remain faithful, for he cannot deny himself." This thought, though true, can lead to laziness. We have to take the preceding clause equally seriously: "If we deny him, he will deny us." If we treat God as a sort of religious

robot,[1] he will show us that he is anything but that—that he is a free, living God who is also the eternal Word, which proves itself to be free and unfettered when we find ourselves "chained like criminals" for its sake. Only "if we die with Christ shall we also live with him".

[C] Twenty-ninth Sunday in Ordinary Time

Exodus 17:8–13; 2 Timothy 3:14–4:2;
Luke 18:1–8

1. "Listen to what the corrupt judge says." As he often does, in today's Gospel Jesus takes the immoral realities of our world as his point of departure. Here it is the corrupt judge, elsewhere it was the servant who defrauds his master, the prodigal son, the foolish rich man, the glutton, the wicked vineyard owner. Beginning with what is familiar, Jesus wants to move up to the laws of the Kingdom of God. Here, as in the parable of the friend knocking at the door at midnight, the point of comparison is the persistence of an importunate but not unjust request. If even the wicked, . . . then all the more God who is good. Jesus wants to make utterly clear to us: God wants men to ask him, even to pester him. If God gives man freedom and goes so far as to enter into covenant with him, then he is not merely concerned about human freedom but has bound himself in a covenant with his partner without giving up his divine freedom: God will always give the petitioner what is best for him, "the good" (Mt 7:11), "the Holy Spirit" (Lk 11:12). Whoever prays in the Spirit of Christ will be listened to without ex-

---

[1] The German word translated here as "robot" (*Automat*) can also mean "vending machine"—TRANS.

ception (Jn 14:12–14). And the Gospel adds, "without delay". God does not hear our prayers at some later date. He hears and immediately responds with whatever best corresponds to the request. A request, however, presupposes faith, which is why the Gospel ends with something for us to mull over: will the Lord "find faith upon the earth" when he returns? It is we, who are listening here, and not just anyone, who are being asked this.

2. *"As long as Moses kept his hands upraised, Israel had the upper hand in the battle."* In the first reading, the portrait of Moses' uplifted hands during the battle with the Amalekites speaks volumes. As Joshua fights, Moses prays—and it is a penance for him, since it is difficult and painful to keep his hands lifted up to God for hours on end. That is how the Christian community is constructed: some fight on the outside while others pray on the inside—in the monastery or a "private chamber" at home—for those who are fighting. The image can be extended: Aaron and Hur support Moses' arms when they begin to droop, and they hold up his arms until evening, so that Israel can win the battle. The hands of those who pray and of those with contemplative vocations in the Church have to be supported, for without prayer the Church cannot be victorious— victorious not in worldly but in the spiritual matters required of her. If the Church is to avoid being routed in the difficult battles of our day, all of us must pray and help others to achieve persistent prayer, rather than depend on external busyness.

3. *"Preach the word, whether or not people want to hear it."* The word of which the second reading speaks is not a word of mere action, as in Joshua's battle, rather, it is equally the word of petitionary prayer, the word spoken by Moses' upraised hands. "Remain faithful to what you have learned", that is, "out of

the sacred Scriptures", which never call people to mere or-thopraxis. Only if the "man of God" is "instructed" by "the Scripture inspired of God" will he be "equipped for every good work". The first "good work" is prayer, which has to be taught to Christians through "tireless and patient teaching".

[C] Thirtieth Sunday in Ordinary Time

Sirach 35:12–18 (20–22); 2 Timothy 4:6–8, 16–18;
Luke 18:9–14

1. "God be merciful to me, a sinner." The Gospel of the two men praying in the temple, the Pharisee and the tax collector, reveals to what kind of prayer penetrates to God. We notice a difference even in their respective postures. The one stands "with unbowed head" as if the temple belongs to him, while the other "keeps his distance", as if he has crossed the thresh-old of a house in which he really does not belong. The first one prays "to himself",[2] really not even praying to God but review-ing for himself the list of his virtues, assuming that, when God himself notices them, he will respect them and marvel at them. Moreover, this man catalogues his virtues as a means of setting himself off from "other men", none of whom have attained his level of perfection. He is traveling the road of "self-discovery", which is precisely the path of "loss of God". The other man can only discover sin in himself, can only find himself devoid of God, which, as he pleads, "be merciful to me", turns into an empty place for God to occupy. No one whose ultimate

---

[2] After making the point that the Pharisee prayed "to himself", von Balthasar adds that the German lectionary translation "tones this down by adding the word *softly (leise)*"—TRANS.

goal is his own perfection will ever find God. Anyone who has the humility to permit God's perfection to take effect in his emptiness—not by being passive but by working with the talent he gives him—will be considered a "justified" person in the sight of God.

2. *"Whoever serves God willingly will be heard."* The first reading confirms this. "The prayer of the lowly pierces the clouds", although we must remember that "lowly" or "poor" here does not mean someone who lacks money, rather, someone poor in virtues, someone who knows he does not meet God's standard. Yet recognizing this void alone is not enough, rather, the text clearly says, "Whoever serves God willingly will be heard." This is service undertaken with the humility characteristic of a "useless servant" (cf. Lk 17:10 [pp. 353–54 above]), but not with the passive waiting of the "lazy servant" who buries his talent. One serves by employing the talent the Lord has given him, which is truly entrusted to him, to make it yield fruit for the Lord. God, the "just judge" will "do right by" this sort of poor man.

3. *"That is how I was saved from the lion's jaws."* In the second reading we find Paul in prison and in court. He is the poor man whose case does not look hopeful from an earthly standpoint. He is close to death and yet, he "has fought the good fight", not only while he was free, but even in his present poverty, abandoned by all during his court hearing. Yet his lonely self-defense before the court becomes precisely his final, decisive "proclamation" of the gospel for "all the nations to hear". By honoring only God (like the tax collector in the temple), he will be "rescued" by the Lord and "brought safely into his heavenly kingdom". The tax collector was "justified", Paul receives "the crown of righteousness"—a crown made up not

of his own righteousness,[3] as he never tires of repeating, but of God's.

[C] Thirty-first Sunday in Ordinary Time

Wisdom 11:22–12:2; 2 Thessalonians 1:11–2:2;
Luke 19:1–10

1. "But you spare all things, because they are yours." The marvelous point of the first reading is that God loves everything he has made, or else he would not have made it. In view of countless evils in the world, many people, Christians included, do not want to believe this. Yet the proof that the Book of Wisdom gives is so simple and convincing that one can scarcely contradict it without either denying God or accusing him of self-contradiction. "You love everything that exists, for if you hated something, you would not have created it." Sin we certainly find in abundance, and it must necessarily be tracked down, but since even the sinner belongs to God, he is not punished according to naked justice, but is "spared" and punished in such a way that afterward he can recognize a call to conversion in the punishment. The astonishing wisdom of this Old Testament book is found in the statement that God loves everyone and thus punishes sinners solely out of love and with the aim of returning them to love.

2. "Do not be so easily agitated or terrified." In the second reading it almost seems as if Paul intends to recall the insights of

---

[3] As noted above (p. 128, note 3), the terms translated here as "justified" and "righteousness" are essentially the same in German (and in Latin, Hebrew, and Greek): *gerechtfertigt, Gerechtigkeit* —TRANS.

the first reading. God, who "rebukes offenders little by little", grants us time "to fulfill every honest intention and work of faith". Therefore one ought not let himself get worked up over proclamations of the imminent end of the world, even if such announcements are supported by prophecies or revelations. Instead, he should calmly and without panic continue his Christian activity. The Lord is not merely someone who threatens to descend upon us from the future ("like a thief in the night"), rather, he is also the One who constantly accompanies us on our way to heaven and, while underway, clarifies things for us through his fellow travelers (as with the disciples on the way to Emmaus), thereby removing all our fears.

3. "Zacchaeus, hurry down." The Gospel sketches a strange picture for us. An extremely wealthy man clambers up a tree to see Jesus. As the "chief tax contractor" he was viewed as a great sinner, yet Jesus specifically wishes to stay at his house. And Jesus knows that wherever he enters, grace enters with him: "Today salvation has come to this house"—precisely "because the Son of Man has come to search out and save what was lost." He stays with Zacchaeus because there was something salvageable there, certainly not because good deeds were done there and he wished to reward them. Instead, he stays with him because "this man too is a son of Abraham", who is not excluded from God's faithfulness and love. Thus we cannot answer the question whether the man's assurance that he will give half of his fortune to the poor is based on something that had happened earlier or whether it was simply his response to the grace extended to him by Jesus. The Evangelist has no interest in that question. All he is concerned with is the salvation that Jesus brings to this household. It is good to know that he also lodges with the immensely wealthy—if they are to be recipients of Christian salvation. His beatitudes for the poor ought to be interpreted theologically rather than sociologically. There are poor men who are rich in the spirit (of lustfulness), and there are rich men who are poor in the spirit (because they "press their resources into service" [Lk 8:3]).

[C] Thirty-second Sunday in Ordinary Time

2 Maccabees 7:1–2, 7, 9–14; 2 Thessalonians 2:16–3:5; Luke 20:27–38

1. "God has given us hope that he will raise us up again." The first reading's narrative of the martyrdom of the seven brothers also contains the sure testimony to belief in the resurrection. The brothers are tortured cruelly: flogged to death, robbed of their hacked-off limbs. Yet to the astonishment of their torturers, they endure all of this by referring to the resurrection that will render their bodies whole again. "God has given us hope", which no one can take away from them, and the limbs loaned to them from on high can eventually be restored. A heroic ideal is being sketched out before our eyes, a picture that is intended to present clearly to us what Paul meant with the words: "For this momentary light affliction is producing for us an eternal weight of glory beyond all comparison" (2 Cor 4:17). This certainly applies not solely to bloody martyrdom but to every sort of burdensome earthly trial, which, despite its load, remains as light as a feather in comparison with what has been promised.

2. "God is not the God of the dead", which is why, in the Gospel, Jesus simply brushes aside the foolish casuistry of the Sadducees regarding the woman married seven times. Of course the resurrection of the dead will be a corporeal resurrection, but since those privileged to experience it will never die again, marriage and the generation of children will have no more meaning (which, however, does not mean that all distinctions between man and woman will disappear). Those who are transfigured in God will have a completely different kind of fruitfulness, because fruitfulness is part of the image of God in men, yet it no longer has anything in common with mortality. It has to do only with the vitality that participates in the living fruitfulness of God. If God is introduced as the God of Abraham, Isaac, and Jacob, that is, of the living, then these, who are alive in God are also fruitful together with God: on earth they are fruitful in their earthly progeny and in heaven they are fruitful together with God in a manner known only to God and his angels.

3. "Brothers, pray for us." In the second reading, we are promised "eternal trust and sure hope"—just like the martyred brothers. More than that, we are also promised an understanding of spiritual fruitfulness already on earth. This fruitfulness derives from Christ and was unknown to the Old Covenant. Men who unerringly await the return of Christ and the resurrection, whose hearts "love God" and receive "strength for every good work and word" from God, can already participate in eternal fruitfulness through their intercessory prayer here below. The Apostle counts on this prayer "so that the word of the Lord may make progress and be hailed by many others" and so that the power of "confused and evil men" might be held back. Christian prayer is like a sluice gate that has been opened up, permitting the water of heavenly grace to flow out into the world.

[C] Thirty-third Sunday in Ordinary Time

Malachi 3:19–20 (4:1–2); 2 Thessalonians 3:7–12;
Luke 21:5–19

SPREAD OUT BEFORE US we have here Jesus' view of world history that will take place after him. The first reading looks ahead to the last things at the end of history, distinguishing between the wicked, who are to be burned, and the righteous, who shine like the sun. Meanwhile, in the Gospel, Jesus looks at the theological constants within history. The promise of the destruction of the temple comes across as only a prelude. As long as it stands, it is the Father's house that must be kept clean for the sake of prayer. But Jesus is not preoccupied with stone temples, cathedrals, or enchanting Baroque churches; hence he need not be concerned with the work of historic preservation connected with these monuments. Only the "temple of his body", which is the Church, matters to him. He predicts three things regarding her future.

1. "Many will come in my name. . . . Do not follow them." Paul spoke of the inescapable schisms, all of which claim the name of Christ when they appear. Jesus pronounces woe to all who give cause for offense (Mt 18:7), yet schisms are unavoidable "in order that those who are approved among you might be recognizable" (1 Cor 11:19). No future prospect could be more painful for the One who pleaded with the Father for the unity of Christians. Can the rifts be healed? Almost involuntarily one recalls the words: "No one sews a patch of new cloth on an old garment . . ." (Mt 9:16). In today's Gospel he simply gives words of guidance: "Do not follow them."

2. Then comes the prospect of wars, with *"kingdom rising against kingdom"*. This is not simply a case of having borrowed apocalyptic language that has no meaning today, rather, it is the consequence of the fact that Jesus came not to bring peace but a sword and to divide even the closest family relationships (Mt 10:34–36). In response to his doctrine the apocalyptic beasts enter history. And the more powerful earthly means of power become, the more absolute becomes the opposition between them and Christ. This is paradoxical in the extreme, since Jesus praised the powerless and peacemakers, yet precisely their presence permits the waves of world history to tower higher and higher. His teaching and his person were unbearable already for men back then: "Away with him!" His audacity in claiming to be the Truth ("He has made himself the Son of God." [Jn 19:7]) faces an ever more infuriated response from world history.

3. Therefore *persecution* will not merely be an occasional episode, rather, it will be an "existential reality" for the Church of Christ and for individual Christians. Jesus speaks of it with formality (vv. 12–17). Persecution will affect "you"—the representatives of the Church who were present—and thus the entire Church. The places where Christians will have to make their witness (*martyrion*) include synagogues and Gentile courts. Arrest, imprisonment, betrayal by one's own family, and hatred are all announced without any attempt to sugar-coat the pill. Yet only "some" among these "witnesses" "will be put to death", which is important to remember in regard to the idea of martyrdom. (In the Book of Revelation we find a similar point: what is required is that one bear witness with his entire life and at the risk of his life—but not necessarily as a blood witness.)

What should a Christian do? In the second reading Paul gives a laconic answer: Work. And work like he works—in both the Church and the world. He has "worked day and night", he has not "depended on anyone else for his food". All that is required of a Christian is that he be engaged in both Church and world. In light of God's providence, "not a hair of your head will be harmed" (Lk 21:18).

[C] Christ the King

2 Samuel 5:1–3; Colossians 1:12–20;
Luke 23:35–43

1. "This is the King of the Jews." The inscription placed above the Crucified One was formulated by Pilate to provoke the Jews. The soldiers who read it mocked Jesus as much as did the "leaders of the people", calling up to him: "If you are the King of the Jews, save yourself." But at least in Luke's Gospel we encounter one man who takes the inscription seriously—one of those crucified with Jesus, who turns to him with the words: "Remember me when you enter upon your reign" (or "when you come with your Kingdom"). Here the inscription tacked to the Cross results in the Kingdom of God being understood for the first time as the Kingdom of Christ. Thus the ancient cry of the Psalms, "God is King", is transformed into "Christ is King." It makes little difference exactly what image of this King Jesus the criminal had; he was at least convinced that this King had the power to help him, a poor dying man. This is the first dawning of the universal royal power of Jesus.

2. "They anointed David king over Israel." The first reading reminds us briefly that David was Jesus' royal ancestor. As a shepherd boy David had been anointed by Samuel at a time when Saul still ruled. In today's reading David is acclaimed by all the tribes of Israel as the shepherd of the entire nation. He is a prefiguration of what happened on the Cross: Jesus was the Anointed One (Messiah) from the very beginning, but on the Cross he was publicly proclaimed King (according to John's Gospel, in the three world languages of the day).

3. "In him everything continues in being, . . . through his blood on the Cross." The second reading expands the criminal's notion into a limitless claim, without sacrificing the core of Jesus' Kingdom, the Cross. All creation is subject to him as King, because creation simply would not exist without him. Creation as a whole has "its existence" in him. From the outset God conceived the world in such a way that it might become the "Kingdom of his beloved Son", and this in such a manner that it was not merely to be taken for granted, but that precisely "everything" should be "reconciled" in him, so that we might have "redemption, forgiveness of sins through him", so that this "peace" among all beings and ultimately between heaven and earth could be "established" in no other way than "through his blood on the Cross". God's whole love for the world only becomes apparent in the Son through this most extreme sacrifice, covered as it was by the mockery of Jews and Gentiles and by the flight and denial of Christians. Thus it is that this divine love can rise, in the form of the Son, to rule over all things in his royal dominion.

SCRIPTURE INDEX

The Sunday and feast day readings are in roman type. Other Scripture references cited in the text are in *italic*.